AMERICAN RELIGIOUS AND BIBLICAL SPECTACULARS

MEDIA AND SOCIETY SERIES
J. Fred MacDonald, General Editor

AMERICAN RELIGIOUS AND BIBLICAL SPECTACULARS

Gerald E. Forshey

Media and Society Series

 PRAEGER

Westport, Connecticut
London

Library of Congress Cataloging-in-Publication Data

Forshey, Gerald Eugene, 1932–
    American religious and Biblical spectaculars / Gerald E. Forshey.
        p.   cm.—(Media and society series)
    Includes bibliographical references and index.
    ISBN 0–275–93197–8 (alk. paper)
    1. Religion in motion pictures.   2. Bible films—History and
criticism.   3. Religious films—History and criticism.   4. Motion
pictures—United States—History.   I. Series.
PN1995.9.R4F67   1992
791.43′682—dc20   91–47578

British Library Cataloguing in Publication Data is available.

Library of Congress Catalog Card Number: 91–47578
ISBN: 0–275–93197–8

First published in 1992

Praeger Publishers, 88 Post Road West, Westport CT 06881
An imprint of Greenwood Publishing Group, Inc.

Printed in the United States of America

The paper used in this book complies with the
Permanent Paper Standard issued by the National
Information Standards Organization (Z39.48–1984).

10 9 8 7 6 5 4 3 2 1

For Florence Amelia,
who after 36 years
is still the sunshine of my life.

Contents

Acknowledgments

This project had its genesis long ago at the University of California, Los Angeles, when I decided that I wanted to be a minister. My mother told me I could never be one because I loved the movies too much. She lived long enough to see me ordained in the Methodist Church, and to have a copy of the 1978 doctoral dissertation that makes up a large part of this book.

The actual project started in the office of John G. Cawelti in Cobb Hall at the University of Chicago, where I talked to him about supervising a dissertation on film aesthetics and authorship. Noting my history in the ministry, he suggested the curious omission of these great big religious films in film studies. I realized that my work and training so far had involved explaining the religious meaning of secular films. He was suggesting that I turn it around and try to find out the cultural uses of religious movies.

Martin Marty helped hone my historical skills in the ensuing years, and Peter Homans gave me valuable help in thinking about the religious experience from a cultural perspective. When it came to putting my thoughts into readable English, Jean Caffey Lyles found the subjunctives and passivity in my writing voice, along with assorted other ills, and made me rewrite and retype it all.

During the research, wonderful people and great libraries assisted me. The Academy of Motion Picture Arts and Sciences, the American Film Institute, the UCLA Theater Arts Library, and the University of Southern California Film Library provided wonderful resources to complement the Regenstein Library at the University of Chicago, the Chicago Public Library, the Northwestern University Library, Cecil B. DeMille and the

Chicago Research Library. Gladys Cole, former secretary, working for the DeMille family, opened up DeMille's scripts, files, and speeches to me. Universal and MGM both let me into their archives. Stuart Kaminsky, then of Northwestern University Radio, Film, and Television Program, made available materials from Charlton Heston (much of which was later published in his book *The Actor's Life*) and an interview with William Wyler.

I have had wonderful discussions with people from the Popular Culture Association, notably Jeffery Mahan, Douglas Kellner, and Horace Newcomb. Jim Wall has been a solid and loyal friend in hundreds of conversations we have had about film and religion in our 30-year friendship. There have been colleagues, such as Robert Jewett and John Lawrence, who have taken interest. John Auer gave me early encouragement, and Martin Deppe read the later version and helped me clarify the focus. Martha Scott has been pressing me to finish this phase as the good pastor and religious counselor that she is.

My teaching of film in the City Colleges of Chicago and at the Garrett-Evangelical Theological Seminary (under the aegis of Dean Richard Tholin) has helped me see more deeply into the art of film than I saw in the dissertation.

Finally, there is Fred McDonald, the editor of this series. University presses had shown some interest in previous years, but it never quite fit their profiles—was it religion or was it film? Fred is convinced that there is an audience for both, and I hope that he is right. I doubt if my mother would have believed it.

AMERICAN RELIGIOUS AND BIBLICAL SPECTACULARS

1

The Religious and Biblical Spectacular

When the 1950s ended, *Variety* noted that in six of those ten years, religious spectaculars had been the most popular films. Starting in 1949 with *Samson and Delilah*, and running consecutively through *Quo Vadis* (1951), *David and Bathsheba* (1951), *The Robe* (1953), *The Ten Commandments* (1956), and *Ben-Hur* (1959), religion as spectacle dominated the screens.

Little attention has been paid to this phenomenon. Most historians barely refer to these movies that so attracted audiences to the box office. There has been no systematic attempt to classify them as a genre. Yet the films remain with us, resurrected at Christmas and Easter in prime-time television and drawing larger crowds than witnessed them at the height of their release. Now new prints of *The Ten Commandments* and *Ben Hur* have been struck, and they are back in the theaters.

In these films, the persistent tensions in American culture are fashioned into popular art. They reveal a great deal about American values.

Most films that focus on religion as a subject also reveal certain inescapable tensions brought on by the Industrial Revolution, with its reliance on science to produce the technology that makes America so economically strong. Because of this clash, three themes dominate religious films.

The first is the relation of a naturalistic world view to religion. Popular religion assumes a physical world of the flesh and an invisible world of the spirit. Over the course of the period covered by this work, the trend was away from this dualistic world view. The depiction of religion becomes progressively a private psychological experience. In the early films of this study, one ending suggests that faith in one's ideals is worth dying for because there is a fulfillment beyond earthly life when the powers of this world will be overthrown (e.g., *Sign of The Cross*). Another ending suggested that evil would be overthrown in this world, and the heroes and heroines allowed to live happily ever after (e.g., *Quo Vadis*).

Later, this fulfillment beyond history and happy endings comes under closer scrutiny. As the idea of a separate spiritual reality decreases, more ambiguity is introduced, and the possibility of living faithfully without any assurance of the triumph of good or of eternal life is scrutinized with much more care.

A second major problem concerned the treatment of miracles. How were miraculous interventions into the natural world to be treated? Scientific methodology based on empiricism and naturalistic metaphysics give no credence to miracles. One option was to portray only those that could be explained psychologically—psychosomatic healings or mass hallucinations. Another was to treat them as rumors and stories that circulated in antiquity. Treatments varied from straightforward depiction to rationalized interpretation, but in each case, the film makers were quite aware of the reasons they were choosing and gambling that they might not offend the audiences' sense of reality.

The second theme is especially transparent in the religious spectaculars that use biblical or important religious eras for their backdrop. In a pluralistic world, ideologies conflict, and claim natural and supernatural justification. Because of the close identification of American society with the "good" society of the religious spectaculars, these films suggest that there are eternal principles to follow, and the hero embodies the values that make a country great as soon as he adopts the proper state of mind. The enemy represents the oppressive forces, and his overthrow suggests God's blessing to the religious values the protagonist is being pulled toward. At times, the forces of evil are within the nation itself—economic depression, militarism, racism. The films explore the options, for example, whether violence or the reckless accumulation of wealth is God's way.

Once again, as the separate sacred realm becomes less believable, the notion that one particular ideology is identified with the will of God is challenged. This growing ambiguity and uncertainty is evident from the late 1950s on.

The third theme involves ethical behavior. The three themes that dominate popular ethics—sex, violence, and success—are constantly explored. The role of sexuality and its relationship to one's duty become the main themes of a series of biblical spectaculars spanning the 1950s. The question of when violence is justified is continually raised. The problem of success is found both in the early films (*The Last Days of Pompeii*, 1935) and the late ones (*Jesus Christ Superstar*, 1973). Since these questions are never resolved in the culture, the films offer continuing comment on changes in attitudes toward ethics in American culture, trying to give some supernatural justification so as to escape the purely subjective decisions of the individual.

Over the years, as American religion struggled with the place of a naturalistic world view, the concept of the righteous nation, and the basis of individual ethics, American film making was changing. At the beginning of the period, film making was an instrument of mass culture, and producers could depend on most Americans buying a ticket at least once a week. After the expansion of television in the mid–1950s and the breakup of the monopoly of production, distribution, and exhibition rights in motion pictures, producers began to change their formulas on the assumption that they now had to appeal not to a mass culture, but to a pluralistic one. This trend toward thinking of the audience in terms of many groups affected the spectacular films, especially because they were so expensive to mount that producers believed they had to represent the widest possible points of view to garner a profit.

There are other films that use religion as subject. A biographical film, such as *A Man Called Peter*, offers a way to look at what was considered the individual ethical problems of an era. *Friendly Persuasion* tries to resolve the tension between claims of the Civil War and the Quaker Religion, whereas *Elmer Gantry*, using evangelistic crusades as a backdrop, explores the American success formula and the emergent sexual revolution. *The Exorcist*, using the concerns of the horror film about the way science dominates our thought processes, raises questions about the ubiquity of evil and our inability to explain it.

Although such films as *The Ten Commandments* celebrated the American era in international diplomacy as a sign of God's blessing, *Hawaii*, made during the American involvement in Southeast Asia, questioned the effect of our cultural dominance.

With the exception of *The Crusades*, the spectacular films chosen are set in the biblical period. The persistent themes of the religious films are found here—justification of the nation, the attack on rationality, and the problem of ethics in a pluralistic culture.

From the beginning, movies were attracted to religion and spectacle. Six years after the publication of *Quo Vadis?* in 1895, the first film version was made. It was remade in 1910, 1912, 1925, 1951, and 1986 (as a television miniseries).

The public's craving for spectacle was probably one of the main influences in the development of the movies. In the silent years, spectaculars were less a set of conventions than the potentiality of the camera to explore human action within the vast physical environment.

Spectacle has always fascinated people. Aristotle, in his *Poetics*, described it as one of six elements of tragedy, admitted that it has "an emotional attraction of its own," but was more dependent on "the stage machinist than that of the poet."[1]

Religious spectaculars grew out of two popular artistic traditions—the spectacular stage melodramas and the popular quasi-religious novels of the nineteenth century. In the early part of the century, the French dramatist Pixerécourt developed spectacular effects for the stage—floods, forest fires, explosions, tall ships with full rigging. By the late nineteenth century, lavish effects, such as the chase across the ice in *Uncle Tom's Cabin* and the chariot race (on a treadmill) in *Ben-Hur*, were being used on the American stage. In the more remote areas of the country, however, these special effects were executed on a modest scale because of inadequate stages, and people who traveled to the big cities were reminded of the limitations. The motion picture offered realistic spectacle. Singling out the chariot race from *Ben Hur* as an example, one theater critic wrote in 1899, "The only way to secure the exact sense of action for this incident in a theater is to represent it by Mr. Edison's invention."[2]

The capacity for spectacle evolved over the next decade in the works of D. W. Griffith and Thomas Ince, but it was not until *The Birth of A Nation* (1915) that the full panoply of spectacular effects emerged on the American screen. Griffith had built on the work of Georges Melies, an amateur magician who discovered the possibilities of illusion. Melies worked magic, creating visual images impossible in the natural world, but had little interest in dramatic structure. Griffith, an actor trained in melodrama, created films that paid attention to such images. With *Judith of Bethulia*, Griffith turned to Sacred Writ (*the Apocrypha*) for dramatic material.

During the last half of the nineteenth century, a number of melodramatic historical novels appeared that were easily adaptable to spectacular effects when they reached the stage. After the development of motion pictures, such novels as *Quo Vadis?, Sign of the Cross*, and *Ben-Hur* were transformed into spectacular films. The Industrial Revolution, which created the modern forms of entertainment and information—mass circulation newspapers, movies, television—offered motifs of escape that have remained a dominant function of these entertainments. The group of plays set in antiquity, using spectacular effects, set a pattern, established a myth, and then became a staple of the film industry.[3]

Over the years, religion has continued to be big box office. *A Man Called Peter* (1955), the biography of Dr. Peter Marshall, pastor of the New York Avenue Presbyterian Church in Washington, D.C., was one of the most popular films of 1955. *The Nun's Story* (1959), *Elmer Gantry* (1960), *Rosemary's Baby* (1968), and *Hawaii* (1966) made headlines in the 1960s. *The Exorcist* was the largest moneymaker of 1974, and the most controversial film of the 1980s was *The Last Temptation of Christ* (1989).

Within the spectacular genre, one can identify three basic categories. Some are mythically displaced—that is, the world in which they exist contains demigods, demons, dragons, and other fantastic creatures beyond the human experience (*Die Niebelungen* (1974)). None ever had a large popular following in the United States. Occasionally there are spectacles in which the natural environment overcomes any other elements present, and the protagonist is pitted more against nature than any adversary (*Lawrence of Arabia*).

Most spectaculars, however, are historical spectacles. These films represent personal dramas set against the events of a particular period. *Gone with the Wind* is set during the Civil War and *Cleopatra* in ancient Rome, whereas *War and Peace* depicts Russia during the Napoleonic Wars. The focus of interest, however, is the personal drama.

Religious and biblical spectaculars differ in their emphases and dramatic constructions. In the religious spectacular, the historical period is of religious significance, and familiar religious figures have roles *within* the drama to lend significance to the dramatic actions. Biblical spectaculars center on biblical figures and/or events. They may introduce fictional characters or portray events from the point of view of one character in the drama.[4] In them, the biblical events and characters are central to the story being told.

The spectacular is not defined by plot, organizations, or character, but by the manner in which all these elements are subjected to what Matthew Arnold called "the grand style." In speaking of Homer's epics, Arnold said that "his manner invests his subject, whatever his subject be, with nobleness." This treatment of the subject matter, rather than the theme, defines the importance of the epic. Arnold argued that Homer invested his subject with "nobleness" by adopting "the grand style."[5]

In somewhat the same way, the scale of the drama and the techniques of the film makers define the spectacular. Penelope Houston, Raymond Durgnat, and Stephen Farber all consider the matter of scale. Houston defines it in terms of its effect on narrative—"big climaxes," "a luscious eye-catching decor," and a "key dramatic moment to round off the first half."[6] Durgnat likened the films to Greek epics, dealing with large-scale enterprises and actions. Human activity is painted against a landscape in which "man matches, in action, the hugeness of the world." They extend themselves to the limit as they stand before a bewildering social and physical environment."[7] Farber discusses the techniques, pointing out what drew people to the movies first "was the grandeur of the medium at its most ambitious or at its flashiest—the dazzle of the exotic, the monumental, the romantic that no other medium could match."[8]

Each is a version of Arnold's "grand style." Even the shot that defines the spectacular is the "boom shot." In the scene at the Atlanta train station in *Gone with the Wind* (1939), the camera opens on a medium-close shot of Scarlett as she implores the doctor to come with her to deliver Melanie's baby. As she walks through the station, the camera booms up, revealing a mass of dead and dying soldiers, which defines Scarlett's insensitivity to the social tragedy enveloping the South.

The physical environment supplies the scale for the drama, a magnifying glass for the eventual victory of the protagonist. Cecil B. DeMille, the most famous director of spectaculars, said that the environment of a spectacular is a frame, and one would not "take a Rembrandt . . . and frame it to conform to the dimensions of a miniature. When the story has been properly framed, it is the story that we are aware of—not the trappings on the screen."[9]

Religious and biblical spectaculars are like other spectaculars in that the historical past is of some importance to contemporaneous audiences, the protagonist suffers trials and tribulations while the villain controls the action, action takes precedence over characterization, and a melodramatic archetype underlies the formula.

In the 1930s, the religious spectaculars reflected the Great Depression or American attitudes toward the gathering world crisis. After World War II, religious spectaculars incorporated the tensions of the cold war into their dramatic structures. Biblical spectaculars, on the other hand, did not really start in the sound are until after World War II. The first cycle of films concerned sex and social responsibility, with the protagonist tempted from his duty by a woman. In the 1960s, the biblical spectaculars explored the basis of ethics through a series of films based on the life of Jesus. These presented special problems, but they attempted to adhere to most of the elements of the formulaic pattern for biblical spectaculars.

As in most melodramatic formulas, the villain of the spectacular controls the action. He energizes the plot, and his strength ultimately leads to his downfall. The more potent his evil, the more heroic the resolution. The villains tend either to be mad (Nero in *Quo Vadis*) or obsessed with power (Rameses in *The Ten Commandments*), and are often connected with perceptions of contemporaneous international leaders. Hitler seems to have been the prototype for the mad leader, the one who incinerates the earth or kills without conscience. Such rulers are weak and licentious. Sometimes an evil woman controls the villain. Sycophants surrounding the villains represent a corrupted social order.

Villains obsessed with power use popular versions of Stalin as a prototype. This character justifies his malevolence by the realities of power. He is without conscience, a self-centered personality attempting to shape an absurd world to his own ends. Characteristically, he requires no people around him, since he is sustained by the Roman or Egyptian social order itself.

The mad emperor appeared most often in the films made during and just after Hitler's reign; after 1954, this type disappeared. By then, those who had accepted the corrupted personality theory—that Hitler had caused the war because he was a lunatic—found their fears giving way to more frightening and more rational kinds of threats from the Communist world.

In the religious spectacular, the villain is either temporarily victorious or is killed; in the biblical spectaculars, there are additional options; for example, a female villain converts because she is "really" a loving woman who has been misinterpreted, or another in which the villainy is generalized into the entire social order of Rome or Egypt.

The hero is subject to the same frailties as the rest of the audience. Often he has roots in the working class, and usually is invested with democratic attitudes. He is a good man, but may be a skeptic caught between conflicting social consciousnesses, usually involving subjugation of others; often this is linked to the fact that pleasure has become the dominant ethical principle in the villain's society. The villain and the protagonist come into conflict, and the hero is subjected to trials that test his spirit. His ability to survive and adopt a new ethical consciousness makes it possible for him to triumph. The hero must decide between seeking pleasure or power and doing his duty. When he adopts a duty ethic, his fate reveals that the world order is actually benevolent, and has been working in his favor all through his trials and tribulations.

In the biblical spectacular as well, the hero typically goes through a prolonged crisis of faith before adopting the new faith. In the Jesus films, this crisis is deflected to one or more characters around Jesus. In films about religion, doubt is as real as faith, but the hero must adopt the faith in order that providence might triumph.

In the religious spectacular, love is often the agent of salvation. The biblical spectaculars are wary of sexual love. In a whole cycle of biblical spectaculars concerning sex and social responsibility, love is played against lust, and the character's fates are related to the choice.

The religious spectacular centers on the hero's conversion to the new consciousness, whereas the biblical spectacular, with the exception of films about Jesus, usually pivots around the hero's return to righteousness.

The main interest of the film is action; the characters are metaphorically stripped for action, making it possible for the larger design of the melodrama to function—the clear presentation of good and evil and the eventual revelation of providence. The characters, though seemingly free, act out the providential design.

The world of the spectacle is often divided into competing urban and rural values. The urban world is frequently characterized by licentiousness and opulence. Its values are skewed, sadistic, and materialistic. The courts at Rome, Jerusalem, and Egypt are viewed as overindulgent and brutal. Urban dwellers go to the arena, a place where human life is subject to the grossest degradation. The loose sexuality found in the courts is a sign that the fundamental cultural institutions are degraded.

On the other hand, rural values are presented as lasting and sustaining. They bear the traditions of Christianity. Rural people, who live close to the earth, even when brought to the city, revere honesty, gentleness, marriage, community, and family ties. They do not have elaborate institutions;

the church is uncomplicated. The films suggest that rural values might be maintained even in urban life, but the pressures of dehumanization are enormous. Though rural values might not prevail in this life, they are bound to triumph beyond this life.

Although these representations of values are caricatures, they reveal some of the deep feelings Americans had about urbanization. By linking religion with the more sustaining rural values and ignoring the negative elements of rural existence, the films are able to represent those values as essential to the Christian faith. In the religious spectaculars, these rural values represent the strength of American life. In the biblical spectaculars, the emphasis is more upon the "personal" adoption of these values to form the basis of ethical norms.

The conflict between hero and villain leads to bloodshed and suffering. The hero's victory is achieved in the face of circumstances that seemed overwhelming early in the film. Very often the nation is overthrown or reformed, as in the killing of Nero or Caligula, and the action ends in the coming of a new social order.

This heroic action reveals the protagonists as "men among men," worthy of respect and emulation. Thus, when they are "saved" from their particular crisis, it is not to a "weak" or "woman's" religion, but to one worthy of a man's respect. Indeed women are assumed to be inferior, though usually more moral unless they are part of the villainy. In religious spectaculars, women are easily persuaded to the faith, often becoming agents of regeneration. The male's physical superiority is a sign of his higher status, and his heroic deeds are symbols of his special worth in spreading the new consciousness.

In the biblical spectaculars, the men are more reflective—often already faithful at the beginning—but tend to be swayed from their duty by other concerns. Eventually, they overcome their crisis of faith and act out the heroic role. In the Jesus films, it is nearly impossible to make Jesus into a sinner; therefore, the crisis becomes that of Judas, who is always shown as close to Jesus.

Religious spectaculars have two kinds of endings: the victory of the hero in death, or the hero's victory over evil and the beginning of a new social order. In those films that end with the protagonist's survival, there is an assurance that good will win out within history. There is a better world to be lived in, here and now, and we sense a "happily ever after" ending. The lovers are united, free to live out their destinies with each other. The old order has either been destroyed or replaced.

In the fulfillment beyond history, the world remains in the hands of the evildoers, but symbolically we are assured that evil's triumph is temporary. Holding on to the faith, even in the most trying of circumstances, is better than living under tyranny. Providence may not yet be ready to show itself in this world, but there is a reward in a world to come.

In the biblical spectaculars, virtue always triumphs in the end. Sometimes this triumph requires the death of the hero at the moment of his victory over the powers of evil, for example, Samson. At other times, the ending suggests the growing satisfaction in the lovers' relationship, as in *David and Bathsheba*. In the Jesus films, the Resurrection comes at the conclusion, contradicting the Crucifixion. The endings define the films' own standards of victory.

From a dramatic standpoint, the alternative endings provide the necessary suspense to keep the film interesting. Melodrama requires the good to triumph and the wicked to fail, which we know from the beginning. The suspense comes from the possibility that the good may fail.[10] In these films, there are different ways of affirming the providential world order—by the overthrow of the present regime or by a courageous willingness to die without compromising principle, an especially satisfying fantasy in a culture that reveres devotion to principle and duty.

Melodrama seemed natural for religious themes, because it emphasized the "workings of heaven justly guiding man's affairs."[11] This providence works within the dynamics of history, and the melodrama shows "how the complex ambiguities and tragedies of the world ultimately reveal the operation of a benevolent humanly oriented moral order."[12] These films dramatized the fantasy that people very much like us would eventually triumph in this world if we stayed close to the principles most familiar to us and most commonly accepted. In the face of a society characterized by less religious certainty, and in a nation whose technological forces and pluralism were challenging the old supports of the social order, that assurance obviously gave comfort and functioned well in reinforcing cultural values that were losing their legitimacy.

If the "grand style" defines its visual and dramatic style, the spectacular's method of approaching history is a key to its interpretation. American culture holds that some historical periods reveal crucial insights into the present. DeMille thought that *The Ten Commandments* needed all the financial and technical resources he could muster to acquire the scale needed to emphasize the social significance of the story for our age.

The historical setting must "look real," in accordance with what the audience pictures as the ancient world. That look changed as visual technology changed, and it became more natural; the difference between the sets of *King of Kings* and *Jesus of Nazareth* demonstrates a strikingly different "realism."

The ancient past becomes significant when we recognize our own attitudes in the ancient world. These similarities suggest that some things are eternal. We see the contemporary world as we imagine it might have been in ancient times. The ancient world must *seem* ancient but still modern, and in doing so, the world of the spectacular becomes a model for modern attitudes.

The use of history in religious and biblical spectaculars serves to keep us aware of our traditions and responsibilities, imparting a sense of identity as both Americans and Judeo-Christians. The task is accomplished so effectively that it is often difficult to distinguish between patriotism and religion.

Popular history relates people to a tradition that may or may not have actually existed, offering interpretations that meet contemporary concerns. For example, concern for the unity of Jew and Arab in the 1959 version of *Ben-Hur* is not found in the 1923 version, for the state of Israel did not exist then and was not a political issue when dealing with a Jewish hero.

Spectaculars combine history and myth. By casting current problems in historical perspective, they suggest that certain problems in the past were solved by faith and moral action; by extension, today's problems can be dealt with in a similar fashion.

History is also shaped to meet the needs of the drama. For Americans, the ancient past is one great sweep of time. The religious spectaculars had less trouble than the biblical spectaculars in shaping history to fit dramatic requirements, because they were not dealing directly with Sacred Writ. For example, according to Roman Catholic tradition, Peter made a trip to Rome at the end of his ministry and was crucified there. Protestants, citing the silence of the Bible concerning such a trip, have argued that Peter never went to Rome. Yet in the religious spectaculars, it seems that Peter made *two* trips to Rome—the first between A.D. 35 and 41 (*The Robe* (1953), *Demetrius and the Gladiators* (1954)), and the second a quarter-century later (*Quo Vadis*), yet the Protestant Motion Picture Council did not refer to it, mainly because the film satisfied many historico-mythic needs.

On the other hand, biblical spectaculars often give dramatic shape to the historical material by combining accounts, adding fictitious episodes, changing the order of the stories portrayed, and emphasizing material authenticity of the sets and costumes. These techniques of reshaping the drama became critical in the Jesus films when the stories were called upon to judge the culpability of the Jews for the death of Jesus. The producers' fear of being regarded as anti-Semitic forced the film makers to consult modern biblical scholarship to solve their problems.

What is presented is a *mythos*, not a history. Americans regularly rewrite history, giving different emphases to events than were given by earlier generations. The precise facts are of little consequence. What is important is whether the presentation coincides with the current generally accepted view, for example, of race, native Americans, women, or labor, as shaped by whatever social forces are at work in the period. In the religious spectacular, this aim is not difficult to achieve, because the general public knows so little of antiquity, and much of this knowledge is shaped by the mass media. In biblical spectaculars, the problem is different, because more people know the stories and accept them both as history and Sacred Writ.

In history, human purposes are decisive, and they shape the selection of events. In the spectaculars, history is used to reaffirm the social values deemed basic to American society. The history and authenticity are there to ensure the plausibility of the *mythos*.

The time chosen is a "strong time," the moment when some great event occurred, investing all actions and values associated with it with special significance. We believe the sacred realm has intervened into the temporal affairs of the heroes and heroines; then their activities become models for us. If the nation keeps the faith—that is, if the individual men and women who witness the move adopt its values—then the nation will be preserved.

Characteristically, the myth has several versions. Its meanings change as the problems faced by the people of different periods change. The myth is stored so that it can be called on periodically: In the case of the spectaculars, it demonstrates how the audience must act in history if they are to receive God's blessing for themselves and the nation.

The films I have chosen represent those that had enough of a following to be deemed "successes." That is true for all but the last film, *The Last Temptation of Christ*, which is treated as a special case, for it is not even a spectacular. Its reception, however, clarifies so many things about Jesus films and their reception that it deserves consideration.

Political, religious, and film history form the matrix in which I discuss these films. Using this information makes it possible to examine the shifting patterns of cultural dynamics and helps account for a film's popularity. When I could find material about the writer's, director's, or producer's visions of the film, I have used the material. In DeMille's case, that was substantial; in other cases, it is far less so. What this gives us is their intentions, whether or not they were realized. Occasionally, script notes clarify these intentions.

In assessing the cultural impact, one must have some information about how the audience reacted. It is impossible to know how people who first saw these films reacted to them, but by getting a wide variety of reviews, it can give us clues. Newspaper reviews include those from major New York and Los Angeles papers, but there are also reviews from other parts of the nation where critics were less influenced by the industry itself and reflected more of what their readers were interested in. The religious press also reviewed the films—from publications written for the Catholic laity to those written for professional clergy. National mass distribution magazines reflecting a wide variety of reading tastes (*The New Yorker, Parents*) were consulted, as were both popular and scholarly film magazines.

In the end, however, these are my impressions as I try to sift through the films themselves and through the responses made to them by the American people.

NOTES

1. Aristotle, *Poetics* 6.1450^b6.16–20 Trans. by Kenneth Telford (Chicago: Henry Regnery, 1961), p. 14.

2. Arthur Knight, *The Liveliest Art* (New York: Macmillan Co., 1957), p. 21.

3. Peter Green, "The Movies Make Hay with the Classic World," *Horizon* 3 May (May, 1961): 53.

4. For example, *Salome* (1953) portrays the conflict between Herod and John the Baptist from the points of view of Salome and a fictional Roman commander.

5. Matthew Arnold, "On Translating Homer," in *Matthew Arnold: Poetry and Prose*, ed. John Bryson (London: Rupert Hart-Davis, 1954), p. 294.

6. Penelope Houston, "The Theory and Practice of Blockbusting," *Sight and Sound* 32 (Spring, 1963): 71.

7. Raymond Durgnat, "Epic," *Films and Filming* 10 (December, 1963): 9.

8. Stephen Farber, "Spectaculars 1967," *Film Quarterly* 20 (Summer, 1967): 12.

9. Cecil B. DeMille, "Forget Spectacle—It's the Story That Counts," *Films and Filming* 3 (October, 1956): 7.

10. John Cawelti, *Adventure, Mystery, and Romance* (Chicago: University of Chicago Press, 1976), p. 46.

11. David Grimsted, *Melodrama Unveiled* (Chicago: University of Chicago Press, 1968), p. 225.

12. Cawelti, *Adventure*, p. 45.

2

The Depression-Era
Religious Spectacular

It has often been argued that movies of the 1930s offered escapism in the midst of the social crisis of the Great Depression. There were, however, films with themes that did deal explicitly with such problems, such as Archie Mayo's *Black Legion* (1936) or King Vidor's *Our Daily Bread* (1934). Even the "frivolous" musicals referred to economic problems, such as the "Easy Street" number from Mervyn LeRoy's *Gold Diggers of 1933*, of that same year. For the most part, however, the themes were sublimated and found their way into the genres, such as the gangster and comedic styles of the period. In assessing them, Andrew Bergman argued that the possibility of individual success was kept alive by finding scapegoats, or the belief that the federal government was going to save everyone. These films reworked the myth of a society without class bias, suggested that hard work would result in personal success, and suggested that personal evil was responsible for the social crisis. The New Deal became "a veritable leading man."[1]

In the religious spectaculars of the 1930s, the basic ingredients of the formula were symbolically reworked to refer to the economic and personal crisis. In order to keep the "grand scale" intact, the individual became involved in a major social catastrophe—such as the burning of Rome or the Crusades.

One myth films spread was that the 1920s were a period of loose morals, and that the Great Depression was the result of the personal and business morals of the era. Film makers were unwilling to suggest that the deep social and economic problems were aberrations in economic institutions and arrangements themselves. To the general populace, these forces seemed like madness. This attitude found its way into the period's films, and both the question of personal responsibility and the question of social chaos appeared in the religious spectaculars. Further, when director Cecil B. DeMille departed from these concerns to international ones, as he did in *The Crusades* (1935), the effects were seen at the box office.

America became an urban nation during the 1920s, with a concomitant shift in values. This shift showed itself in the backdrops of depression films. After World War I, the American moral tone relaxed as Americans abandoned Victorian standards. Arthur Knight noted that Hollywood was out of touch with the values of the people in the towns and villages across the country, who were shocked by the sophisticated sex, drinking, divorce, and drugs presented to them as fashionable.[2] Still a sizeable constituency both enjoyed and condemned the films' portrayal of decadent life.

The urban style was part of a melting pot of European immigrants, mass production, the spread of universal education, the creation of mass transportation, and a host of other changes going on in American society. In the movies, however, it symbolically focused on materialism and a looser sexual morality. Films spread those images across the whole of the population. Margaret Thorp attributed it to DeMille:

Glamour as we know it today was really invented, or better, discovered by Cecil DeMille . . . [who] noted that the two chief interests of men and women during the postwar boom were sex and money, and proceeded accordingly. Everybody was . . . interested in ways of spending money. The new rich . . . wanted to know all about high powered cars, airplanes, ocean liners, yachts, villas, exotic food, wine, jewels, Paris dresses, perfect servants; and DeMille told them. His were really the first educational films.[3]

The urban-rural conflict affected both the censorship and the content of films. The struggle over censorship was temporarily resolved by the establishment of Will Hays as czar of Hollywood moral codes in 1923 and the adoption of the Production Code in 1934. DeMille sensed early the new circumstances, realizing that the American people were questioning materialism and moving toward the virtues with which they were raised. DeMille's brother William wrote: "Having attended to the underclothes, bathrooms and matrimonial irregularities of his fellow citizens, he now began to consider their salvation."[4]

In his movies, Rome and its heroes begin to look suspiciously like the proponents of the urban lifestyle, whereas the Christians seem to exemplify the values of the rural nation. Virtues, such as hard work, restraint, and moderation in all things, made their way into the movies. The protagonist of religious films becomes the man in the middle, torn between the indulgent (urban) life and someone he loves who represents Christian (rural) values. The story ends with the victory of rural values, presented as a new consciousness (Christianity).

For the movie business, 1932 was the worst of years; the depression finally reached California, and box office receipts were down more than 50 percent. Thus, when DeMille and Paramount agreed to make a picture after an unhappy three-year separation, there was cause for celebration. A great many people would be going back to work.

DeMille's interest in *Sign of the Cross* (1932) went back to 1923. He saw it as the completion of a trilogy that had started with *The Ten Commandments* (1923). "*The Ten Commandments* had been the story of the Giving of the Law. *The King of Kings* was a story of the Interpretation of the Law. *Sign of the Cross*...would tell of the Preservation of the Law."[5]

The play had been written after playwright Wilson Barrett had met Robert G. Ingersoll, the great atheist advocate of the era. They talked religion, and Barrett announced that he would write a play to appeal to the same classes as Ingersoll, except that his would show the "beauty and strength and purity of the faith." Half a century later, DeMille had the play adapted for the screen.[6]

The film begins with Nero's decision to blame the Christians for the burning of Rome. Marcus Superbus, prefect of Rome, falls in love with the young Christian girl, Mercia. Poppaea, Nero's wife, wants Marcus for a lover.

Marcus is torn between the attractions of Nero's court and the Christian community. He is powerful, sexually prolific, and uncommitted. This is the Roman side, the urban side, of his nature. DeMille establishes the corruption of the court in the beginning scenes when Nero frets over the broken string on his lyre while Rome is burning. We meet Poppaea taking a bath in goat's milk.

Charles Laughton commented, "Nero was nuts. I play him straight." He is both childish and monstrous, appreciating the sadistic cruelties of the arena, watching through his emerald *lorgnon*.[7] In one scene, he casually caresses a near-naked young man as one would a pet, suggesting he was also homosexual.

In the opening sequence, Nero rationalizes his persecution of the Christians. He tells the captain of his guard, Tigellinus, that despite their persecution, the Christians continue to grow. They accept another God other than the Roman emperor, one who exalts meekness. Finally, they decide to blame the Christians for the burning of Rome.

Nero is dangerous but rather passive. Tigellinus, who wants to usurp Marcus' place, and the lustful Poppaea easily bend Nero to their wishes. His evil is weakness rather than willful depravity. The idea of a new consciousness playing into the hands of a madman is found here for the first time, defining the way Nero was played for two decades.

Marcus' decency is stimulated by the persecuted Christian community. They must practice their religion secretly; a reward of 30 pieces of silver

will be given for their capture. Mercia and her young brother Stephanus
are classic movie Christians. DeMille draws parallels—the good woman is
balanced by an evil woman, the childlike emperor by the manlike child.
Their parents had been used as torches for one of Nero's orgies. "They
died like hundreds of others—holding to the truth," Mercia says.

Stephanus, her younger brother, fails the community when he is tortured.
Just as he is about to be led into the arena, Mercia tells him, "It was your
body that was weak, not you!" Flesh and spirit are juxtaposed as the
fundamental human choices. Power, especially over life and death, ema-
nates from the flesh. Spirituality and love form the other side.

Marcus tries to seduce Mercia to the side of the flesh. The opening run
program is quite descriptive about Marcus' intentions at the orgy:

Mercia is brought to Marcus' own apartment . . . a snow white lily—in a dung heap
. . . her purity fascinates him . . . vainly he pleads with her . . . love him and he will
save her . . . every luxury . . . every honor will be hers. Every honor . . . except one,
she reminds him. By force he seeks to bend her to his will and wish . . . she evades
him. A laugh . . . and Ancaria stands in the door.[8]

Ancaria performs the "Dance of the Naked Moon." The script describes
the music as "an Oriental whine with a lascivious rhythm." Cut onto the
soundtrack, however, are the songs of the Christians in opposition to the
"barbaric dance rhythms." Marcus yells for the orchestra to drown them
out, for a "love song is stronger than a fanatical dirge." Having failed in
his attempt to seduce Mercia, Marcus renews attack, but Mercia tells him
that she wanted his love "as a man, not as an animal."

For DeMille, the scene was important as the proof of Mercia's virtue.
He argued that the dance was necessary "to bring out by contrast the
greater strength and purity of Mercia's faith."[9] Will Hays, upon the advice
of Martin Quigley of the Legion of Decency, tried to have the scene excised,
but for DeMille, the Roman Catholic church was attempting to interfere
with his freedom of expression, and he refused.

Later scenes include more than a half-hour of atrocities in the arena—
people burned in oil, pygmies skewered on tridents by Amazons, women
and children eaten by lions, human bodies crushed by elephants. The
church was willing to accept the violence but not the sexuality.

DeMille chose Elissa Landi for the role of Mercia because "she combined
mysticism and sex with the pure and wholesome."[10] The church seems to
have sensed the ambiguity in DeMille's work—that a woman of Christian
virtue is not very interesting unless she is also sexually appealing.[11]

As Mercia is going to her death, Marcus comes with one final plea that
she recant her faith and save her life. He tells her that all gods are a fantasy.
"Yours is a mistaken belief." Mercia, who has helped her brother and
guardian through spiritual crises as they faced death, experiences one of

her own. "To know that you loved me is all I can have." His decision to die with her, unlike the motivation in the original play, comes not out of faith but because of love. "I shall go with you," he tells her, "you can teach me your hymns, your faith. Some day I will understand."[12] It does not seem to bother him that he will not have time to learn them, since in the final shot they walk out into the arena while a Christian hymn swells on the soundtrack.

Variety commented, "Religion over paganism. And the soul is stronger than the flesh. Religion gets the breaks, even though its followers get killed in this picture. It's altogether a moral victory."[13] The combination of spectacle, violence, sex, and the moral victory of religion was popular with moviegoers, who often paid their admissions with IOUs when they did not have the cash. The eventual triumph of the good for those who hold fast to the "true faith" was a concept attractive to people experiencing hard times. The rural values are associated with Christianity, and Marcus' rejection of the licentious urban attitudes intensifies the enjoyment.

DeMille said, arguing for the epic romance, "The world is coming out of its hangover. It wants to cure the headache it gets every boom period by a long cool dose of the simple spiritual things in life."[14] In DeMille's imaginary world, romance was the driving force behind history. In *The Crusades* romance causes King Richard I to go on the Third Crusade and agree to a successful compromise to the bloody warring. It also provides the motivation for the building of the transcontinental railroad (*Union Pacific*, 1939), the winning of New Orleans (*The Buccaneer*, 1938), for ending the conspiracy of unscrupulous captains and salvage masters who were sinking the boats off North Carolina (*Reap the Wild Wind*, 1942)— and even for the Exodus (*The Ten Commandments*, 1956).

On that scale, history is a clash of impersonal forces and personal commitments. DeMille sees history working out for the good because great leaders' romantic aspirations lead them into commitments that have very specific historical and political consequences. One individual decision is ultimately significant, even that of casting away one's life for love, especially if there is a heaven waiting for the lovers.

Sign of the Cross was swathed in controversy. Some believed that the film was more concerned with sin than redemption, and that DeMille was "more happy with a dissolute and decadent Nero than with the more heroic representatives of pristine Christianity."[15] Another suggested that DeMille was appealing to the people who wanted to watch the sadism of the arena and the pious who wanted a "beautiful and noble message."[16]

DeMille had cast the mold for the religious spectacular. The forces of evil are pitted against the forces of good, with good the ultimate victor. Evil is depicted as hedonistic materialism, based on power, wealth, and the corruption of accepted sexual morality, for example, with the morality of Rome. Good, on the other hand, is spiritual and based on a new consciousness that will ultimately prevail. In this world, evil might prevail, but not beyond history. Sexuality outside of marriage is depraved, whereas sexless romance or marriage is exalted. The audience is invited to identify not with the powerful Romans, and especially not with the ruling class, but rather with the powerless, downtrodden Christians, whose strength is in their commitment to a divinely ordained morality, for which they are tortured and die, though eventually they are triumphant in heaven.

DeMille saw parallels between his film and the Great Depression.

Do you realize the close analogy between conditions today in the United States and the Roman Empire prior to the fall? Multitudes in Rome were then oppressed by distressing laws, overtaxed and ruled by a chosen few. Unless America returns to the pure ideals of our legendary forbears, it will pass into oblivion as Rome did.[17]

His characters show the inequity between the rich Romans and the poor Christians, a weak and vicious emperor swayed by outside forces that use him for their own interests, and a Christian community that survives the most terrible trials and emerges victorious. One can find much similarity between these views and the faith of pre-Rooseveltian America.

The religion is so broadly conceived that it is really not a faith at all, but a few vague ideas that would offend no one. The Roman Catholic journal *Commonweal* summed up the problem:

Their faith has little to distinguish it from the monotheism of the Jews. There are some references to a sort of diluted Christ as "Master" but nothing to indicate that, to the minds of the Christians themselves, He is more than a human teacher of beautiful ethics and brotherly love.[18]

The campaign to sell *The Crusades* was atypical for DeMille. Instead of a fashioned screenplay, he pitched the film as an interpretation of historical events. That may be a major reason it lost $700,000 in its first run, before rereleases made it popular.

In the opening montage, the cross on the sepulcher is pulled down, sacred books are burnt with flames consuming a picture of the Virgin and child, men are herded into dungeons, and Christian women are sold on the slave market under Saladin's direction. When threatened by the Hermit (a combination of Peter the Hermit and Bernard of Clairvaux), representing the wandering monks who exhorted Europe to join in a Crusade, Saladin tells them to inform the Christian kings that "you have seen the walls of your Holy Land crumbled and fallen, your women sold as slaves, your knights trampled beneath the hoofs of our horses, your gospels cast into flames, the power of your cross broken forever."

DeMille has the Hermit reply what he thought would sell to American audiences: "The cries of these Christian women sold into slavery will be answered by Christian chivalry."

Having established these atrocities, DeMille turns the Saracen into a gentleman. As one newspaper noted, Saladin emerges as the real hero, his "suave and generous behavior to the Christians in startling contrast to the lumberjack whoopings of Richard and the chicanery of allied chieftains."[19]

Instead, Conrad of Monferrat becomes the villain though not the antagonist. The Christian kings continuously bicker, and in a famous scene in which Saladin appears before them (using his scimitar to cut a scarf floating in the air), they seem more likely to fight each other than to unite against him.

DeMille's portrayal of the political situation of the Third Crusade is drawn from the international situation of 1935. Following World War I and into the 1930s, Americans did not want to be entangled again in European politics. In 1935, with Hitler and Mussolini firmly entrenched and with Stalin shipping people from the farms to the cities, the United States wanted little to do with the leaders of France, England, and eastern Europe who were faced with foundering political bases because of the worldwide depression. The 1934 Johnson Act prohibited financial transactions with any foreign government in default on its obligations to the United States, many of them former allies of World War I. A year later, the Neutrality Act attempted to insulate the nation from the gathering clouds of war on the European horizon. Many thought that the League of Nations "encouraged European nations to enlist us in the name of Higher Morality in their perpetual feuds,"[20] almost a reference to the film.

These feelings appeared in American films and became part of the religious landscape. During a period when the traditional systems of meanings were undergoing a radical shift, Laughton's mad Nero was a plausible villain. The failure of the old order is experienced as disorienting, and madness is its metaphor. In an age of lingering depression, people were fearful of being drawn again into European politics, and DeMille thought that bickering kings and small-time profiteers might be more recognizable in the context of religious history.

When Saladin visits the kings, they are a potentially powerful force. Richard tries to demonstrate the power of his sword by slicing a steel mace, but Saladin cuts through the veil—a clever and impressive demonstration of the difference between might and finesse. Accustomed to noble heroes and black-hearted villains, audiences seemed unprepared when DeMille gave them a noble antagonist, an ambiguous hero, and a scheming but weak villain.

From the beginning, Richard's character is a problem. Other kings might be less than noble, but Richard spends the early part of the picture running away from Alice. He goes on the Crusades because the Hermit says that "all other earthly promises are wiped away," and he is thereby freed from his prearranged betrothal. He marries Berengeria to feed his troops. On his wedding night, after sending his troubador to marry Berengeria by proxy, Richard sings and jokes with the troops through the night. The bedroom scene in Richard's tent outside Acre, where Berengeria chases him with his sword, is slapstick.

Yet the fundamental story is of Richard's redemption. The Hermit warns him that he will be brought to his knees for his pride. Richard is ready to abandon the Crusade for love. When Berengeria asks if he would let their love stand in the way of the whole world, Richard answers, "In the way of heaven if need be." Even when he has assaulted Acre and Jerusalem, losing half his troops and his old friend Hercules, he can only pray, "If you—if you are really there—receive this old man's soul." When Richard refuses Saladin's offer to make him king of Jerusalem on grounds that he fights for the cross, Saladin tells him, "You have no faith in that cross." Richard can only reply weakly that the men who died had faith in the cross, and he will not break faith with them.

Ultimately, only love is important. Again, romantic love is at the core of DeMille's religious sentiment. Berengeria tells Richard after he has been offered the truce of Allah that their pride is the cause of their suffering. "We have been fighting God, instead of seeking him. Oh, what if we call him Allah or God? Shall men fight because they travel different roads to Him? There is only one God, His cross burns deep in our hearts. There is only one way. Peace. Make peace between Christian and Saracen."

When Saladin refuses him permission to pass the gates of Jerusalem, making it impossible for him to lay his sword on the tomb of Christ and consummate his marriage, Richard is ready to fight again, but Berengeria intercedes, telling him that he must sacrifice his love for the world's peace. Personal love can be fulfilled only if it is in service to a higher cause.

Yet DeMille was not ready to impose the solution he had in *Sign of the Cross*. Richard, fulfilling the Hermit's prophecy at the beginning of the film, is bought to his knees. Frustrated in love and bound to his chivalric vow, he prays for pity, noting the Hermit was right. "I'm no longer king, I've no pride now, no glory, I kneel to my God. Grant me your mercy and give her back to me. Have pity on a penitent fool." His prayer is answered when Berengeria places his sword on the tomb.

The critics pounced on this solution. One accused him of studying "the sex motive in history," and that the battle between Christianity and Islam, led by Richard and Saladin, was "chiefly concerned over the hand of Loretta Young."[21] Others were unconvinced by Richard's regeneration in his humiliation.[22] Such massive killing would seem to call for a more significant ending than the uniting of two lovers.

The romantic myth behind this is powerful: The struggle of individuals for love is as important as a divine mission, rooted in the belief that love and marriage are the foundations of society. It links divine providence to our basic emotions. DeMille believed that the story of Richard and Berengeria "held the audiences' interest and perhaps conveyed too the *truth* that the men and women of the history books were men and women of flesh and blood."[23] For history to have meaning, it must connect with contemporary values, which for DeMille meant romance.

DeMille had become enamored of Harold Lamb's book *Iron Men and Saints*, which he described as "sound scholarship combined with stirring and colorful writing."[24] Lamb could provide him with the justifications he needed to combat the inevitable criticism of historical inaccuracy.

The expected attacks came. The *Catholic World* spent three pages of its review discussing the Third Crusade in historical detail before even mentioning the film.[25] DeMille seemed to worry far more about whether the music was similar to that of the period than about whether the battle of Acre took two years rather than a single night to wage.

DeMille called his method "telescoping history." He felt free to change the facts to suit his dramatic purposes. Historical accuracy would be impossible in two hours of film, leaving audiences confused, bored, and angered. "Audiences are not interested in dates: they are interested in events and their meaning. We chose the year 1187 as the focal point for our story, but did not hesitate to bring in elements from other Crusades before or after that time."[26]

In this context, "truth" and "meaning" become interchangeable. To obtain historical "truth," he had to produce a "stirring and picturesque drama," welding together many diverse elements to "obtain verity as well as verisimilitude."[27] An uneasy tension exists between "verity" (truth) and "verisimilitude" (historical accuracy). The controlling purpose in both instances is the dramatic structure; education (and presumably religion) is a byproduct that must serve the drama.

There is no way to separate history from its symbolic interpretation. Humans project what they consider significant events back into the past, choosing similar events. Meanings are constantly adjusted to fit the changing mores of a society ("relevance"). As economic entities, films try to influence the emotions, and DeMille tied his history to romance. *The Crusades* was not trying to educate; it was trying to make money, and to do so, it used the existing values. The times were there not for themselves, but to give a sacred time frame for the love story.

The Crusades does not attempt to deal with the depression when international events were of little importance to Americans. As Hitler and Mussolini began to take on increasingly menacing proportions in 1936 and after, American newspapers and magazines began to pay more attention. *The Crusades* became a moneymaker several years after its initial release, drawing audiences during and after World War II, when international events were of primary importance to audiences.

Neither does the film pose an urban culture against a rural one. Such settings as Rome and Pompeii carry strong urban imagery, especially in terms of sexual licentiousness. Dramatically, they provide the cultural support for the villain. In *The Crusades*, the villainy is more the corrupt kings using the Crusades for their private goals than that of a decadent social order.

In the end, *The Crusades* became a paean to extol love as the driving force in history, to exalt individuals above the events, to resolve the tension between the emotional lust for violence and the intellectual desire for peace, and to call for unity in successfully integrating the nation into a world community, by sacrificing our personal goals for the greater good.

Insofar as these intentions were confused by the presence of other elements—an ambiguous hero, quarreling kings, a noble adversary, a petty villain, and a historical setting that was not well-defined in the audience's mind—the film's initial failure seems explainable. In the next decade, DeMille would devote himself to making films extolling America, before merging his biblical interests with his patriotic urges in *Samson and Delilah*, and more prominently in his last film, *The Ten Commandments*.

Merian Cooper and Ernest Schoedsack were known for *King Kong* and its spectacular effects, so that when they started making *The Last Days of Pompeii*, in which there was to be a volcanic eruption, much publicity and excitement ensued. The picture had nothing to do with Sir Edward Bulwer-Lytton's popular nineteenth-century novel, but Cooper lamely explained "we felt that because of its contribution to the photoplay a certain acknowledgment was due to the famous work."[28]

This film almost explicitly refers to the problems of the depression. Money is the root of sin, but when used wisely, money becomes the route to salvation. In the beginning, when Marcus stops a slave from running away and is offered a reward, he replies that he has enough money, telling Gaius, "I've a wife who loves me and a baby son. I work hard, eat hearty, and sleep sound. What more could I have?" His fall begins when he takes the *luxury* of using the reward to buy a ball for his son, who loses it in the street and is run over, along with his mother, by a patrician's chariot. To save them, Marcus goes into the arena, where he kills a man—a bagful of gold is clinked in front of him by a patrician in the stands. Having killed and thus stained himself, he finds his wife and child dead. He learns his lesson. "I've lost all I loved because I was poor. . . . Money is all that counts. All you have to do is—kill."

The point is stressed repeatedly—when Gaius tells Marcus how much money he was won on his killing, when slaves are bought, when the injured Marcus becomes a slave trader, when he chooses money over the life of Jesus, and when his values are contrasted with those of Flavius, his adopted son. Marcus tells him, "Don't worry how I make the money and I won't worry how you spend it."

The film's religious themes relate to economic themes. After curing Flavius, Jesus refuses Marcus' money, who cannot understand because Jesus is poor. Peter says, "He's the richest man in the world," totally confusing Marcus. As he enters Pilate's house, Pilate is washing his hands and confides that he has been forced to condemn a man. Pilate advises Marcus, "Pin your faith to gold," and Marcus replies, "I chose it long ago."

At a dinner for Pilate in Pompeii, just before Flavius is captured, Marcus tells Pilate that neither God nor man can takes his treasure from him. Most of his statements about money are ironic.

Flavius acts as a champion of the poor and the persecuted, but Marcus, who has spent years trying to blot the memory of Jesus from Flavius' mind, feels that Jesus was a failure. He asks Flavius where he would be "if I'd listened to his teaching. He said, 'Sell all you have and give it to the poor,' "—a counsel Flavius is following.

After Flavius is captured and condemned with the Christians, Marcus' money will not buy Flavius' freedom. Marcus uses his money to save a woman and her son, showing that, freed from pecuniary considerations, he can finally be redeemed.

The film uses a class analysis to draw parallels to the Great Depression. In the opening scene, Marcus knocks out the escaping slave. Gaius tells him, "For a peace-loving man, you're a handy fighter." The allusion is to boxing, which had long been a way for the poor to acquire wealth. (*Time* even called Marcus "the Joe Louis of Pompeii.")[29] *Variety* noted, however, that Marcus is "more a victim of a fierce semi-barbaric environment than of any personal cruelty trait."[30]

The *Photoplay Study* for teachers and students pointed out that:

Augustus emerged from years of strife as the greatest of Roman leaders, and gradually replaced the democratic institutions of ancient Rome. In their stead was built up a powerful centralized state with himself as the fountainhead of law and order. He was popular, energetic, and an able organizer . . . Commerce and industry flourished once more.[31]

The description could hardly have been more obvious if Franklin Roosevelt's name had replaced that of Augustus.

It moralizes that Marcus "is the symbol of humanity's many falls but gradual progress toward a shining goal where men not only preach but practice the pure principles of unselfishness and self-sacrifice taught by Christ."[32]

Optimism was growing at the time. Cases challenging Roosevelt's National Recovery Program and congressional criticism reflected the country's ambiguity toward the New Deal. The fragmented power that resided in private interests and in the states and municipalities was being consolidated by Roosevelt and brought under centralized authority. *Photoplay Studies'* comments about Augustine centralization connote some fear. Herbert Hoover continuously criticized the New Deal as a "stupendous invasion of the spirit of liberty."[33]

The religious counterpart of this optimism was found in the Christian idealism of Schleiermacher, Ritschl, and Rauschenbush, which had taken root in the American "personalist" movement in theology. These theologies gave humans a larger role in social transformation than the older orthodox theologies. *Photoplay Studies* presented these ideas in a secular context by talking about "gradual progress" and the "pure principles of unselfishness and self-sacrifice."

It is not surprising that in a country faced with decisions about wealth and success, film makers would cast sin and salvation into those terms. Marcus was described as an "upright character who becomes tarnished by worldly success," and becomes cynical.[34] His salvation comes when he decides to set aside his commitment to gold and to act on behalf of those whom he loves. By turning his back on the oppressive system, he is saved.

The notion that the decadence of the cities is the result of urban dwellers' material wealth is reminiscent of the suspicion that the crash of 1929 resulted from a failure of spiritual values, especially those that came from an urban society. Moral rather than economic arguments are used; it is not seen as a structural weakness in the economic system. In contrast to the wealthy urban decadence is a society of workers, slaves, and other powerless people, who, like Marcus, are victims. They hold to the utopian dream of a better world where material values do not dominate, and traditional values will triumph. In Christian terms, they are the meek who will inherit the earth. As in the two DeMille films, love saves Marcus, though this time it is parental rather than romantic love. Flavius is led to his religious faith by his personal experience with Jesus and his love for a Christian woman, Clodia.

The stereotyping of good and evil is not quite so clear here as in other films. Pilate confesses that for years he has not been able to blot the day of Jesus' death from his memory. Money, with its devaluation of human life (symbolized by richness, decadence, and the arena) is opposed by Christianity, with the poor inheriting the earth and finding freedom from their poverty and oppression. Because he is a worker, Marcus' spiritual salvation is implicit from the beginning.

Once again, there is a problem with history. Most reports put the date of Christ's death between A.D. 26 and 33 and the eruption of Vesuvius in A.D. 79. Yet Flavius ages only about 15 years during that period, and Marcus only reaches middle age. Producer Cooper recognized the problem and asked the indulgence of the film audiences for the ages of the characters in the picture, ascribing it to dramatic necessity. "In playing the story in one lifetime, rather than in two generations, we were able to effectively condense the action and still retain the great power of the theme."[35] In the popular mind, the requirements of dramatic unity are more important than ancient dates. Through the 1950s, any story of antiquity had to refer to the Judeo-Christian tradition, or it did not fall into the province of "strong" time.

Not only does providence work itself out in "gradual progress," but it uses a natural cataclysm, the eruption of Vesuvius, as its agent. Flavius is about to be eaten by a lion when the games are interrupted by the explosion, demonstrating that nature itself is on the side of righteousness. Marcus and Leaster, Flavius' slave teacher, save the younger generation. Marcus' friend Burbix carries children to the boat. A woman who rejects a small child while riding on her litter is swallowed up by the earth. The cataclysm works for the good of the people who have not been hopelessly corrupted and lets some of them show their innate goodness through self-sacrifice. The films of the 1930s were filled with disasters that demonstrated the goodness of men and women in trying circumstances, and often they happened at the most propitious moment, as in *Hurricane* (1937), *In Old Chicago* (1938), *San Francisco* (1936), or *One Million B.C.* (1940). Volcanoes generally erupted just in time to save the worthy people.

This demonstrates an uneasiness with the scientific view of the world. Though Marcus is interested only in saving his son, the Christians are also saved by this natural disaster. The volcanic eruption would not occur again in religious spectaculars, being replaced by other variations of the formula. It does suggest, however, that in some minds, righteousness and God's control of nature are linked.

This vision of the world can be applied subliminally to social reality. Though the disaster of the depression was presumably caused by love of money and overindulgence, it remains the work of God, but only those who are wicked or unrighteous will be lost, whereas many can find salvation, symbolically escaping to "an island in an unspoiled world."

NOTES

1. Andrew Bergman, *We're in the Money* (New York: Harper and Row, 1971), p. xvi.

2. Knight, *The Liveliest Art*, p. 111.

3. Margaret Thorp, *America at the Movies* (New Haven: Yale University Press, 1939), pp. 68–69.

4. William De Mille, *Hollywood Saga* (New York: E. P. Dutton & Co., 1939), p. 242.

5. Cecil B. DeMille, *Autobiography*, ed. Donald Haynie (Englewood Cliffs, N.J.: Prentice Hall, Inc., 1959), pp. 305–6.

6. Program Book, "The Sign of the Cross" (Hollywood: Paramount Publix

Corp., 1932), p. 18. Apparently Lew Wallace wrote *Ben Hur* because of the same kind of confrontation with Ingersoll.

7. *New Yorker* 85 (December 10, 1932): 85.

8. Program, *Sign of the Cross*, p. 12.

9. DeMille, *Autobiography*, p. 323.

10. *Time* 20 (December 5, 1932): 32.

11. Cf. Chapter 5 for a full discussion of this theme.

12. Program, *Sign of the Cross*, p. 13.

13. *Variety*, December 6, 1932, p. 14.

14. *Cincinnati Enquirer*, February 12, 1933, Sec. III, p. 3.

15. *New York Herald Tribune*, December 1, 1932, p. 14.

16. *Dallas Morning News*, February 8, 1933, p. 8.

17. Quoted in Charles Higham, *Cecil B. DeMille* (New York: Charles Scribners' Sons, 1973), p. 165.

18. *Commonweal* 17 (December 2, 1932): 45.

19. *New York Times*, August 22, 1935, Sec. III, p. 21.

20. Edwin Borchard and William P. Lage, *Neutrality for the United States* (New Haven: Yale University Press, 1937), p. 344.

21. *New York Herald Tribune*, August 22, 1935, p. 12.

22. *Variety*, August 19, 1935, p. 6.

23. DeMille, *Autobiography*, p. 345.

24. Ibid., p. 342.

25. *Catholic World*, 142 (October, 1935): 86.

26. DeMille, *Autobiography*, p. 344.

27. *The Crusades, Photoplay Studies* 1, p. 5.

28. *Last Days of Pompeii, Photoplay Studies* 1, No. 4 (October, 1935): 5.

29. *Time* 26 (October 28 1935): 52.

30. *Variety*, Oct. 18, 1935, p. 6.

31. *Last Days, Photoplay Studies* 1, No. 4: 6.

32. Ibid., p. 9.

33. Quoted in George Mowry, *The Urban Nation* (New York: Hill and Wang, 1965), p. 101.

34. *Seattle Post-Intelligencer*, November 1, 1955, p. 7.

35. *Last Days, Photoplay Studies* 1, No. 4: 5.

3

The Cold War Religious Spectacular

At the end of World War II, America had to cope with a different set of circumstances. The war had healed many of the emotional scars of the depression, but there were new worries. Industrial capacity had vastly increased, but it was no longer necessary to make war materials. People had relocated to the urban centers for the war effort and still remained in the cities. Immigration had shifted from Asians and Catholic Europeans to displaced persons from all over Europe and Latin America. Women, as a result of their work status during the war, were beginning to understand themselves differently. Blacks had also become increasingly self-conscious; having fought for America, they began to think they had a right to share in its fruits, and their focus shifted from survival to equal opportunity. Products of industry changed from war materiel to consumer goods.

These factors reshaped America's self-perception. The nation, no longer able to pretend that it was an isolated fortress, readily accepted its role in international affairs, especially in the formation of international alliances and support of the United Nations. The vast "Marshall Plan" to rebuild Western Europe soon extended to Japan and created enormous potential for economic growth, making it possible for the United States to become the first "affluent" society. With the enormous growth of the middle classes came the expectation that most Americans had a "natural" right to own a home, a car, and varying creature comforts.

As Americans increasingly became middle class, they also began to equate their creature comforts with the blessings of God, a theme present in American culture throughout its history, and formalized in Jefferson's claiming of "God-given" rights in the Declaration of Independence. In a world where Christian nations had been at war with each other for more than a generation, the idea of America as a chosen nation had already appeared in war movies.

As the war ended, Americans were faced with the clash of rival ideologies. The Soviet Union blockaded access to Berlin, and the United States had to airlift supplies into the city to avoid a war. China became a Communist country; the Nationalists and America's protege, Chiang Kai-shek, fled to the islands of Formosa and were protected by American warships. The United Nations intervened in an invasion of South Korea by North Korean Communists, and the United States found itself in its third war in a third of a century. Americans could not ignore international concerns, yet it was difficult to believe that this was the reward God had given a righteous nation.

In the religious spectaculars of the period, the theme of the "righteous nation" took precedence. The films followed the ebb and flow of America's concern with international affairs. The earliest postwar spectacular, *Quo Vadis*, looked back at the transforming influence of Christianity on the unrighteous nation, with Christianity representing the possibility for transformation of an evil society.

As the image of World War II faded and the emergence of the Soviet Union's nuclear capability dominated the international scene, the villains of the films, who had been madmen, became less frequent and rulers obsessed with power began to appear. The protagonists, on the other hand, were very much like the returning veterans—skeptical, burnt out, worn out, perpetually in a crisis of faith. These men were puzzled by the emergence of Christianity and disenchanted with the power of their nations. By the time of *Ben-Hur* (1959), the hero was not saved from his skepticism until the last reel. Also, in *Ben-Hur*, the villain is no longer a ruler, but rather the conspicuously atheistic ideology of Rome. Such themes represent a shift from the evil personality theory as the key to history.

In the 1950s, production values became preeminent. Movie screens were filled with expensive properties, extensively researched for accuracy. The epics demonstrated the studio's resources, which they believed television could never achieve.[1]

These major production values, however, were also dramatically useful in making ancient history seem contemporary. The sets and costumes transported audiences to a time strong in significance. Audiences knew these trappings from other movies, and because the attitudes conveyed are equally familiar, the era seemed much like our own time. The action, because the setting seemed vaguely contemporary, became a metaphor for contemporary America's struggle to define its role in the vast international arena.

The films often portray antitotalitarian sensibilities, reinforcing the audience's bias. When in addition the story is set in and around the period of Jesus and the early church—the films suggest that these stories, and their actions and attitudes, are based on universal truths.

The treatment of miracles raises the problem of interaction between a scientific world view and the Christian faith. Often the miracles are noticeable by their absence. For example, the Crucifixion, but not the Resurrection, is depicted in *The Robe*. The writers sensed that much in the claims of Christianity revolved around attitudes toward miracles, but they also recognized that mainline Protestants and Reform Jews had modified their thinking (and even their biblical research), trying to find some form of accommodation between dualistic and naturalistic metaphysics. Thus the trend was to include those miracles that could be expressed in terms of psychological attitudes and wishes.

This created problems for the endings. One of the staples of Hollywood theology was that, although the evil of Rome controlled this world, it could not retain control in perpetuity. Many martyrs to the faith found their fulfillment beyond this life. As the decade progressed, however, many Christians and Jews were having trouble reconciling life after death with a scientific world view, and others were demanding that their moral fantasies be fulfilled in this life. Thus, there is a curious mixture of martyrdom for some of the lesser characters along with wish-fulfillment for the major figures. The stories, though laden with historical associations, take on nonhistorical endings—lovers are united and living as Christians, while Rome apparently becomes benign in its persecution.

The growth in church membership during the 1950s is not reflected very strongly in the films. The image of the church suggests a reprise of the urban-rural conflict of the 1930s. The Christian community is always seen as righteous, a bit odd, sustaining strong values of honesty, integrity, courage, sexual continence, and familial loyalty. The Christian community in films acts as a foil to Rome and as a surrogate for American middle-class values. The church never appears as an established institution but always as an embattled community attempting to do what is right.

Beneath it all remains the major concern of power in an international community, power's moral uses, and what constitutes the righteous citizen in the righteous nation. In the continuing struggle between nations, there is a belief that a nation's pursuit of power may lead to moral weakness and its eventual downfall unless it has the proper values. Americans, who had revered both national strength and national morality, found in the struggles that swept across the giant screens sublimated metaphors for those questions.

The Sign of the Cross presented its audiences with the bestialities of the arena, and when it was rereleased just after World War II, with Paramount tacking on an opening shot of a bomber flying over the Eternal City and a comment linking ancient Rome with the fascists, Americans once again flocked to see it. It signaled that there was still money to be made from the spectacular. The arena scenes did not seem so far removed from Ilsa Koch's lamp shades made of human skin or the latest installment of the *Reader's Digest* "Lest We Forget" series, detailing the sexual atrocities of the Japanese.

When DeMille decided to make *Samson and Delilah*, a ready-made audience seemed assured, but Paramount was not excited about the prospect. In 1945, the federal government started an antitrust action that eventually forced studios to divest themselves of their theaters, making it impossible for their films to obtain automatic play dates. America had become an urban nation since the birth of the feature film, and films in the cities had to be assured of somewhat longer runs. Movies were no longer the only means of seeing and hearing dramatic presentations, because the radio networks had expanded into television, and Americans were buying TV sets in the burgeoning postwar economy.

So DeMille was greeted with less than enthusiasm when he unveiled a project that he had been researching since 1936.

A biblical story, for the post–World War II generation? Put millions of dollars into a Sunday School tale? Anticipating this familiar chorus . . . I asked Dan Groesbeck to draw a simple sketch of two people—a big brawny athlete and, looking at him with an at once seductive and cooly measuring eye, a slim and ravishing attractive young girl.[2]

DeMille noted that the executives saw the sketch as "boy meets girl—and what a boy, and girl!" He then announced that his project was *Samson and Delilah*, to which they responded, "Oh, if *that's* what you mean . . . You see, we thought . . . But that's different . . . That's okay."

Sex, violence, and religion in one lavish package! When *Samson and Delilah* topped the box office charts, *Quo Vadis* became a logical remake. It had been made five times, but never in sound. The novel had won a Nobel Prize, and it had all the ingredients for a spectacular. MGM, the richest and most famous studio, had the funds to embark on such a venture. Moreover, the time was propitious. In response to its enforced divestiture of theaters, MGM had made both wage cutbacks and layoffs in 1949, and was ridding itself of the expensive star system, which cost more than exclusive rights were worth. Both psychologically and economically, the studio was in need of a production in the "grand style" that would win the market back to the theaters.

After the war, there was a return to religion. There was far more commonality than difference among the major faiths. By 1955 Will Herberg was saying that American religion was more secularist than religious, but it was a "secularism of a religious people."[3] This blend of secularism within religion is a key feature of the religious spectaculars of the 1950s.

The studio publication "The Story Behind *Quo Vadis*" describes Marcus Vinicius as "a type of the pagan supremacy so soon to be confronted by a Gospel of love and pity—and destined to be overthrown by that gospel at last."[4] Having made Lygia his slave, only to have her escape, Marcus meets the Christians at Rome, who include "people of all classes who have gladly embraced the gospel of peace and good will toward men." Lygia returns his love, but when he learns that she intends to remain a Christian, he rushes off to the lascivious empress, Poppaea.

Nero burns Rome to the ground as an inspiration for his songs and blames the Christians. In the arena, Ursus, Lygia's protector, kills a wild bull with his bare hands. The Legion revolts; in the end Marcus and Lygia are together, while Nero and Poppaea die. The studio release completes the story with: "A great new light is breaking on the world. A new era is being born."[5]

Without significant alterations, Marcus Vinicius could become DeMille's Marcus Superbus, Lygia could become Mercia, and the plot line would only need their death to become an update of *Sign of the Cross*. The formula remains, but the nuances are significantly changed.

The story is about the struggle for Marcus' soul. Director Mervyn LeRoy and scriptwriters John Lee Mahin, S. N. Behrman, and Sonya Levien were not nearly so interested in sex as DeMille, and nothing approaches Ancaria's "Dance of the Naked Moon." Marcus Superbus dies without adopting the Christian faith. Marcus Vinicius adopts the Christian faith without dying. At the crucial moment, when Ursus is grappling with the bull, a giant closeup of Marcus intrudes and he prays, "Christ, give him strength," at which point Ursus snaps the neck of the bull.

Few moviegoers noticed or cared that LeRoy had taken great liberties with the historical record—that in fact the persecution of the Christians, the burning of Rome, and the deaths of Nero and Poppaea did not all happen in the same week. Nero lived to rebuild the city again and remarry before he committed suicide.

The struggle for Marcus' soul is a well-developed theme. When Marcus is first stationed at Plautus' home, the apostle Paul visits and tells Lygia, "Those two fine vital men [referring to Marcus and his lieutenant, Nerva], they *are* Rome. If we could teach them, we could teach the world."

Paul's advice leads Lygia to discuss religion with Marcus. He wants to unite the world under one power, but she talks of a gentler way. She tells him that Paul envisions a world where there would be no slaves to which he replies, "That beggar-faced philosopher shouldn't be stuffing your luscious little head with such nonsense."

From the film's opening image—chained men wending their path down the Appian Way—slavery characterizes Rome. That a beautiful patrician woman who happens to be a slave could be a pacifist seems incredible to Marcus. He assumes that a single power must rule, and that war brings peace. While we are invited to accept Lygia's version of a "gentler and more powerful way," in fact, the situation resembled that of the United States, which had just fought a war for "freedom." The idea that a totalitarian power must rule the world was a code for the Nazi's eschatological Third Reich.

Later, Marcus follows Lygia to her secret meeting place, where they hear Peter.[6] Nowhere in the spectaculars considered does one find a more comprehensive statement of the popular theology that underlies these films than in Peter's speech. In its length and revisions, American values and theological concepts are blended so that it speaks the commonly accepted values of the culture.

Peter's sermon transcends sectarian lines, because it depends more on biblical story and American ideology than on Christian doctrine. After declaring himself the rock on which Jesus was to build his church, he launches into a list of values widely held among both religious and secular people, using biblical phrases for naturalistic claims—that Jesus fights against poverty, gives hope and peace, and overcomes the pain of death.

After more of his own story—his betrayal of Jesus, the Crucifixion, and the Resurrection—he repeats the Beatitudes, then gathers several passages from various books of the Bible, and interprets them so as to provide a contrast with the Roman style:

Jesus asks us to obey the commandments which God gave to the prophet Moses. Obey those who govern you and the laws by which they govern. Even though, under them, you suffer cruelties and witness maliciousness beyond your mind's dimension, make no threat of violence in return. For so it is with the will of God— that with well-doing and noble thought you may raise a mounting wave that will silence the ignoble acts of foolish men.

Peter concludes by warning them to stand fast in the faith in their coming days of trial and repeating the "love your enemies" passage from the Sermon on the Mount.

The Romans are offended by Christian ideology. The new religion is more the fantasy of American's hearts than the actions of their lives. It was not love that won World War II, but the American industrial capacity and its soldiers. Marcus' response is in fact much more descriptive of the way Americans practice their values: "I heard a childish old man speak in riddles." Lygia urges him to hope and pray that the "image of Christ will appear in your heart"—something that happens when she is helpless in the arena, but Marcus is not impervious to the dangers of this new consciousness. He wonders if she wants him to love "all the rest who want to put a blade through my ribs." He calls her God "a whining beggar," one for slaves, aliens, and outcasts. He recognizes the message's threat to Roman law and pledges himself to Rome. The dual value systems remain the same as in *Sign of the Cross*—cruelty versus charity, the power of the state versus the power of faith.

The idealism echoed postwar America. In a nation that had been through World War II and was engaged in a cold war in Europe and a "police action" in Korea, with weapons of destruction so awesome as to call up visions of apocalyptic horror, the listing of Parthians, Egyptians, and Persians invoked images of NATO, the United Nations, and the Marshall Plan, which most Americans trusted and used to exemplify the difference between Western and Eastern Europe. The blockade of Berlin by the Soviets was proof that America was pursuing the right course, and the idea of loving the "whole human race" did not strike people as absurdly as it did Marcus.

Having destroyed the Axis war machine, Americans believed that their success was the result of divine approval of American goals and values. The conversion of Marcus signifies the possibility of evangelizing the former enemies—a secular popularization of the general American belief in universal salvation, and certainly in line with what had happened in Germany and Japan. Exempted, of course, from this universal salvation are the unrepentant, such as Nero and Poppaea.

Nero intrigued the critics. He peers through a red glass and is constantly surrounded by sycophants, including the intellectual Petronius, whose attitude toward him is coolly ironic. When we first meet Nero, Marcus salutes him as he might Hitler. During the triumphal march into the city, amid the shots of opulence and a spectacular crane shot of the court of the Vestal Virgins, a laurel bearer keeps repeating into Nero's ear, "Remember that thou art only a man."

When Nero first sees Lygia, he is about to claim her himself, but Petronius saves her by saying, "She is too narrow in the hips." Nero, afraid of being scorned by the intellectual, repeats that judgment as his own. Having established that Nero is weak, the film establishes that he is also insane. The burning of Rome is seen from the balcony of Nero's palace, where he shows Petronius his model of Neropolis, which "will spring from the loins of the fire." He worries about writing a song to compare with the sacking of Troy. Crosscut with these scenes are shots of the populace hysterically trying to escape the fire.

Nero's last scenes emphasize both his cruelty and his madness. When he kills Poppaea, he looks off into space with a glazed stare, and the camera shoots the scene in a low-angle oblique shot to emphasize both his power and his madness.

The comic treatment of Nero is preserved from *Sign of the Cross*, but there it was used to suggest the corruption of a system headed by a madman, whereas in *Quo Vadis* it seems more personal. The question of how a madman could rule a rational people was a far more realistic one after World War II than before. The sardonic humor, charm, and weakness present a complex and ambiguous character that audiences did not really know how to respond to. This uncertainty is apparent in the reviews.

The confused reaction is understandable when we look for prototypes among the former enemies. Mussolini obviously had been too much a pawn of the Nazis. Tojo was too oriental and opaque, whereas Joseph Stalin was too cold, logical, and deceptive. Stalin was still remembered sitting with Roosevelt and Churchill as an ally. If the character were to be credible to a mass audience, the only available model was Hitler, who was thought of as a madman, had incinerated the earth, had overreached himself for power by convincing himself that he belonged to "the Master Race," and whose actions were both horrifying and subtly intriguing. With American attitudes changing toward Germany as a result of the Marshall Plan, the cold war, and the passage of time, however, the Hitleresque Nero comes off as too mad for credibility and not attractive enough for his hold over the people to seem plausible.

In the end, the Romans overthrow Nero and thus are partially redeemed. The lines given to Marcus and Nerva at the end of the film apply as much to Germany as to Rome:

Marcus: Galba has a task ahead of him—to rebuild Rome, and bring back Roman justice.

Nerva: I fear the glory that was Rome is never fully to be reached again, Marcus.

Marcus: Babylon, Egypt, Greece, Rome . . . what follows?

Nerva: A more permanent world, I hope. Or a more permanent faith . . .

Marcus: One is not possible without the other.

By the end of the film, faith and national destiny are indissolubly linked.

In contrast to Nero, Petronius was the intellectual, the one who knew enough to feel guilty about what was happening, yet was still captive to the luxuries of Nero's court. His mind was pagan, and his temperament was ironic because he could see what was happening. He bears a resemblance to the American intellectual left, which would not give up its fascination with liberal social programs despite the cold war. Though he was witty and a pagan who had no faith in anything, he could see the consequences clearly. He was without courage, but not a coward. His final insults to Nero, when he strikes at Nero's detestably pedantic poetry, are an emotional high point of the film. His suicide redeems him, but in fact, he is helpless because he has no faith in or commitment to anything.

The spectacular religious films of the 1950s and 1960s discuss "freedom" in terms of "faith." Even the advertising and reviews refer to them. The studio said that it wanted to make a film that "would carry a message of beauty and inspiration to the people of the earth." It pairs love and faith, courage and terror, lust and luxury, tyranny and freedom.[7]

The link between tyranny and freedom is made in the opening narration:

Imperial Rome was then master of the world. Her conquests radiated to Greece, Spain, Africa, Asia Minor, Germany, France and Britain . . . With power came corruption—corruption unsurpassed. No man was sure of his life. The individual was at the mercy of the states. . . . High and low alike became Roman slaves, Roman hostages. There seemed no escape from the whip and the sword. That any force on earth could shake the foundations of this pyramid of power and corruption, of human slavery, seemed inconceivable.

At this point, the screen, which had been filled with the Roman standard, now shows the cross Christ is carrying. The narration continues:

On a Roman cross in Judea, a man died to make men free—to spread the gospel of love and redemption, and bring new hope. Thirty years later, the anti-Christ, known to history as the Emperor Nero, undertook to crush this hope. This is the story of that immortal conflict.

The key phrase was "the individual was at the mercy of the state." Americans organized their values around individualism. They had elevated free speech to near-sacred status. Not being able to speak one's opinion was conceived to be the chief fault of totalitarian societies.

Ten years of war and cold war, however, had substantially eroded popular support for free speech. The recision of Japanese Americans' civil rights in 1942 was a wedge, but Joseph McCarthy, following President Truman's lead, led the nation through a period of abridgement of the rights of free speech. For Truman, the world was divided into two parts, "the free world" and "behind the Iron Curtain." Truman expected that "history will remember my term in office as the years when the Cold War began to overshadow our lives . . . the conflict between those who love freedom and those who would lead the world back into slavery and darkness."[8] Such definitions form symbolic links with all struggles for freedom. In *Quo Vadis* and its successors, the invisible world of the Christians ("the free world") and the "captive nations" are pitted against totalitarian Rome.

Such values were lost neither on the makers nor the viewers. The American Jewish Committee said, "Unless we have faith in our ideals, such a possible death will be an animal snuffing out such as suffered by the populace during the burning of Rome."[9]

"Faith in our ideals" is the answer. There is an assumption that religious faith and national ideals are the same, connected by "freedom." Yet the word meant different things to different segments of the political spectrum. As a code word for American values, however, it had remarkable unifying power.

The Southern California Motion Picture Council extolled the virtues of this freedom: "Never has the hope of eternal life been so impressively shown as in the manner in which these early Christians meet death."[10] Thus freedom is linked with faith, and freedom acquires supernatural approval, especially when people are willing to give their lives for it. The nation that defends "freedom" is sacred, and its people are the chosen of God. Whatever the merits of the film, the struggle between "one nation under God" and the "godless materialists" suggests how important the ultimate victory of the faithful was to American audiences.

Newspapers in major cities reviewed *The Robe* on their front pages when it appeared. Virtually every review started not with *The Robe* but with CinemaScope. For weeks the ad campaigns had been trumpeting "a revolutionary new process," and below the title the ads said: "in the modern miracle of CinemaScope."

The process started as a reaction to television. Weekly theater attendance had dropped more than one-third, profits were down more than 20 percent in the industry. In September, 1952, *This is Cinerama* opened in New York. The Cinerama process utilized a curved screen and three projectors. A month later, *Bwana Devil* opened; this three-dimensional movie was photographed through stereoscopic lenses and required polarized glasses for viewing.[11]

Twentieth Century Fox went to a third method of projection—the anamorphic lens, developed by Henri Chretien for use in tanks during World War I. It squeezed the image onto a 35-mm frame, and then, with the use of another lens, projected it onto a wide screen. The screen-size ratio, which had remained at 4:3 for nearly 60 years, was almost doubled to 2.55:1 in the CinemaScope screen. It required only a single projector, an adapter lens, and a new wider curved screen, and that made it attractive to theater owners. To assure its continuing use, Fox announced that it would make all subsequent films in the process.

The choice of *The Robe* as the first production to be filmed in CinemaScope was important to its success. *Cinerama* had no story, and *Bwana Devil* had a trivial one, yet both fared well at the box office. The film rights to *The Robe* had been bought in 1942 before the novel had been completed, yet the film had never been made. *Variety* opined that the size of the image was about to force a new set of aesthetic choices on film makers, and that epics rather than small *boudoir* comedies would fit the large screen best with CinemaScope's large realistic values and stereophonic sound.[12] In virtually every review, some attempt was made to assess the relationship between the film and the process in order to predict CinemaScope's future.

With the success of the biblical spectaculars and earlier religious spectaculars, Hollywood producers reached out for stories of a spectacular size; religious themes were perfect for that purpose. The *New York Times Magazine* rhapsodized that "in addition to spiritual strength, the Bible offers many stirring narratives—of clashes of battle, of epic human conflicts and rivalries, of sacrificial and profane love—all eminently suited to the movie medium."[13] *Harpers* pointed out that *The Robe*, as a popular novel using biblical history, would have been a major production at any studio. "What CinemaScope gives it is a newly experimental vigor, as though the film industry were back in a this-is-how-it's-going-to-be-folks frame of mind."[14]

Philip Dunne—who wrote *David and Bathsheba*, the film that bailed out Darryl F. Zanuck's weakening position at Fox in 1951—was given a script by Gina Kaus to adapt. Although the film program says that Dunne's "only regret is that Lloyd C. Douglas did not live to see the film version," Dunne believed that it was a job that he did not "love enough," partly because Lloyd Douglas was "rather simple-minded."[15]

The Robe dealt more with the problems of religion in the modern world than any previous spectacular. Whereas the others seemed to be metaphors for national and international concerns, with making American life and values sacred, *The Robe* centered on the question of conversion and faith, and the difficulties imposed by the choices.

The story follows the dissolute Marcellus Gallio, who wins Christ's robe and becomes "possessed." He is sent back to Jerusalem to find the enchanted robe, joins the Christians, returns to Rome, and eventually confronts the emperor Caligula.

The political metaphors in the film are plain, but the character of Caligula is even more confused than that of Nero in *Quo Vadis*—he has none of Nero's charm.[16] Caligula represents enormous power in the hands of a madman, but the plausibility of a mad emperor was no longer easily established in the public mind. The secondary figure of Tiberius mitigates the villainy of the state. Tiberius has abdicated from everyday politics, but is a wise and crafty observer of human nature, and realizes that Caligula is unfit to rule.

The political themes are brushed in with the broadest strokes. Marcellus, on trial for his life before Caligula, says:

If the Empire desires peace and brotherhood among all men, my King will be on the side of Rome and her Emperor. But if the Empire and Emperor wish to pursue the course of aggression and slavery that have brought agony and terror and despair to the world—if there's nothing for men to hope for but chains and hunger—then my King will march forward to right these wrongs. Not tomorrow, sire. Your majesty may not be so fortunate as to witness the establishment of His kingdom, but it will come.

Although that may seem preachy today, *The Hollywood Reporter* thought that in "a divided world struggling for salvation, for something in which to believe, the vocabulary of faith . . . is as fresh and pertinent today as it was when it was first espoused."[17]

With both East and West having atomic capability, with the Americans and Chinese still negotiating at Panmunjom over the fate of Korea, it would be odd if such themes did not insinuate themselves into the period's formulas. Moreover, the "something in which to believe" would naturally be American values.

Although the salvation of Marcus Vinicius had nationalistic significance, and DeMille's heroes come to salvation through love and suffering, the formula is given a new twist in *The Robe*—first Marcellus is converted, and then his loved one. Before he can bring her around to his faith, he must go through a long and searching journey to find it.

Philip Dunne seems to have more influence on the finished film than director Henry Koster, and he is not charitable about the finished product. Zanuck had to convince him to "put the script into English" from the "imitation DeMille." The problem was to avoid the religious cliches and "obvious religiosity." Dunne thought that the moment Jesus appeared on the screen "everyone is stunned and overwhelmed," but Dunne explains that he "took Jesus, as he took himself, as a man."[18]

The structural change in the script, Dunne says, was to delay the conversion of Marcellus, who in the novel and in earlier scripts had become a Christian "almost immediately after the crucifixion." This timing suggested that the garment had magical qualities, and Dunne emphasizes that he wanted to avoid the use of miraculous occurrences in the film. He cites dramatic reasons for that decision, but the tortured quest for faith is also found in his scripts for *Stanley and Livingstone*, *David and Bathsheba*, and *Demetrius and the Gladiators*.

What bothered Dunne was that the novel examined religion simple-mindedly and too directly. He wanted an oblique look. Thus he made Marcellus a cynical playboy with a sense of justice instead of the hardened, battle-weary soldier of earlier spectaculars. In the opening sequence in a Roman square, Marcellus' sarcastic voice narrates his doubts about Roman culture:

Some say we are only masters, that we create nothing. But we have made gods, in our own image of course, for what god could be nobler than a Roman?

Fine gods—and goddesses—who make love—and war—huntresses—and drunkards. We don't thank them for our good fortune, for the power lies not in hands of marble, but in ours of flesh . . . Could any god offer us more?

The answer is the dramatic emphasis of the film—what more the Christian God has to offer.

Demetrius, having seen Christ on Palm Sunday, announces that "He wants me to follow Him." Stopped by a man in the streets, Demetrius is told that Pilate has ordered the arrest of Jesus. When asked why, the man replies, "Because men are weak. Because they are cursed with envy and cowardice. Because they dream of truth but cannot live with it. So they doubt. . . . Why must men betray themselves with doubt? Tell them to keep their faith . . . They must keep faith." The man is Judas.

There was some criticism of the scene because of its melodramatic force, but it is consistent with the religious theme. Marcellus, having no faith in anything, gives himself to pleasure. Judas is a sign of the cost of being "faith-less." Doubt leads Marcellus to salvation, but one must doubt pleasure and self-indulgence if one is to be saved. Judas doubts the wrong things.

With the Crucifixion, the theme of guilt emerges, having been set up in Marcellus' cynicism and his giving Paulus 30 pieces of silver to find out where the "elusive trouble-maker" is. Demetrius asks Marcellus to intercede for Jesus. At Golgotha, Marcellus leans on the cross and finds his hands bloodied. As he raises his eyes, Jesus' voice says, "Father, forgive them—they know not what they do." When the storm hits Golgotha, and he tells Demetrius to put the robe around him, it is as if he is possessed by demons. Demetrius angrily announces that he is claiming his own freedom, curses the Roman Empire, and runs off with the robe.

On the galley returning to Capri, Marcellus awakes from nightmares of a hazy Christ and a pounding hammer, and screams, "Were you out there?" a reference to a popular Christian hymn, "Were You There When They Crucified My Lord?" whose refrain—"O-o-o-oh, sometimes it causes me to tremble"—describes what is happening to Marcellus. It is, however, also a clue to his eventual conversion.

On Capri, Tiberius hears Marcellus' story and lets him believe that the robe is bewitched. He commissions Marcellus to find out about the new cult and to retrieve the robe, but notes, "When it comes, this is how it will start—some obscure martyr in some forgotten province. Then madness, infecting the Legions, rotting the empire, then the finish of Rome." Tiberius calls it the greatest madness of them all, "man's desire to be free," noting that Marcellus is the most effective physician he could have sent, a madman.

In a series of sequences where Christian virtues are portrayed, Marcellus goes to a village as a spy buying homespun, but Justus makes the townspeople pay back the money he has overpaid. He hears how Jonathan's crippled foot was healed, and when he gives the boy his donkey, Jonathan gives it to a crippled child. Hearing a paraplegic woman singing, he asks why Jesus did not heal her.

Miriam: He could have healed my body—and then it would have been natural for me to laugh and sing. And then I understood that he had something even better for me . . . He had left me as I am, so that all the others like me might know that their misfortune wouldn't deprive them of the happiness of his kingdom.

Marcellus tells her it is irrational to believe that way. When she laments that Marcellus never met Jesus, he tells her that he did indeed. Noticing his troubled expression, she says: "Sometimes it's a comfort to learn that others too have felt confused and lost and have found their way. The way is never easy, but it's a path good men must take." Marcellus, who had told Miriam earlier that "power is all that counts," is disturbed.

Dunne wanted no miracles in his script. He wanted rational explanations that would not offend adherents of other faiths. He intended to give "an oblique view from one of His potential enemies instead of a head-on view of people convinced of His divinity."[19] Dunne portrays nothing that transcends either science or psychology.

Marcellus is transformed by his confrontation with the Christian community. When the Roman detachment kills Justus, he switches his allegiance. The night before Demetrius refuses to burn the robe, but neither can Marcellus. Demetrius tells him that the spell is "in you," and at the depths of his despair and anger Marcellus is healed.

Having made the journey through guilt to healing to allegiance, Marcellus is urged to enlist in the Christian legion. When he confesses to Peter that he is the one who killed Christ, Peter relates his own denial and tells of his sense of forgiveness. The "potential enemy of Christ" pledges his sword, his fortune, his life, and his honor as a Roman to the service of Christ.

Beneath the obvious story, the film presents what is probably the most positive image of the church in any of the spectaculars. Justus tells Marcellus that "the new ideas he espouses have a way of growing—like children." Marcellus is converted by the Christian community, rather than to a specific ideology. In earlier spectaculars, the protagonist is converted by his love for a Christian woman, but in *The Robe*, he is converted because he has found something worthy of emulation. In the end, he enlists in the evangelical mission of the church—to spread the gospel to Rome, the crossroads of the earth.

His most notable convert is Tiberius' ward, Diana. She is confused by Marcellus' new religion. To Marcellus' plea for her to have faith, she answers:

Faith in what? In this new god of yours? How can he help you? He couldn't save his own son. They crucified him and they'll kill you too. . . . Does this dream of yours mean more to you than our love? Marcellus, what you have told me is a beautiful story, but it just isn't true. Justice and charity—men will not accept such a philosophy. The world isn't like that. It never has been and it never will be.

Although Dunne explicitly abhorred the idea of using miracles for conversions, it is through a miracle that Diana changes her very modern and pragmatic mind. When Demetrius is dying in the Gallio household and Peter comes, the door is shut, and the scene cuts to Marcellus outside praying for Demetrius. The script and film seem to suggest that there is a limit to science, a popular notion that lies behind much of public acceptance of faith-healing in films. The "miracle" thus is acceptable as an expression of the power of faith over the power of nature.

Diana is converted by the miracle. In the last scene, Diana chooses to join Marcellus in death, telling Caligula, "I have no wish to live another hour in an Empire ruled by you. . . . That *you* should be Caesar! Vicious—treacherous—drunk with power—an evil, insane monster posing as Emperor. As for me, I have found another king. I want to go with my husband—into His kingdom."

For all Dunne's efforts to keep the story on a naturalistic plane, the film undercuts itself with its last shot. Marcellus and Diana walk proudly to the Field of the Archers to be executed, leaving behind them the court, handing the Christian slave Marcipor the robe to be delivered to Peter. Amid a rising chorus of alleluias, the world dissolves, and they walk into blue skies and fleecy clouds. Life is not fulfilled in this world, but in a supernatural afterlife.

Most of the newspaper reviews saw "immense themes of faith, love and sacrifice . . . blended amid the depictions of the pomp and pageantry of Rome."[20] The forces remain in contention—Rome and Jerusalem are still natural enemies. In *The Robe*, however, Rome is not nearly so evil a place as DeMille or LeRoy had depicted. It is a place where "faith, love, and sacrifice" are possible, and the redemption of the land is feasible.

Part of this difference in interpretation might be attributed once again to Dunne, who more overtly identified Rome with America than did earlier spectaculars. He said, "Romans were people very much like us and faced, as historians are fond of pointing out, some of the problems that Americans face in the modern world,"[21] mainly that of being the custodian of world order.

Thus, although the film attempted to portray Marcellus' conversion and his effect on those around him, it also dealt with themes of national consciousness. Faith and citizenship are placed in opposition. Although affirming that faithful citizenship is possible, it displays an uneasy relationship between the complexities of urban Rome and the simplicity of small-town Palestine, where Marcellus is converted. The tension between urban and rural life discussed earlier remains even into the 1950s.

Despite an intelligent script and a treatment that is less than sensational, the film is defeated by CinemaScope. The properties of that new technique had to be displayed. *Time*'s reviewer asked, "Can CinemaScope be used for anything except ponderous spectacles and chorus lines?"[22]

The medium was big enough for a large theme, but the CinemaScope screen required movement and passion to fill it. The serious discussion of faith in the modern world was lost in the overall effect. Stereotypical characters fare better here, for the story is in the action, not in the mental struggle.

The film expressed many of the doubts that were later to strike so fiercely in secular thought. The dualistic world view, that there was both a world of physical happenings and another equally real spiritual world, was being questioned. Dunne had perceived it in his treatment of the miracles, but that discussion was largely restricted to the intellectual community and had not yet struck with the forcefulness that would cause many Americans to revise the way they thought about their religion. It had already caused major revisions in Reform Judaism and the Unitarian and Universalist denominations. However, in an age when there were doubts about the nation's righteousness, when Senator Joseph McCarthy was pointing out that many Americans were disloyal, when the United States was stalemated in a war for the first time since the War of 1812—for the audiences of such an era, Diana's conversion was comforting because it rejected participation in an evil system.

Faith had become an object—something to "have." Martin Marty described it as a "revival of faith in faith," in which "no particular deity is a deity, and the worship accorded such a deity is also religion."[23]

In *The Robe*, the triumphant victor is the sense that things will ultimately turn out all right. Providence had become an assurance that even if this world is in the hands of a Caligula, and even if eventually one comes up against Roman authority, those who hold on to their integrity, who abstain from seeking power and pleasure, will be triumphant. The only way to live with integrity is to believe and act—and die, if necessary—for something larger than ourselves, for a new consciousness that has justice and charity as its operating principles. In an America that had accepted a theory of containment against the evil forces of Communism, *The Robe* assured rational men and women of their ultimate victory, though the temporal world be in a stalemate.

Demetrius and the Gladiators was in production even before *The Robe*'s premiere, the studio labeling it as the story of "Christianity's first backslider . . . [who] becomes disillusioned with the inheritance of the meek and gives himself to excesses."[24] Most reviewers regarded it as inferior to its predecessor, but Philip Dunne, who wrote both, liked it better.

Dunne was interested in "doing the reverse half of *The Robe* story."[25] The film picks up as *The Robe* ends, and is set into motion by Caligula's attempt to understand why Marcellus and Diana were not afraid to die.

Dunne wondered what might happen if a Christian refused to fight. He says: "Early Christians were opposed to killing—Christians today not only kill but call down the blessings of the Lord on those who do."[26] He wanted to demonstrate other ways to prove one's courage.

Demetrius falls from grace when he is faced with "an event that really shakes his faith." The rape of Lucia reminds him of the cry from the cross, and the deaths of Marcellus and Diana. His intercessory prayer in the cell is an expression of the age-old Jueo-Christian problem of theodicy: "If you *are* God, help her," he cries. Since Lucia has supposedly been murdered, Demetrius concludes that there is no God, and gives himself over to revenge and lust.

In an earlier conversation, Claudius asks him about his belief in eternal life. Demetrius replies that he does not expect to live forever in this world, but Claudius is skeptical. Demetrius says this world is a better place because Jesus lived in it, to which Claudius notes the emperor would disagree because the Christians cause him trouble. Demetrius asks if they steal, lie, fight, or are drunkards. Claudius replies that if they did, they would not be noticed.

Americans have always equated religion with morality, which has become imbedded in the culture.[27] Little of the religion in American movies deals with agonizing over the limits of life or with philosophical speculations, as in the films of Ingmar Bergman or Robert Bresson. Religion in American movies usually deals instead with sustaining a moral commitment. Thus, when the question of evil arises, the rebellion takes the form of a reversal of morality. When Demetrius resists the seduction of Messalina, he cites the Ten Commandments. Messalina shifts the moral principle from duty to pleasure. "A commandment for everything . . . don't look, don't touch, don't fight, don't breathe, don't live . . . don't listen to the heart . . . the blood. Is there nothing human in your religion?" The dichotomy between flesh/pleasure and spirit/duty remains central as in earlier films. When Peter confronts her, Messalina tells him that Demetrius will always choose her because she can give him the world. When Peter asks Demetrius to turn from his dissolute life, however, he bases it on a change of consciousness:

Peter: Anything that was base, Jesus could make noble . . . he found the leper and made him clean . . . he found death and made life . . . he found you a slave and made you free . . . Now you've won a great victory over him, haven't you, Tribune? You've made yourself a slave again.

Demetrius, having faced evil and not having received a miracle, gives himself over to murder and lust, but becomes a slave to the flesh. Peter's belief in the miracle of the Resurrection bothers Demetrius because of his residual guilt. Facing Peter and angrily recounting his loss of faith in "this God who turned His face from me when I begged Him to save an innocent girl," he is disturbed when Peter tells him: "You talk as if you still believe in Him."

Lucia has the robe, and Demetrius must take it from her. Peter tells Demetrius that in her catatonic state she finds comfort in it. He asks if her sacrifice was of no avail, because "the man she worshipped now reviles and ridicules God?" Her cure is psychological, as is her injury. There is nothing here to contradict psychology or medicine. In the meantime, Demetrius has killed all her violators. Both emotional poles—revenge and repentance—are thus achieved.

The serious question of believing in God's existence is avoided by Lucia's restoration with the explanation that Demetrius did not know she had survived. Messalina and Claudius's reformation is not only historically suspect, but as a parallel to Demetrius' experience, suggests that there is really nothing to be learned from conversion.

The Messalina story poisoned the story of faith. The Christian press, which had so enthusiastically hailed *The Robe*, was less enthusiastic about *Demetrius*. They believed that the violence and sexuality were "seized on as a means of giving a piously righteous veneer to screen materials of proven popularity but extremely low edification content?"[28] The religious response had far less to do with the question of the plausibility of belief in God than with morality. In scene after scene, the film deals with doubt—that of Glycon, Messalina's fear that Christians' beliefs are true, Caligula's attempt to understand death, Claudius' careful questioning—but reviewers seemed not to notice.

The Christian community does not play a very large part in the film. In an urban setting, the Christians are persecuted, and they hold the same values of family and honesty that were present in the depression era spectaculars. There is, however, no effective counterpart in the Christian community, as in *The Robe*. From *Demetrius* on, the religious community looks more like American culture than like a body of people to be emulated for their religious values.

Demetrius was the first American spectacular to raise seriously the question of doubt. Perhaps the reason for the inclusion of this theme is to be found in a symbolic attachment to national concerns. Metaphors for the nation are conspicuous by their absence. The mad Caligula does not touch any of the archetypes. Messalina is a tepid vamp.[29]

If there is a reference to the nation, it can perhaps be found in Claudius. He is a gentle, subservient pagan, not given to the bestiality of the arena. At one point, Messalina finds him picking up the pieces of a broken figurine and says:

Messalina: Why don't you send for a slave to do that? Or do you feel more comfortable on your knees?

Claudius: With a tyrant, it's better to live on one's knees than to stand erect—and die.

The words are reminiscent of the "better dead than Red" debate, which raised questions about the place of national pride in a world where both the United States *and* the Soviet Union had nuclear weapons. Generally, however, the character of Claudius stands between the mad emperor figure of previous spectaculars and the powerful rational figures of subsequent spectaculars.

The nation, having ended the Korean War without the use of nuclear weapons, was returning to normality, and this may account for some of the interest in the film. A different feeling suggested that the danger of World War III was receding. President Eisenhower expressed this attitude when he said: "We have arrived at the point . . . [where] there is just no real alternative to peace."[30]

The "sacred nation," with its divine-mission motif, made less sense, and it left room for personal doubt. With the loss of exclusive possession of the bomb, Americans did not feel as blessed as they had and, moreover, found that owning the bomb did not make it possible to win all wars just by threats. Instead of a victory, a war had been liquidated; the lofty righteousness of our cause was not confirmed by an unconditional surrender. People were demobilizing and turning their attention back to domestic society and more personal concerns. In such an environment, there seemed room for a film in which "the test of Christian faith is told not in terms of multitude, but more in the restricted vein of one man's fight against temptation."[31]

With the exception of *The Egyptian* (1954), *Sign of the Pagan* (1955), *The Prodigal* (1955), and *The Ten Commandments* (1956), the spectaculars of the next few years were secular, but MGM, in financial trouble again, was anxious about the future. *Around the World in 80 Days* (1956), *Oklahoma* (1956), *South Pacific* (1958), and *War and Peace* (1956) all received spectacle treatment, though only *War and Peace* was shaped to fit the formula. Looking at its lagging profits, MGM decided to film a new version of its moneymaker of the silent era, *Ben-Hur*. The studio already owned the property, and they had Karl Tunberg's script in hand, its language reworked by S. N. Behrman and Maxwell Anderson. Sam Zimbalist, the producer, convinced William Wyler to make his first spectacular.

The spectacles were popular because they were the one thing studios could do that television could not match; as such, "they were the last grand flings of the studios."[32] Spectacle had originally attracted people to the motion picture from the stage,[33] and in the years since *The Robe*, many of the technical problems of the large screen had been solved. For television watchers, who had to put up with fuzzy definition, snowy pictures, and lack of color, *Ben-Hur* proved quite attractive. The movies had lost 53 percent of their weekly audience in seven years, and *Ben-Hur* offered the studios a chance to show people what they had missed. As Michael Wood noted, the epics were about money. Their excess was "conspicuous production." Their logic suggested that the big screen needed big events, such as the burning of Rome or Atlanta, as well as gigantic casts to go in giant sets, "and all this means ingenuity and authority and money quickly becomes the almost overt subject of these films."[34]

Nor should one underestimate the importance of religion as subject. By 1957, religion had developed a high visibility in the mass media. Billy Graham had appeared on the cover of *Time*, and his crusades had filled coliseums in London, New York, and Los Angeles. Fulton Sheen, the Catholic bishop, had a highly popular television show whose audience cut across denominational lines. Such religious films as *The Ten Commandments* and *A Man Called Peter* drew well at the box office.

Ben-Hur tells of Judah Ben Hur's attempt to restore his family after he had been sent to the galleys and his mother and sister were imprisoned, because he had refused to help his boyhood friend Messala put down Jewish resistance.

Christ is a reference point for the story. Wyler said that his intention was "not to show the face or his person at any time, but rather show the effect on other people." The influence of Christ is also in Esther's conversion, her comforting of the leprous mother and sister, in Judah's conversion, and in the miraculous healing of Tirzah and Miriam. When Judah considers revolution after being told that his mother and sister are dead, the influence of Christ suggests another alternative.

As in other religious spectaculars, the story concerns the salvation of the protagonist. Judah begins the story as a privileged Jew, gains character through his trials, finds his revenge empty, falls into despair, toys with the idea of becoming a revolutionary, and finally is converted to faith—a turning point that, it is suggested, *causes* his mother and sister to be healed.

The film consistently downplays sexuality in favor of violence. When Messala enters Jerusalem, the camera tracks him through a row of spears. When he and Judah meet, they throw javelins at a crossbeam in a scene that suggests that the two men are equally capable of committing violence; their toast is "Down *Eros*, Up Mars!" The scenes aboard the galley are particularly grisly, especially when the ship is rammed and men are virtually tearing the flesh off their legs to escape their irons.

At the same time, *eros* is played down. The love interest between Esther and Judah had little of the romantic interest usually found in spectaculars, both religious and biblical, and the idea that Judah would embrace Christianity for the love of a woman is inconceivable in the film's context. Yet this motivation had been a staple of almost all previous religious spectaculars.

The chariot race is the key scene in developing the theme of violence. Although the scene lasts only ten minutes on the screen, over 180 hours of film was exposed. The race becomes the classic clash between good and evil. Messala has a whip and a Greek chariot with saws on the hubs; he uses them effectively, crushing the Corinthian chariot. One after another, the chariots go out of the race, carrying their bloodied drivers with them.

At one point, after Messala has whipped Judah and his horses, Pontius Pilate says, "Messala brings no honor to Rome today." Messala forces Judah into two wrecked chariots, but Judah's team jumps over it. In the final duel, with everyone else out of the race, the hub of Messala's chariot breaks, and he is dragged under his own chariot through the arena.

Considering that he did not want to do the film and that he offered to do the chariot race without pay or credit, Wyler's reaction to the race is revealing. In a note dated nearly a year before the film was shot, he wrote that "the whole story goes out the window, just as it did with the galley-ship bit. What is happening that matters to Ben, other than he's going to drive a team of white horses? Who cares?"[35]

Wyler makes a good deal of sense out of it with the following scene, whose purpose is to offset the emotional satisfaction of good's triumph over evil. The good versus evil theme of the chariot race pulls the spectator into the action, but the melodrama is reversed in the next scene between Messala and Judah. Messala has the final revenge, mocking Judah:

Messala: Triumph complete—the race won, the enemy destroyed.

Judah: I see no enemy.

Messala: There is enough of a man still here for you to hate. They're not dead.

Judah (grabbing his body): Where are they?

Messala: Look for them in the Valley of the Lepers if you can recognize them. The race is not over.

In order for the film to move beyond the revenge motif of the chariot race to a Christian climax, it was important to have such an emotional scene.

Violence is also highlighted in the final scenes involving the Crucifixion and Judah's conversion. During the Crucifixion scene, Wyler cuts to a close-up of the nails being pounded into Jesus' hands; then the camera swings overhead as the cross is raised and settles in the hole dug for it. This horror converts Judah. The contradiction between the peace-loving man who was strong enough to give Judah a cup of water in defiance of a Roman soldier and the man now being put to a violent death by the state makes a peaceful man out of Judah.

Wyler also removed much of the film's suggestion that revolution was a viable alternative. In the version edited for television, this element has almost entirely disappeared. Originally, in the shooting script, Simonides tells Judah that failing to find his mother or sister, "If one principle fails, it is good enough to have another. And that principle could be the liberation of your people."[36] Wyler dropped the line. In another deleted scene, Judah tells Esther, "Every man of Judea is unclean and will stay unclean until we've scoured off our bodies the crust and filth of being at the mercy of tyranny. No other life is possible, except to wash this land clean."[37]

In the 1926 version, Judah went from the chariot race to "organize the Galilean soldiery in the larger Jewish national hope of seating the Messiah on a temporal throne."[38] In the 1959 version, Judah refuses Pilate's suggestion that he take Roman citizenship, telling Pilate that his mother and sister are lepers "by Rome's will." In another reference that might be construed to suggest revolutionary sentiment, Judah tells Messala early in the film, "Rome is an affront to God. Rome is strangling my people, my country, the whole earth, but not forever. And I tell you this, the day Rome falls there will be a shout of freedom such as the world never heard before." These references, however, are not strong enough to lend credence to revolution as a serious alternative to Christianity.

Wyler is clear that Rome is hated because of its tyrannical rule. In rejecting Pilate's offer of Roman citizenship, Judah tells him that Rome destroyed Messala "as surely as Rome has destroyed my family." Jew and Arab both cheer Judah's victory in the circus. In the scene where Sheik Ilderim comes to collect bets in the Roman baths, he is told that a Roman is worth four to one over any Arab or Jew—to which the sheik replies, "Very bravely spoken." Wyler, commenting on this scene, says: "The Jews and the Arabs were together, were allies and the Romans were the invaders, the aggressors."[39]

One problem of the film is its treatment of Rome. There is Messala, the friend turned enemy, and on the other hand, Arrius, the enemy turned friend. Some reviews found Messala unconvincing, because he was "an evil man whose villainy and lust for power were not clearly motivated." Bosley Crowther noted that "Ben-Hur [is] strong, aggressive, proud and warm—and his nemesis, Messala, has those same qualities inverted ideologically." In other reviews, Messala was variously described as a psychopath, one dedicated to the Roman, and "wrapped in the sophistries of patriotism."[40]

Even if one agrees that Messala's motivation for such a monstrous change is problematic, there is little doubt about the object of his commitment. When Sextus asks him how you control Jewish minds, Messala replies, "You asked how to deal with an idea. I'll tell you how: with another idea—with Rome."

For Messala, Rome is not an abstraction. "Fate chose us to civilize the world," he tells Judah. "Roman law, architecture, literature are the glory of the human race." For Messala, the world has no god, and "in an insane world, there is only one sanity—the loyalty of old friends." That world, then, is ruled by the power principle, and Messala seems to be drawing on Machiavelli when he says that the emperor (as Rome) is "the only god. He is power. Real power on earth. Not . . . (gestures at sky) not that!" Violence is the way in which power is exercised, and morality derives its norms from power. If Judah insists on a world in which morality is related to eternal principles, then he is the mortal enemy of those who work out of the power principle.

Arrius sounds suspiciously like a despairing atheistic existentialist. He tells Judah, who is chained to a galley oar, that his god has no more power than the images he prays to. "Religion is necessary as long as men fear death. . . . My gods will not help me. Your god will not help you." Later Arrius explains his atheism. "It is a strange stubborn faith you keep, to believe that existence has a purpose. A sane man would have learned to lose it, long before this." When Judah asks him what made him lose his faith, Arrius tells him, "It died with my wife and son."[41]

Arrius is redeemable because he is not seeking power; he wants an answer to the question of why the innocent suffer—the same problem that drove Demetrius away from the faith in *Demetrius and the Gladiators* and the same problem that Judah must face when he learns his mother and sister are lepers. Arrius has redeeming virtues because he is capable of love; Messala cannot love because of his monomaniacal drive for power.

Arrius and Messala represent the two sides of atheism. Messala dies as he has lived, filled with hate, but Rome, built on atheism, is not the den of evil portrayed in the earliest films. There is an ambiguity about it that makes the city more difficult to identify with any particular nation. Rather, it warns against any nation's pursuit of power.

One of the factors that persuaded Wyler to make the film was the story's political implications. He thought of the film in terms of the Egypt-Israeli 1956 war, which Eisenhower refused to support. He was attracted partly because *Ben-Hur* told the story of Jews fighting for their freedom. "What had changed in 2000 years? Instead of Romans, it was now Arabs, but the fight for a homeland hadn't changed."[42]

Others related it to different political events. Now in the hero's conversations with Messala, one can hear echoes of the horrible clash of interests in Nazi Germany. In the burgeoning hatred in Ben-Hur, one can sense the fierce passion for revenge that must have moved countless tormented people in Poland and Hungary. And in the humble example of Jesus . . . one can feel the general spiritual movement toward the brotherhood of man.[43]

Using concepts of "master race" and Nazism, Bosley Crowther looks back past the cold war to an earlier, more easily definable villainy. He is not, however, impervious to linking the World War II rhetoric to the Polish and Hungarian rebellions against Russian domination.

Others were more inclusive, noting that "there were two tyrannies in the immediate past, and one (Russia) still with us."[44] Judging from reactions to *Ben-Hur*, the themes of freedom and nonviolence were lauded, but the enemy no longer appeared clearly definable.

In the final version, Wyler's film tried to have both revenge and for-giveness. Judah's revenge proved the moral superiority of the oppressed. The chariot race is what the audiences remembered, not just because it is spectacular, but because it is so emotionally satisfying. The final confron-tation between Judah and Messala does not undercut the revenge motif sufficiently to give key emphasis to the Christian theme that concludes the picture.

The last hour of the film centers on the redemption of Judah from his revenge. Christopher Fry reworked the Crucifixion sequence at least four times, but Wyler was satisfied with none of the versions. He dropped a long theological dialogue between Balthazar and Judah. Wyler's puzzle-ment over how to end the film is expressed in this comment:

So in the end Ben-Hur and the chariot race—and his fight with Messala and his closeness to Pilate, and his position as a Roman citizen—none of these things involve him in the story of the Crucifixion. So what had it been all about? He's just another innocent bystander who happens to hear of OS [off screen] events and who talks about them.[45]

The film was to end with the voice of God saying, "These things I have spoken to you that in me ye may have peace. In the world ye shall have tribulation, but be of good cheer. I have overcome the world." Wyler's exasperation shows in his note: "What voice? WHOSE VOICE? Get cast-ing office to find 'Voice of God.' "

Wyler tried to resolve the problems visually. As the sequence begins, we see the blood of Christ dripping into pools formed by the rainstorm, running across the barren land. Judah goes home and tells Esther, "Almost the moment I heard him say 'Father, forgive them' I felt his voice take the sword out of my hand." His mother and Tirzah are seen in a long shot. They come to him, and Judah and the three women cry and touch each other's faces. The final image fades to three crosses silhouetted on a hill, as shepherds and sheep walk in front of Judah and the women, with the soundtrack rising into an alleluia.

The healing of the women is treated almost psychosomatically. After peace settles on Judah's face, the rain begins and the film cuts back to Tirzah, who declares that she is no longer afraid; at that point, she and Miriam are healed.

The healing is a miraculous occurrence in a film that scrupulously avoids such phenomena. Advanced cases of leprosy are not psychosomatic. The viewer is left with a single impression—that nature was disrupted and Judah was rewarded with his heart's desire for turning to Christ. That this inter-pretation offended the sensibilities of Fry and Wyler is suggested by the numerous rewritings of the sequence. The conception was dissatisfying, but it stemmed from the problem of the miracle's implausibility in a naturalistic setting.

The *Boston Globe*, in commenting on this sequence, said:

The shattering scenes when Christ is nailed to the cross are seen at a merciful distance, but they leave the audience shaken with emotion. There is a different reaction to the big chariot race—the big adventure thrill of *Ben-Hur*. Everyone knows that it is Ben-Hur who wins over the cruel Messala . . . *Ben-Hur* has a double appeal—that of faith and divine love on one side, and the action of a courageous man fighting adversity and tyranny on the other.[46]

Doubtless, most of the audience wanted the nonviolent, miraculous ending to succeed, but as the *Chicago Tribune* remarked, "The final scenes seem to drag."[47] It is the "courageous man of the chariot race" who came to symbolize *Ben-Hur*, decisively winning over "faith and divine love."

Ben-Hur was the largest, most expensive, and most seen of the religious spectaculars. It was also the last popular one. In 1954, two religious spectaculars—*The Silver Chalice* (1954) and *Sign of the Pagan* (1954)—did not do well at the box office. Neither had the feel of "the grand style," and *Sign of the Pagan* was further hampered by its historical setting of the Gothic invasion of Rome and by featuring Attila the Hun.

The failure of *The Silver Chalice* was somewhat more unexpected because the novel had been a bestseller. Five years later, *The Big Fisherman* (1959) would surprise its producers for the same reasons. Critics found both *Chalice* and *Fisherman* boring; Paul Newman was so distraught by his performance in *Chalice* that eventually he took out an advertisement apologizing for the film. *The Big Fisherman*, instead of filling the screen with action and having a clearly definable conflict between good and evil, grafted a revenge melodrama on to Peter's call to discipleship. The film lacked focus, and a clear villain was never established, weakening the melodramatic archetypal pattern.

Barabbas (1962) received good reviews but not large audiences. The film, written by Christopher Fry, interspersed its action with anguished philosophical questions about the meaning of existence. It also failed to undergird itself with a melodramatic archetype; Rome was too general to be an adequate villain.

The religious spectaculars that did draw mass audience response traded heavily on national moods. In the first half of the decade, Rome's villainy was to be found in its rulers and its decadent aristocracy. Caught between them and the persecuted Christian community was the protagonist, a man of action capable of existing on either side. Eventually, he sides with the Christian community because of its eternal values. Such films represented the hope of the future. The values of righteous people would triumph over the warlike tendencies of countries that, like Rome, valued pleasure and power.

Ben-Hur succeeds almost in spite of itself. It preserves the melodramatic archetype by its superbly produced chariot race; Messala's evil is reprehensible, and Ben-Hur's trials are so hopelessly difficult that the chariot race becomes the classic confrontation between good and evil. The last hour, however, becomes unfocused, and the relationship to Christ is tenuous. When Judah forswears violence, it is after his accounts have been settled. He is a difficult model to follow, and the providence that cleanses his mother and sister hardly seems like the providence that made him successful in the chariot race. Moreover, the "good Rome" is virtually indistinguishable from the "bad Rome," and the film both celebrates Judah's violence and forswears it. The film represents a great achievement not in its moral insight, but by showing the complexities of a great nation concerned with power and trying to sustain a moral framework of peace.

The secular spectaculars took over the nationalistic themes of the religious spectaculars in the next few years. Films such as *Fall of the Roman Empire* (1964) explored the possibility of a *Pax Romana* and the equality of all citizens under a single government. *El Cid* (1961) focused on the necessary qualities for moral leadership of the nation, whereas *Spartacus* (1960), in its slave rebellion, suggested that a nation could not have an outcast society without disruptive consequences.

After 1960, the shared sense of national purpose underwent radical changes. No spectacular attempted to make pluralism sacred. Since the blending of God, nation, and individual was central to the religious spectacular, when the sacred element was dropped, the films reverted to historical legitimation. Historical legitimation of the state's ideals is a secular enterprise, based not on conceptions of God's will, but rather on ideas of what composes human virtue. The providential agent in the melodramatic archetype passed from godly righteousness to "ideas whose time had come."

In the 1970s, the theme of the "righteous nation" became an examination and indictment of the "unrighteous" nation. In large-scale films, such as *Hawaii* and *The Sand Pebbles*, Americans were portrayed as abrasive and destructive elements in a foreign culture. There was little room left for the "grand style," and even the biblical spectaculars that had shakily survived the 1960s began to speak in a less assured voice.

NOTES

1. Michael Wood, *America in the Movies* (New York: Basic Books, 1965), p. 169.

2. DeMille, *Autobiography*, p. 399.

3. Will Herberg, *Protestant—Catholic—Jew* (New York: Anchor Books, 1955), p. 3.

4. Metro-Goldwyn-Mayer, "The Story Behind *Quo Vadis*" University of Southern California Film Library, Los Angeles, California (Unpublished).

5. Ibid., pp. 3–11.

6. It is significant that there was no serious outcry from Protestants, who did not believe that Peter had ever visited Rome. The *Protestant Motion Picture Council* gave it a backhanded review: "The whole of Christendom does not believe that Peter was ever in Rome. The novel is built upon this legend, so we are considering fiction with its romantic overtones and religious emphasis in its fanciful and historic frame." Quoted in *Unbiased Opinions*, December 8, 1951, p. 3.

7. MGM, "Story," p. 3.

8. Quoted in Peter Jones, *The USA: A History of Its People and Society Since 1865* (Homewood, Ill.: Dorsey Press, 1976), p. 668.

9. *Trade Show*, November 1, 1951; *Unbiased Opinions*, December 12, 1951, p. 3.

10. *Unbiased Opinions*, December 12, 1951, p. 3.

11. A good discussion of the search for perceptual depth is found in Kenneth MacGowan, *Behind the Screen* (New York: Delta Books, 1965), pp. 447–63.

12. *Variety*, September 22, 1953, p. 6.

13. *New York Times Magazine*, October 11, 1953, p. 32.

14. *Harper's* 207 (November, 1951): 92.

15. Philip Dunne, tapes on his film scripts, University of Southern California Film Library, Los Angeles, California.

16. He was variously described as "something out of Peter Ustinov and Charles Laughton in their most hyper-histrionic moments," and an "evil effeminate prince regent." *Variety*, September 22, 1953, p. 6.; *The Nation* 177 (November 17, 1935): 38.

17. *Hollywood Reporter*, September 7, 1953, p. 3.

18. Dunne, tapes.

19. Dunne, tapes.

20. *Atlanta Constitution*, October 1, 1953, p. 34.

21. Dunne, tapes.

22. *Time* 42 (September 28, 1953): 110.

23. Martin Marty, *The New Shape of American Religion* (NY: Harper & Bros., 1959), p. 31.

24. *New York Herald Tribune*, June 18, 1954, p. 4.

25. The film was made largely because of Fox's fear that it had invested too much in *The Robe*. Since the costumes and sets were readily available, using them would help recoup possible losses.

26. Dunne, tapes.

27. Robert Handy, *A Christian America: Protestant Hopes and Historical Reality* (New York: Oxford University Press, 1971), p. 22.

28. *America* 91 (June 26, 1954): 345.

29. "By implication, her less desirable traits of character are attributed to her being a crazy mixed up kid in a bad environment." Ibid.

30. Eric Goldman, *The Crucial Decade* (New York: Vintage Books, 1960), p. 262.

31. *Los Angeles Daily News*, June 17, 1954, p. 32.

32. Wood, *America in the Movies*, p. 169.

33. Farber, "Spectaculars 1967," p. 12.

34. Wood, *America in the Movies*, pp. 169–72.

35. Wyler's notes in alternate script. UCLA Theater Arts Library, Los Angeles, California.

36. Alternate script, *Ben Hur*.

37. Ibid.

38. *Ben-Hur* program (1926), no credits given. UCLA Theater Arts Library, Los Angeles, California.

39. Wyler interview, July, 1976.

40. Commonweal 71 (December 11, 1959): 321; *New York Times*, November 19, 1959, Sec. II, p. 50; *Dallas Morning News*, December 18, 1959, Sec. II, p. 10.

41. In some versions that played in theaters and on television, this has been excised.

42. Axel Madsen, *William Wyler* (New York: Thomas Crowell, 1973), p. 339.

43. *New York Times*, November 22, 1959, Sec. 4, p. 12.

44. *Dallas Morning News*, December 18, 1959, Sec. 2, p. 10.

45. Alternate script, *Ben-Hur*.

46. *Boston Globe*, November 29, 1959, p. 26.

47. *Chicago Tribune*, December 24, 1959, Sec. 2, p. 1.

4

The Biblical Spectacular: General Considerations

Religious spectaculars emphasize the "grand style," and reshape political, social, and cultural history to meet the needs of the screenplay. They portray two consciousnesses—one symbolizing American values (identified with religion), the other symbolizing an opposing value system that is passing away. In the end, the providence of God wins over the forces of evil, suggesting the victory of duty over power or pleasure.

Biblical spectaculars tend to be different. In the religious spectaculars, the central focus turns repeatedly to the struggle for the individual to become or stay righteous in an immoral society that holds the power. The biblical spectacular focuses on how ethical principles affect society. The problem of sexuality, for example, is the major interest in the 1950s films *Samson and Delilah, David and Bathsheba, Salome, Solomon and Sheba.* Here the emperor's duty clashes with the woman's sexuality to explore the tension between duty and pleasure.

The three Jesus films done in a spectacular mode—*King of Kings* (1961), *The Greatest Story Ever Told,* and *Jesus Christ Superstar*—examine the difficulties that arise when the Jesus myth becomes the basis of contemporary morality. *King of Kings* explored the problems of violence and nonviolence. *The Greatest Story Ever Told* examined the way a modern world view deals with morality based on the Jesus story. *Jesus Christ Superstar* reversed the formulas and looked at Jesus through the eyes of Judas, with Jesus becoming a liberal reformer rather than the founder of a divine morality.

The Bible attempts to go beyond the spectacular formula. In *The Bible* familiar norms disappear; the well-known stories become absurdist myths and do not provide a foundation for any moral standard. *The Bible* presents an Old Testament deity in grotesque contradistinction to the commonly held American image of the deity. The film alters the formulas, works from a new archetype, and uses the traditional myths to suggest the impossibility of a morality based on sacred norms.

In these films, one plot device services a central interpretative function. In the religious spectaculars, the key figure was the villain. In the biblical spectaculars of the 1950s, the woman gives force to the plot, whereas in the Jesus cycle and *The Bible*, the central element is the treatment of miracles. Liberal Christianity and Reform Judaism attempt to interpret the miracles in a manner that does not offend science or psychology, often providing rational explanations for miraculous events. Although many conservative Christians and Jews believe in the literal "inerrancy" of the Scriptures, film makers considered these groups negligible because they had a long history of being opposed to motion pictures per se.

At the heart of this treatment of miracles is the relationship between myth and history—between the time of sacred events and contemporary political, social, and cultural time. Film makers developed a "could have happened that way" philosophy. For instance, it "could have been" that a blind man just "thought he could see" after his encounter with Jesus in *The Greatest Story Ever Told*, or it "could have been" that Samson actually killed the entire Philistine army with the jawbone of an ass, especially if the men had to approach him threading their way one at a time through a narrow passageway.

To deal with the conflict between science and religion, and between myth and history, expensive systems of research were used for justifications of the plot line. DeMille even published Henry Noerdlinger's book, *Moses in Egypt*, about the research on *The Ten Commandments* and sent it to major university libraries across the nation. By the time *Jesus Christ Superstar* was made, virtually no research was being done, and the author of *Superstar* fashioned the musical from his memory of the traditions.

In popular religion, these stories are usually cast within the framework of melodrama, with its struggle between good and evil. With the exception of *Jesus Christ Superstar* and *The Bible*, the formulas of melodrama prevail. In those films, the pattern is altered, changing both the dramatic action and the meaning.

Even the grand style changed in the period from 1949 to 1973. The destruction of the temple of Dagon in *Samson and Delilah* emphasizes physical detail and depends on the audience's suspension of disbelief. The immense desert and temple ruins in *Jesus Christ Superstar* are no less spectacular, but the film is substantially different in tone, feeling, and dramatic purpose. The crowd scenes are restrained. The boom shots, instead of capturing masses of people in frenetic motion, show isolated individuals against a bleak background. The scenery is no longer realistic;

on the contrary, it is designed to look like a stage—bleak ruined buildings and stage props making up large parts of the design.

Between the end of World War II and 1973, the urban mentality overcame the cultural lag of ruralism, changing social and political attitudes.[1] The postwar boom in mainline religion tended to homogenize differences and values. Traditions became identified with "the American Way of Life," against the "communist menace and for the 'free market,' " and equated these with "Christ's mission in the world." Ecumenical moderates, on the other hand, became identified with cultural pluralism. In their attempts to break away from provincialism and chauvinism, in their demand for tolerance, they severely undermined the divine support for Christian and Jewish worship and ethics.[2]

This pluralism led the film makers to shape their dramas to reach wide numbers of people; consequently, they downplayed particularism that might offend people and offered ambiguous doctrine that could be interpreted in several ways.

The concern about sexuality that dominated the spectaculars of the 1950s gave way to anxiety about social change, affluence, militarism, and racism in the 1960s. These issues linked themselves to a religious quest to find a divine basis for morality. In this way, the issues found their way into the Jesus cycle.

The 1960s and 1970s led to what Martin Marty calls "identity constriction" of Protestants, Catholics, and Jews. In Israel's struggle for survival, Vatican II, and the freedom and antiwar movements, the major groups of the American religious spectrum directed their attention outwardly toward the world and inwardly toward survival.[3] As the mainline denominations blurred their religious identities during the 1950s and 1960s, as they adopting secularity and relativism as appropriate standards for religion in a pluralistic society, they unwittingly undercut the divine basis for ethical standards. In such an atmosphere, the biblical spectacular, which focused on the role of ethics from a religious perspective, no longer had a role.

Other Jesus films came on the scene, causing no great ripple, until Franco Zeffirelli changed the definition of the spectacular. The "grand style" was transferred to television, now making its own movies. Instead of wide vistas and authentic detail, the style now was important by the very fact of its length—its piling of incident on incident, detail on detail. *Jesus of Nazareth* became a monument in itself, lasting over six hours (without commercials) and spread out over four nights, culminating at Easter, but conservative forces on the horizon, notably the archconservatives at Bob Jones University, raised questions, and eventually General Motors pulled out of its sponsorship.

The mid–1970s were a time when the conservative churches became politically active. Within a few years, two groups, the National Federation for Decency and the Moral Majority, were prominently discussing film and television concerns in public forums, as well as getting financial support from the same sources as President Ronald Reagan. Their world view traded on some alternative to the growing consciousness of scientific methodology, which they identified as "secular humanism." The battle was waged across the political and cultural spectrum, including libraries and abortion clinics.

The loss of divine supports for ethics had seriously compromised the sexual morality that they identified with. The women's movement, the two-income family, divorce rates, and the decreasing birthrate, along with a steady increase in affluence, had changed the cultural landscape. The Vietnam War had redefined the nature of political authority and morality, making individuals more responsible for deciding whether or not to support a foreign adventure because the government willed it.

Into this atmosphere came a modest film by noted film maker Martin Scorsese based on a book written 30 years previously, Nikos Kazantzakis' *The Last Temptation of Christ*. Well before the film emerged, a spectacular public debate opened worldwide, led by many of the conservative churches and fueled over television by evangelist programs.

The evangelists had lost much of their financial base because of revelations of sexual and fiscal impropriety of two leaders of their programs—Jim Bakker of the PTL Club and Jimmy Swaggarts—along with the failed Republican candidacy of Pat Robertson, and Oral Roberts telling his audience that if enough money did not come in, he would be "called home." They found new causes in Scorsese's film and the trial of Colonel Oliver North for selling arms to the Iranians to fund the Contra guerillas waging war with Nicaragua.

The reaction against *The Last Temptation of Christ* was largely confined to its treatment of Jesus as human, confused, and sexually obsessed with Mary Magdalene. At the heart of the controversy was the long-standing feud between the scientific mindset, which made humans an accident of nature (thus having to define their own morality), and that of the Bible, in which humans are special creations (therefore seekers after a supernatural righteousness). The mainline religions, questing after a human Jesus who could provide a model for their own humanness, were thrust into competition with the conservative evangelicals, who believing that this world is unremittingly evil, wanted a Christ to save them from their humanness. Thus, the battle continues unspectacularly into the future.

NOTES

1. Mowry, *The Urban Nation*, pp. 196–97.
2. Martin Marty, *Righteous Empire* (New York: Dial Press, 1970), p. 250.
3. Martin Marty, *A Nation of Behavers* (Chicago: University of Chicago Press, 1976), Chap. III.

5

The Sex and Social Responsibility Cycle

Cecil B. DeMille, reading the signs of the times, persuaded the studio heads to make *Samson and Delilah*. Its basic concern is to explore sexuality and social responsibility.

Henry Wilcoxon, traveling to promote the picture, said that filmgoers wanted "more adult subjects" because they "feel that Hollywood is writing down to them," and that they were "glad to see controversial subjects attacked properly."[1] DeMille, always sensitive to the public mood, knew that people were ready to explore his favorite themes—sex, religion, and nationhood.

The film tells the story of Samson, judge of the Danites, and how he betrays his covenant with God by lusting after Delilah, a Philistine woman.

One biblical commentator noted that although "always brawling and excelling all rivals in muscular strength, this uncouth fellow is no match for feminine wiles."[2] DeMille seized on this, giving Samson an American flavor, replete with values Americans were ready to explore.

Even the religious reviewers thought that the love story provided the chief interest of the film. "It is indeed safer to present Samson as a warning than as a type to be imitated. He was governed largely by selfishness and passion."[3]

In *Samson Agonistes*, John Milton had described Samson as "a man who divulged the secret of the gift of God to a deceitful woman." The film program notes make Samson and Delilah prototypes of sexual conflict: "Whenever a beautiful woman tempts, loves, then destroys, she is Delilah. Whenever a man of enormous spiritual strength is tempted, loves and is destroyed, he is Samson."[4]

From the beginning, DeMille's Samson is a flawed hero. A judge of his people, he is scolded by his mother. At the well when an old man is bullied by Philistine soldiers, young Saul boasts that Samson will punish them. When Samson appears on screen, the camera angle emphasizes his giant size from the back, but he is more a playful child than a heroic judge.

His judgment is flawed; he wants to marry Semadar, a Philistine woman, rather than the good and faithful Danite woman, Miriam. Sexual desire causes Samson's downfall.

His religious function is virtually tribal. One review complained that Samson's "position as a God-appointed leader of his race who forgets his mission is never clearly stated."[5] DeMille was not primarily interested in a political message. Lust was on DeMille's mind. When this love triangle reappears in *The Ten Commandments*, it is strongly linked to *both* the political and sexual themes.

When Delilah first appears, she is a young, seductive woman. The script describes her as having "all the wisdom of a young sphinx, coupled with the fascination of a hooded cobra." This deceptive serpent image from Genesis is reinforced when the Saran says, "The girl has the wisdom of a serpent." In discussing elements of the film that could be exploited by the distributors, *Boxoffice* described her as "the seductive, sexy, scantily-clad and ravishingly beautiful siren. . . . It is Lamarr who gives the picture its Sex—with a capital 'S'—quotient."[6]

DeMille told his staff: "We'll sell it as a story of faith, a story of the power of prayer. That's for the censors and the women's organizations. For the public, it's the hottest love story of all time."[7]

DeMille had found an old novel, *Judge and Fool*, by Vladimir Jabotinsky, which identified the unnamed younger sister of the Philistine woman as Delilah. "By that simple, plausible and entirely legitimate device, the story came together as a drama rather than a narrative."[8] DeMille has the younger sister rebuffed, thus giving her a motive for destroying him. DeMille's former executive assistant Phil Koury provides a more graphic description of the script conference:

He's stepping pretty high, this punk from the hills, coming in there and marrying a high-born Philistine girl. So the younger sister sees something here, a way to break up the love match. Her sister, she figures, can get the answer to the riddle out of Samson if anyone can. The younger sister has no motive in the world, except from the bottom of her feet to the top of her head, her body tingles when she sees him, and she wants him. She's never had a man, but, boy, she's ripe—and she wants that Samson. Now there's nothing in the Bible about all this, but it could give us the motive we need.[9]

Samson's motive is personal revenge. His morality is "an eye for an eye." When Semadar dies in his arms, he tells the wedding guests that they were invited out of respect but that he will be blameless for all that he does to them.

Delilah's motive is similar. In a scene that seems inspired by the desolate Tara in *Gone with the Wind*, she looks upon her loss of family and fortune, and she vows to "make him curse the day he was born." When her servant asks about the sort of strength she has against him, Delilah replies, "It is greater than a lion's and softer than a dove's." At her vow of vengeance, the background fires appear to leap forward, so that her head is surrounded by flames. This is another indication of the serpent temptress theme, allying her with the powers of hell.

This personal vengeance theme provides the central dramatic focus of the film. Samson, regarding his loss as a personal rebuke by the Philistines, resists and punishes them, raiding their caravans and stealing their wealth. When the Philistines retaliate against the Danites, Samson delivers himself into their hands, but once convinced that he has paid his debt, he destroys their army.

Samson does not take into account the power of sexuality. Delilah, now the courtesan of the Saran, offers to trap Samson and to deliver him helpless. The Saran, a political realist, does not hesitate to release his favorite sexual partner in order to rid himself of the Danite menace.

DeMille's treatment brings back the rural-urban clash of values. Samson is tempted to urban culture and is helpless in the face of temptation. Though endowed with the qualities of the superhero, he is helpless before Delilah.

Samson feels powerless before her even though he suspects a trap. Pleasure is pitted against duty. Samson abandons his people and their rural values in order to seek his own pleasure. He rejects Miriam, one of his own, in favor of the Philistine woman. Those who go whoring in the enemy camp fail in their duty to their own people. Finally, with Delilah, as he had in the riddle with Semadar, Samson betrays his secret for love.

Samson is an innocent in a world he does not understand. He is blind to Delilah, blind to his duty to his people, and blind to the oppression of the Philistines. His mother warns him that "a man's heart can be blind," but he pays no attention. Only when he becomes literally blind can he repent of his ways.

One review suggested that the film displayed a "naivete . . . and a fond nostalgia for the innocent past,"[10] but that is a better description of the character Samson himself. There is nothing naive about the Saran or Delilah. Innocence is doomed before the forces of the modern urban world— and the unrestrained libido is potentially the agent of destruction.

Delilah is more complex than she seems at first glance. From the beginning, she controls the action. She schemes to steal Samson from her sister— by her behavior on the lion hunt, by inviting the 30 guests to the wedding party, by appealing to Ahtur's racial pride so that he will persuade Semadar to find the answer to the riddle, and finally in arranging for Semadar to marry Ahtur. She brings Samson to his knees, and then having humiliated him, tries to tempt him to accompany her to Egypt. In the end, she brings him to the stone pillars so he can defeat his enemies.

Delilah's feelings are usually ambivalent. At first, she is angered by Samson's rejection of her. In the scenes at the temple ruins, where she pries Samson's secret from him, however, it is never clear whether she is planning to betray him or run off with him. Miriam comes to remind Samson of his duty, and Delilah declares that she loves him "as a man of flesh and blood." Samson sees through the ruse at the beginning of the meeting, declaring it to be "the oldest trick in the world—a silk trap baited with a woman!" Delilah responds that it is the best trap because men always respond. Delilah is stunned when Samson asks her to marry him, but when he starts to leave, Delilah misinterprets his act not as one of responsibility, but as his rejection of her for another, Miriam. "I cannot fight against his God," she says, "but no woman will take him from me."

Even as a conspirator in Samson's destruction of the temple, she remains jealous of Miriam. One cannot tell if she is following Samson's plan out of love for him and belief in his mission, or to prevent her rival, Miriam, from having him. In the death scene, Delilah lies near Samson, her lips touching his hand, kissing him as she promised, with her dying breath.

Although Samson's repentance is necessary from a dramatic standpoint as well as biblical accuracy, there is no such necessity for Delilah's repentance. Samson grieves that he has failed his people as a judge. When Saul tells Samson that he has come to take him home, Samson replies that "there is no home for a leader who fails his people."

When the vengeful Samson destroys the Temple of Dagon, his redemption comes in the final fatal exercise of his strength on behalf of his people. In the last speech of the film, Miriam tells Saul that people will be telling Samson's story for 1,000 years. His redemption is in his being remembered by the community of faith for his great deeds.

There is no biblical justification for the transformation and redemption of Delilah. Her redemption comes when she realizes that nothing can return Samson's sight as she finds him praying while he pushes the grist mill around amid the taunts of the Philistines. Her guilt drives her to despairing belief, leading her to pray for the return of his sight at the cost of her own.

Symbolically she divests herself of her sexuality, appearing at night to the blind Samson dressed in black. The next day at the temple, she resumes her seductive dress, wearing a dress made of peacock feathers in order to dupe the Saran. Her sexuality is now in the service of Samson's revenge. Her decision to die is, as in DeMille's *Sign of the Cross*, a sign not of her faith, but of her love for Samson.

DeMille's decision to redeem Delilah seems based on the need for film heroines to be saved from their wicked ways. This theme regularly recurs in the portrayal of villains and temptresses in the biblical spectaculars, with the notable except of Neferitiri in *The Ten Commandments*. Even the Saran, hardly an evil force of the magnitude of DeMille's Nero or Rameses, has the good grace to drink a salute to Delilah while the temple is tumbling about him. By acknowledging his defeat and Samson's victory, he becomes a "good sport."

Indeed, it is the ruler's lack of power that constitutes an important difference between the religious and biblical spectaculars. There are numerous references to the political intent of the film—the chained Samson is described as "conquered freedom"; the opening narration reminds the audience that "deep in man's soul still burned the unquenchable will for freedom"; Miriam and Saul make reference to Samson's duty to his people. This theme, however, is secondary to examining the social and personal consequences of sexuality. In DeMille's universe, sexuality must be placed within the framework of the duty principle, or it will lead to destruction.

Changes in dramatic construction reflect the American value system. Samson, for instance, does not kill the people from whom he steals the garments to pay off his debt as he did in the Bible, or tie brands to the tails of foxes, which would be cruelty to animals.[11]

Once again, DeMille used the "could have been" principle. One of the writers noted that "since there is nothing in the Bible to indicate that the unnamed girl could not have been Delilah," DeMille seized on the device as motivation.[12]

The tale follows the classic pattern of salvation—Samson begins in innocence, sins, repents, and finally is redeemed.

For all its disdainment of a political theology within the drama, DeMille uses the opening narration to outline one. Humans, in the face of their weakness before nature, become superstitious, which leads them to idolatry. This lures them to the false gods used to enslave other people, but in the souls of the enslaved, God has planted a dream of freedom, and from time to time, a single individual changes the course of history. This dream of freedom and the appearance of the special individual sets history into motion.

Judging from the film, if the dream of freedom initiates historical progress, the appetite for sex inhibits it. Samson follows a "crooked path," but though he strays, he eventually returns to his duty. God, having invested him with power, does not abandon him but uses Samson's weakness to strike a blow for human freedom.

When Samson reveals his own gift to Delilah and tells her of God's ubiquity, she asks whether she can share Samson's power. He tells her that it is a gift that makes humans better than themselves, stirring the soul to music or reading the truth in men's hearts. For him, it is his strength. When Delilah asks if he will always possess this strength, Samson replies: "If I keep faith with the Almighty."

Thus, the cutting of his hair symbolizes his loss of faith—his straying

from the sacred bond. It also suggests emasculation. Sexuality is dangerous—not because it is intrinsically evil, but because it weakens him to
divulge his sacred tie with God. Sex weakens his spirit, and his divine
protection leaves with the spirit. It is only as he labors at the grist mill,
saying the prayers and psalms of his faith, that he regains his strength. The
suggestion is clear: When the leaders of nations lose their faith, their power
is diminished; unrestrained sexuality has national consequences.

The makers of the first three biblical spectaculars—*Samson and Delilah*,
David and Bathsheba, and *Salome*—avoided portraying miraculous feats.
DeMille would face the problem squarely in *The Ten Commandments*, but
significantly, he chose a story that "could have happened" without straining
the credibility of a scientific world view. Most of his changes were for
dramatic purposes, but the slaying of the Philistine army posed a problem.
As violence, the scene had considerable force, but if Samson were to push
over great stone pillars, the slaying of the Philistine army was needed earlier
in the film to establish his strength, as well as to meet the expectations of
moviegoers. DeMille once again resorted to "filling in the missing gaps."
He staged it in a narrow defile, turned over the chariot ahead of Samson
to deny access to the soldiers ahead of him, and grabbed the skull the
jester had been taunting him with. With access limited, the chariot in front,
and his back to the wall, he could meet them one at a time.[13] Ahtur explains:
"He fought within a gorge so narrow we trampled upon the dying to attack
him. And those behind pressed forward—and those forward were forced
back upon the blades behind them." DeMille, however, did not want to
strip the story entirely of its supernatural setting, so he brought in a wind
machine and lit the set so as to suggest a storm.

Why should anyone choose a spectacle for the exploration of the themes
related to sexuality? The spectacle's main power lies in its hugeness—its
grand scale. It had been ten years since *Gone with the Wind*, and nearly
four years since the end of World War II.

The innocent Samson, though self-indulgent and parochial, was caught
up in the salvation of his people and the eventual salvation of the world.
In a letter to DeMille, Rabbi Max Nussbaum wrote:

The Germans have had their Siegfried now for many centuries and that, living in
the age of the State of Israel, its [*sic*] about time to give the Jewish people back
their Samson. To this I say, wholeheartedly, "Amen," because aside from all other
considerations, the picture is even new in subject material: The invincible power
of a Jew who derives his strength from the unshakable faith in an omni-present
God.[14]

The predicament of Samson was not unlike that of an America that
thought of itself as innocent. The innocent and powerful Samson did not
stand a chance in the changed world. In America, the forces unleashed by

World War II and the emerging technocracy were rapidly reshaping human values. The impulsive withdrawal of the self into the pleasure principle was seen as leading to destruction and slavery. In the biblical spectacular, the forces of evil are found not only outside in an evil world, but they are instinctual as well. They are mighty, raw, and powerful, capable of overwhelming the strongest of men. The entire social order depends on the control of such appetites. In reviewing *Samson and Delilah*, the Protestant Motion Picture Council made the connection: "When the carnal nature rises above the power of the spirit, compromise with sin and downfall inevitably ensue, with the possibility of subsequent pardon following repentance."[15]

Television succeeded the movies as the primary mass communication instrument. Despite the success of *Samson and Delilah*, Hollywood soon found itself trying desperately to attract audiences. The Production Code, appropriate to the values of 1934, was perceived as a form of bondage rather than as self-discipline. DeMille had always known that in a Christian America, no one would dare censor the Bible. If an assault were to be made on the Production Code in the interest of freeing up what could be depicted on the screen, a biblical spectacular was an auspicious way to start. *Samson and Delilah* began the assault; *David and Bathsheba* soon followed.

The Production Code forbade pictures that "lower the moral standards." It decreed that audience sympathy should be with the righteous, not with "criminals, wrong-doers, evil or sinful people." With reference to sex, the Code says the "triangle" should not imply sympathy for adultery.[16]

The 1934 Production Code came about because of the fear of censorship more than for moral reasons. The Production Code assumed that films were a major factor in the spread of morality, and that "correct entertainment raises the whole standard of a nation," whereas "wrong entertainment lowers the whole living conditions and moral ideals of a race."[17] The pressure exerted by the Production Code Administration was directed at studio heads, because censorship before the investments were made was more economical.[18]

By 1950, attacks on the Code were mounting. Gilbert Seldes argued that the Production Code created a "sexual morality which no morality, no great religious leader, no church has ever tolerated."[19] Creative artists found it difficult to challenge the Code and its administration. The studios were committed to the idea of family audiences and the notion so often expressed by Eric Johnston, president of the MPAA, (Motion Pictures Association of America) that the Code existed to protect the producers.[20]

Television made that thinking obsolete. Instead of buying two tickets a week regardless of what was playing, people had to be attracted to individual films. Andrew Dowdy noted that "moral ambiguity, a central theme in much modern art in the twentieth century, was proscribed in the Code's commitment to a medium which 'builds character, develops right ideals, inculcates correct principles, and all in attractive story form.' "[21]

Most film historians credit Otto Preminger's *The Moon Is Blue* with cracking the Production Code. The film was condemned by Cardinal Spellman of New York, and a tame little comedy that used the word "seduction" became a legend as people flocked to see why the Production Code had failed to give it its Seal of Approval.[22] *The Moon Is Blue* was the first major studio motion picture to be released without the Code's Seal of Approval, but the first tentative steps had been taken in the biblical spectaculars.

In 1951, *Time* noted that *David and Bathsheba* sent Hollywood "back to the bible for another censor-proof tale of a strong man's weakness for a beautiful woman."[23]

The story details the incident in the Bible where David has an affair with the wife of one of his generals, and then has him killed in battle, only to be accused by the prophet Nathan.

David is guilty of both murder and adultery, yet he is not punished. In an interview, director Henry King was asked if this was not a violation of the Production Code. He commented that the Breen office had some qualms, but "they had to agree with us that we had no right to change the Bible to fit the Code."[24] The Code, anchored in a religious consciousness, was defenseless before the Bible.

Screenwriter Philip Dunne hardly knew the story when Darryl F. Zanuck called him. Zanuck had a DeMille-style spectacular in mind, but Dunne was unwilling to write in that style. Dunne became intrigued with the character of David as he read the Chronicles. By the time he conceived the film treatment, he was thinking of David as "an extremely sensitive religious boy who became king and in the hurly-burly of the king business began to lose his faith and in the end recaptures it."[25] Obviously, this led to the later script for *Demetrius and the Gladiators*, which had many of the same interests. He and Zanuck decided to tell the whole story of David's life in terms of his romance with Bathsheba.

The decision shows that Zanuck believed that the key to audience interest lay in David's sex life. *Catholic World* noted that there were three periods that might make him close to our human frailties: his love and grief for Jonathan, his repentance over the Bathsheba scandal, and the tragedy of his son, Absalom. Zanuck and Dunne chose the Bathsheba incident.[26]

In contrast, the 1976 television special, *The Story of David*, emphasized the political conflicts stemming from David's relations with Saul and later with Absalom. Also, the Bruce Beresford 1985 version, *David the King*, focused on the primitive qualities of the whole story. In 1951, however, the public's interest was in the Bathsheba story.

Dunne made David into a modern man, focusing on the contradictions within his character. "It would have been possible to make him entirely pure and righteous or an exceptional villain or a poetic dreamer or a forceful warrior, and each of these characters would have good authority in the scriptures."[27]

In the film, David has lost his enthusiasm for war and is not even sure of its righteousness. When old friend Joab tells him, "We fought for God—and still fight for Him," David wearily remarks, "So we tell ourselves." He tells Michal that they were married for political reasons—to unite the Northern Kingdom. In his quarters, he confides to Abashai that he has learned "that life can offer no new experiences—no excitement—that power becomes a prison for him who achieves it." Duty offered no personal satisfaction.

David seeks to cure his despair by his affair with Bathsheba. In explaining the effects of the Production Code, Gilbert Seldes noticed that "while men may at times derive pleasure from sexual love, women never do." At the same time, the movies presented endless variations of the "siren who lured men to their destruction, following some obscure purpose of her own, revenge perhaps, or ambition, or desire for power, but not for the ecstacy of passion or the simple pleasure of getting into bed with a man."[28] The studio press materials suggested that it was not pleasure, but power that attracted her.

Such an interpretation is supported only by ambiguous evidence. She confesses that she bathed so that the king might notice her. Dunne said he took license with the Bible in making Bathsheba "aware of the royal peeping Tom and deliberately exhibited herself."[29] She almost does not marry David, however, because he has neglected her, and she angrily tells him, "I'm not a beggar, David." David, of course, feels guilt because he has had Uriah killed.

David and Bathsheba are both victims of loveless marriages. David tells Michal, "We're past the days of our passion, love, or hatred or anguish. Even cruelty. Why should we torture ourselves?" Shortly after David brings Bathsheba to his quarters, she tells him that she has been married for only seven months and that she has seen Uriah only six days during that time. David asks: "Then six days is the sum total of your love?" She amends that: "Of our marriage." When Uriah is brought home to become the putative father of the child of David and Bathsheba, Uriah insults David by saying that Bathsheba is nothing beside his duty, and that if she strays because of neglect, it is his "duty" to condemn her.

Yet these scenes are undercut by scenes in which David calls Uriah home. When Bathsheba complains that since David has called her his wife, he can scarcely expect her now to sleep with her legal husband, he answers that "there is no act so violent that I would not commit it to save my love." Dunne called the scene a "bitter, dirty sequence."

When Uriah arrives, David attempts to inflame his passions with dancing girls, lascivious music, and wine. These scenes give moral insight into David's plight, and serve to compromise him by thwarting his desire to keep both Bathsheba and Uriah alive. The solution he proposes is, as Michal says, "a clever trick—worthy of the son of goatherds."

David and Bathsheba, however, are not innocent. Bathsheba tells David in their first encounter that "if the law of Moses is to be broken, let us break it in full understanding of what we want from each other."

The complications of this love affair are both political and cosmic. Nathan tells David that the people say he is no longer himself, that "he neglects his duty, that he is often away from the city," and that even when he is there, he is not hearing the petitioners. Moreover, Absalom foments rebellion, capitalizing on David's distraction. "The king forgets that he too is the servant of the Lord," Nathan announces. In attending to his own personal happiness, David neglects his duty as a monarch.

The drought is seen as a sign of God's displeasure with the affair. Their marriage sequence is crosscut with a series of shots showing the effect of the drought on the people. On Mount Gilboa, a shepherd and his son come upon a sour well and claim that "the hand of the Lord is heavy upon this land." Later, sheep die; a tornado and a dust storm follow. When the storm reaches the city, the scene cuts to the dying child born of David and Bathsheba's adultery. By neglecting his duty and by insisting on the fulfillment of his own needs, David brings a cosmic punishment on the land. Individual moral decisions have national and cosmic effects.

The film suggests numerous parallels to the political and cultural situation of the 1950s. Faced with a cold war in Europe and an all-out war in Korea, many Americans who had expected a respite from war after 1945 were disillusioned. By June, 1951, after the Chinese invasion of North Korea, Truman's popularity in the Gallup Poll had fallen to 24 percent. There was talk of forcing him to resign, and Congress had turned recalcitrant. The stalemated war in Rabbah, the displeasure with the king, the talk of Absalom's rebellion, the border problems with Egypt—all these seemed like ancient reenactments of modern problems.[30]

Dunne's concern with providing naturalistic motives for biblical supernaturalism is as evident here as in his scripts for *The Robe* and *Demetrius and the Gladiators*. When confronted with the death of a soldier who died when he touched the Ark in order to steady it, David suggests that the sun was hot, the man had been drinking wine, and that the excitement of the Ark falling might have affected him.

Some of this same naturalism pervades Dunne's concept of God. David tells Bathsheba of how he had conceived of God in childhood:

I saw Him in the hills, in the trees, in the miracle of the birth of lambs. I felt His mercy when the wolves had fled and my flock was safe, when spring broke the grip of snow and ice, when the cool wind blew after the heat of the day. I saw His splendor in the flowers blazing on the hillsides and the stars burning in the sky and knew His hand in everything.

And now Nathan has found Him for me. But not the God of my early days. A God without mercy. A God who thinks only of his justice.

David's speech trades heavily on naturalistic proofs of God at a time when neo-orthodox theologians were stressing the otherness of God and citing revelation as the chief characteristic of the divine-human encounter. After David's loss of childlike innocence, however, God is now revealed in the wrath visited on Israel.

Nathan's judgment is set forth in the parable of the ewes; he asks David what would happen if a man with many sheep took the sheep of a man who had only one and killed him. David's righteous answer is that the man should be killed. Nathan responds: "You are the man!" It is not David's life the people ask for, however, but Bathsheba's. She is ready to give it because she knows in her heart how Uriah died, and "I wished him dead. God sees into our hearts, David." The entire redemption theme seems more in keeping with the New Testament than the Old Testament, although Dunne maintained that he found his ending in Psalm 23, "in which David sings of a merciful, forgiving God."[31]

The climax is not in the book of Samuel, and is a curious mix of faith, fury, and mysticism. David goes to the Holy of Holies.[32] He confesses that his life has been a "terrible waste" and that he has been a "faithless shepherd." After noting, however, that "the sacrifices of God are a broken spirit" (Psalm 51), he prays that God will lift his hand from the Israelites "who suffer for my crimes." Finally, he prays that God "look not on the sinner who stands before thee," but on "the boy he was, who loved thee and would have died for thee. . . . Let the boy live again in his innocence."

The scene dissolves back to the anointing of David, and then further back to the Goliath episode. David is a child again in his faith. Outside, raindrops begin to fall, the chants of Psalms 1 and 23 are heard on the soundtrack, and David returns to Bathsheba. The last image is of a smiling shepherd boy.

The Catholic monthly *Extension* argued that the film was about religion, but not "religious." It was particularly critical of the sexuality, which it thought was "arrestingly translated to fit the modern thought pattern in which the illicit is confused with the explicit until love, as the movies present it, appears to provide a perfect and natural excuse for any kind of behavior." It was horrified that the religious stories were being written by nonreligious (specifically non-Catholic) authors, and that the film was "soft-pedaling scriptural history, dogmas, and all traditional Christian principles and authoritative teachings . . . 'leaning backwards' to effect evasive or indifferent treatment of religious matter."[33]

What constitutes a religious film is a matter of definition on which there is no general agreement. Dunne surely was a rationalist. He said of the film that he wanted to "avoid didacticism that says that my religion—or the Christian religion—is the only true one and all else is false. . . . I never say in the script that this has to be the audience's faith. We're only talking about David's faith."[34]

Faith appears as a return to innocence, something that neither Jews nor Christians believe is possible in a fallen world. In the light of the skepticism and alienation of the Davidic character, the ending seems contrived. The dilemma is solved by exchanging the naturalistic emphasis for a miracle.

Dunne wanted to write what he called an "interior drama." His hope was that the characters would be "well rounded, well fleshed out," and David himself was to be a "modern man—aware, intelligent, and sensitive." Dunne was aiming at something more than a melodrama. What emerges as the antagonist is a strictness of spirit, which denies that the individual's free conscience is greater than the Law.

Given the "grand style" of interpretation that King gives the film, the film becomes a somewhat more urbane *Samson and Delilah*. The religious questions of justice and mercy are raised within the framework of personal pleasure and national duty. David forsakes his duty in order to seek his own happiness. The American Jewish Committee spoke of the interweaving of "moral and democratic values, [especially] the rights of the people to be heard and the obligation of the powerful as well as the lowly to obey the Law."[35] In light of that comment, David's confession in the tabernacle becomes not only a religious act, but also a political one. In disobeying the Law, he brings drought, and in confessing, he liberates the people from it.

Though Dunne provides alternative explanations for almost every other supernatural phenomenon, he does not try to suggest one here. Moreover, not a single review in 32 major sources challenged the connection between repentance and the end of the drought. Yet most reviews noted the connection between David's repentance and the lifting of the curse. One suspects that the film was touching a deep subliminal guilt in the audience. In the yearning for innocence, there seems to be the hope of returning to a less complicated world. *Books and Authors* suggested that

perhaps we need more plays with a biblical background as a reminder of our past and a lesson to the outside world that America has not lost her soul. Out of the beauty and the pathos of the picture with its windswept hills and pastoral people issues the familiar assurance that "the Lord is my shepherd." In a new atomic world, that assurance will be welcome.[36]

Audiences were hardly prepared for the arrival of *Salome*. This film seemed more transparent about its double intention. *Variety* opined:

Neither the seventh veil in Salome's famed dance nor the picture come off with the anticipated impact. The first, of course, has to do with the Production Code. The second lies primarily in the fact that the picture is more a thoughtful Biblical drama, produced with good taste by Buddy Adler, than the sex show many expect.[37]

Rita Hayworth had been an archetypal sex symbol since her World War II pinup photographs and the 1946 film *Gilda*, in which she did a dance that, although it did not go very far as a striptease, gave every indication of her cynical sexuality. She had followed this role with more elaborate portrayals of a similar character in *The Lady from Shanghai* and *The Loves of Carmen*. In this film, she becomes a "good girl," and given the sexual content and the ads, it thoroughly confused the patrons.

The film turns Salome from a cynical Palestinian banished by the emperor because of her love for his nephew to a follower of John the Baptist, and conspirator in a plot with a Roman legionnaire to save him.

The first controversy about *Salome* broke out over the use of a billboard in Los Angeles. Variety quoted the city council, prohibiting its use to advertise *Salome* because it "tends to offend public morale and decency." It showed Hayworth's dance, while across the billboard, Stewart Granger, in Roman regalia, seemed to be looking lustfully at her. No such shot ever appeared in the film. By today's standard, the billboard seems hardly worth mentioning, yet the story was picked up by the wire services and made all the major movie gossip columns.

What touched a raw nerve was probably not the advertisement, but the exploitation of Rita Hayworth as a sex symbol. In an extensive discussion of Hayworth as a sex symbol, Michael Wood argued that "down there among the image and artillery of lust," Hayworth projects "neither guilt nor innocence, but an innocence lingering in the midst of guilt."[38]

Salome capitalized on this double image. Herod lusts after her, and Claudius loves her. She is loyal to her mother, even though she cannot understand her mother's hatred. John confuses her; he preaches justice for her mother but saves Salome's life. Yet she blatantly uses her sexuality in trying to save John's life, and no other film had made sexuality quite so explicit.

Biblical spectaculars used incidents or characters from the Bible as the central focus, whereas in religious spectaculars, such incidents and issues are ancillary. By such a definition, *Salome* is a biblical film. A close scrutiny shows that the amount of time taken up by biblically based incidents is proportionally more than in *The Ten Commandments*. John the Baptist is featured in several scenes; the dance of Salome is a long segment; the attempt on John's life and his arrest by Herod (including his interview with the monarch) are biblically substantiated. So too is the final scene, the Sermon on the Mount.

Jesse Lasky, Jr., author of *Samson and Delilah* and a major scriptwriter for *The Ten Commandments*, provided the story for the film. Harry Kleiner, the writer, noted that the previous biblical pictures dealt with flawed biblical figures. This was, however, a New Testament film that dealt with the sacred figure of John the Baptist and, in two scenes, Jesus Christ. Since the film also involved incest and adultery, censorship was not the only problem, but also one of "maintaining a delicate, tasteful balance between the sacred and the profane elements finally dictated the character of Salome herself."[39]

Kleiner is disingenuous. The definitions of incest and adultery are not the contemporary definitions. In the film, John speaks of Herodias as an adulteress living in an incestuous relationship, but from a twentieth-century point of view, marrying one's brother-in-law does not constitute either adultery or incest. In Roman Catholicism, the remarriage would make Herodias an adulteress, but in contemporary morality only a blood relationship defines incest.

On the other hand, for Herod to have intercourse with Salome would constitute both adultery and incest, since she was his niece, the daughter of his brother, and therefore consanguineous. It is difficult to believe that the audience was very interested in that aspect, since the heart of the screenplay concerned whether Salome was going to use her sexuality to destroy John.

Kleiner also suggested that she could have been portrayed as a "Biblical Lizzie Borden," but "the leading character inevitably sets the tone of the dramatic piece." *Film noir* had regularly used women leads as villains (e.g., Barbara Stanwyck in *Double Indemnity* and Hayworth herself in *The Lady from Shanghai*), so there was nothing secular that *required* Salome's redemption within the Hollywood conventions of the time. The spectacular genre, however, required redemption, unlike Richard Strauss's opera or Oscar Wilde's play. The failure of *The Sign of the Pagan* (with Atilla the Hun as protagonist) proved to studio executives that Kleiner's decision not to use a villain as protagonist had been the correct choice for marketing the film.

Salome's redemption not only fulfills a dramatic function, but allows both the sexuality and the innocence of Rita Hayworth's image to be exploited. When she is introduced in Rome, Hayworth is dressed in a simple white garment, an allusion to her innocence. As she moves towards Herod's palace, her dress and demeanor become more visually complicated, but we are always aware of the duality—the sexuality and urbanity on the one side, and the innocence and simplicity on the other.

There is no such duality about Herodias, the real villain. Left alone with Micha, they scheme to use Herod's attraction to Salome as a means of killing the Baptist. She changes from one guise to another—the terrified mother, the shrew, the dutiful wife—but we are always aware that she is a disguised viper.

When Herod first appears, he is illuminated from below, giving him a demonic look. His weakness is sexual licentiousness, but this is undercut by his fear that John is the Messiah. He is terrified by the prophecy that Ezra repeats:

Never forget the deed of your father [the killing of the Innocents], . . . Remember the strange illness that came over him, the unbearable pain that held him, his mind and body became his own torture chamber. Your father suffered agony, agony without relief.

When he meets the Baptist face to face, Herod says that his judges have pronounced the sentence. John tells Herod, "The guilt is yours and yours alone. You have made a mockery of justice by trying a righteous man."

In this quartet of people, the formula is reversed. Once again we have a woman who is sexually attractive, and therefore dangerous, but she does not try to sway the ruler from his duty. In fact, her intent is the opposite. The emperor must struggle with his own lust to save the Baptist from Herodias. Herodias, in turn, must corrupt the innocent daughter to persuade her husband to abandon his duty, which he is doing out of fear rather than from a moral basis. Those with weak faith are prey to lust; it inevitably brings about the corruption of political duty and self-destruction.

The opposite principle is embodied in Claudius. A Roman, he suggests that he might disobey Caesar for Salome; this makes him the antithesis of Fabius, who gives her up to please Caesar. A compatriot of Pilate, he is also a follower of John. He uses his power *for* the Baptist. Herod lusts for Salome; Claudius loves her.

Claudius appeals to Pilate saying that "we must recognize that a new force is coming into the world." It is a force for peace, one that can "win men where Rome could only conquer them." When Pilate tells him that Caesar is the only faith for a Roman, Claudius predicts the eventual triumph of the faith, and "your name will ring down through the years. Pontius Pilate, the first champion of a new religion!" Pilate rejects the notion.

Claudius presses on, but Pilate has common sense, telling of a carpenter who claims that he is the Son of God, who is doing miracles. "I will not tolerate anyone denouncing Rome under the cloak of religion. And this your prophet does. . . . I can't understand a brave soldier and brilliant officer turning to treason." Claudius replies that he has "a greater loyalty than Rome—humanity."

The new consciousness counteracts Rome without setting up a new government. It is a new consciousness, not a new institution. Institutional questions (even theocracies) are omitted from the discussion, yet Rome feels threatened.

Kleiner uses irony with Pilate; infamy is a kind of memory. Claudius understands the nature of freedom, yet he is not forced out of the army as a traitor, though he is tacitly accused of being one. In the end, he will have the girl, yet not be personally stained by Roman corruption.

The picture avoids miracles, because they are dramatically irrelevant. There is one scene in which Jesus' shadow passes over a blind man, who then announces that his sight has been restored. The other miracles, however, are recounted merely as tales. Since the story is carefully limited to events concerning Salome and John the Baptist, the miraculous does not become a problem.

Claudius' report to the imprisoned John that he had seen the raising of Lazarus causes the Baptist to confess: "My kinsman, Jesus—the Messiah. When I baptized him, I heard a voice from heaven, 'This is my beloved Son, in whom I am well pleased.' " This statement led *America* to note that the picture contained, "among other rarities, a forthright acknowledgement of the Divinity of Christ."[40] The evidence, however, is hearsay, since Claudius did not see Lazarus dead.

The film has unresolved ethical dilemmas. The controversial dance seems gratuitously tacked on to the film, and Stewart Granger's dialogue, "I bring you strange tidings," seems quite appropriate. One wonders what might have been the outcome had Salome used Herod's lust to save John's life, exchanging adultery for murder, and Claudius' rescue attempt, in which he presumably kills some of the Roman soldiers, raises the problem of treason.

The film was a curious and wandering tale, appealing simultaneously to the religious sensibilities and the prurience of the audience. One report of a preview audience said that the audience gave the picture its attention "most likely out of respect for its religious theme, and it was not until Salome went into her strip dance that any ripple of reaction started running through the audience."[41]

No serious attempt was made to create a historically recognizable Herod or Herodias. The disillusioned Salome, who has never really been evil, is redeemed, and the soldier who has been good all along remains that way. A curious stasis seemed to have come over the ethical world. The sex symbol finally attempts to use her sexuality for good, but she is subverted by the power of evil.

Unlike the heroes of the two earlier films, this hero has no power; it resides in other hands. The irresponsible Judean emperor and the responsible Roman were unlike any other film to that date. In the end, however, the good man is unable to change destiny. John is still executed.

Metaphorically, the hero is impotent—a symbol that may have been appropriate to the American mood of late 1952 and early 1953. It was an uncertain time when Americans were changing presidents and liquidating a war, but it was also a time when the public did not stay away from a motion picture whose screenwriters felt free to alter the biblical record in order to redeem the heroine. Sex was still drawing at the box office, but so was salvation.

By the time *Solomon and Sheba* (1959) reached the screen, this form of the biblical spectacular of the 1950s had passed its zenith. *Solomon and Sheba* appeared at the same time as *Ben-Hur*, and although it did not make nearly as much money, it returned enough to pay for United Artists' investment.

This was to be the last of the "popular" biblical spectaculars that dealt with sexuality, though *The Story of Ruth*, *Esther and the King*, and *Sodom and Gomorrah* would try to trade on the formula as had *The Prodigal* earlier. None did well at the box office. Though there are probably several reasons for these failures (poor execution, resistance to changes in the formula), sexuality was no longer a spectacular theme. The Production Code had been broken, and with that development, American films could explore sexuality in more personal terms across a variety of genres. America had recovered from the trauma of World War II, and other ethical questions seemed more appropriate for spectacular treatment.

The film follows the tension between Solomon and Adonijah over the kingdom left by David. Sheba comes on behalf of the North African allies to bring Solomon down by bringing discord in the united kingdom that Solomon has put together, and almost succeeds.

Sexuality was still a major interest for American popular culture. Films starring sex symbol Brigitte Bardot received wider distribution than any previous foreign releases. *Peyton Place*, a novel focusing on the sex lives of the people in a New England town, became America's all-time bestseller. Vladimir Nabokov's *Lolita*, a comic novel about a middle-aged man's sexual obsession with a 13-year-old girl, stayed on the bestseller list for months. Also, the attempt to import D. H. Lawrence's *Lady Chatterley's Lover*, which had been barred on grounds of obscenity for more than two decades, occasioned a widely publicized court case.

Solomon and Sheba was the most explicit American film to date. *Life* featured a full-page photograph of Gina Lollobrigida in a diaphanous white garment; she had gained status as one of the reigning foreign sex symbols. Although nudity was still prohibited, the costuming of Lollobrigida came as close to the state of undress as possible. As one review put it, "Deep reading in the Holy book will give you no idea of Solomon's temptation when the queen of Sheba arrived. Miss Lollobrigida wears costumes that even Ziegfeld, inventor of stage nudity, would not have dared."[42] Marjorie Rosen pointed out that "as boxoffice receipts plummeted, movies earnestly went about standardizing the desirable female."[43] She relates this development to the larger trend of what she calls "mammary madness." Designers emphasized the feminine figure during the 1950s, arguing that unlike the 1920s and 1940s, periods of feminist progress, the 1930s and 1950s were reactionary, and with women back in the home, the media "dominated *them*, and rechiseled their priorities and notions of beauty."[44] Rosen, however, also sees in Brigitte Bardot "an uncontrollable anger," a woman who used her body to "taunt, punish, and reward at *her* whim."[45] The character of Sheba seems cast in this mold.

From the beginning, Sheba is the self-directed woman. Unlike Delilah, she is not interested in revenge, and unlike Bathsheba or Salome, she does not seem to need a man. Her concern is with power. In her first scene, she scars Adonijah. Later, as she discusses Solomon with her advisor, Baltor, he explains Solomon's monotheism and suggests that "it teaches that all men are equal and none are slaves." Immediately Sheba senses a threat to her power, commenting that if it were to become widespread, she, along with all monarchs, would lose their thrones. When she meets with the other rulers in Egypt, she bargains to win a port for her country, hinting that she is willing to use sex for political gain.

When she meets Solomon, she tells him that she intends to "bind you in soft chains [her arms] so that I may do with you as I will." She plies Solomon's sister Abishag for the secret of Israel's unity, the source of its strength. When confronted by her love for Solomon, she chooses her "duty"—to betray him rather than to succumb to her feelings.

Sheba follows the syndrome of what psychologists Martha Wolfenstein and Nathan Leites called the "good-bad girl."

On the one hand, there are sexual impulses, which a man may feel to be bad, and which he may find it hard to associate with a woman whom he considers admirable. . . . A good girl is the sort that a man should marry, but she has the advantage of not being sexually stimulating.[46]

There are several strategies to satisfy the contradictory impulses—such as the "good girl who appears to be bad" (Salome). Sheba is perfectly understandable as a sexual woman who functions as a servant of her state; she subordinates her personal desires for her nation's advantage. She is the reverse of Solomon, a leader who cannot control his passion and thus almost brings disaster on his nation. Sheba is neither good nor bad. She is what psychiatrist Harvey Greenberg calls the "madonna-whore"; the feminine image is split in two, but she is redeemed when she learns to relate to her "natural" role,[47] marriage. When she accepts that role as God-given, she is redeemed. Her role as a ruler imposes a false "duty" on her.

The means by which she is changed from sex object/ruler to marriageable love object is the classic pattern of Christian redemption—confession of sin, confession of faith, acceptance of penance, and forgiveness, the same pattern as Delilah and Bathsheba. After Solomon professes his love and offers marriage, Sheba betrays him on behalf of her "duty." Nonetheless, her "real duty" is to be loved, rather than be a ruler who uses sex to solidify her power. When the temple is destroyed and Solomon has lost influence with the people of Israel, her "duty" has been carried out, and presumably she should move on. In most biblical spectaculars, however, the heroine must be redeemed.

Personal guilt overcomes Sheba. She becomes confused about her own beliefs, and the "good woman" begins to surface. When told she can be proud of her victory over Solomon, she bitterly replies that her political goals have been satisfied. "But I have betrayed a great man, who trusted— who loved me—beyond all else."

Solomon takes responsibility for his own downfall, telling her, "I have known from the first where you would lead, where I would follow." What he cannot understand is why she did not leave. She tells him she stayed because she loved him, and that he should "do with me what you will." Her confession of sin and confession of love are identical.

The next step in her redemption is to transfer her belief from pagan deities to Jehovah. As Solomon goes out to meet Adonijah and the Egyptian armies, Sheba prays for his victory, promising to return to Sheba, and "build a tabernacle to Jehovah." In accepting Jehovah, she strikes a bargain, and Jehovah shows Solomon the way to defeat the Egyptian army.

She must not escape unscathed however. Adonijah incites the crowd to have her stoned. The scene contains elements of both revenge and mercy. Her building of a tabernacle in her capital suggests the expansion of the democratic/religious ideals everywhere.

Thus, not only is she redeemed from lust to love, but also from being a scheming "bad woman" to become a faithful "good woman." She finds her redemption by denying herself a life based on the pleasure/power principle and accepting her "natural" function. Yet even here, she chooses celibacy and rulership to marriage as expiation for her sins. This renunciation is made sacred by belief in Jehovah; that is, in accepting a new consciousness.

In comparison, Solomon is noble to the core. He assumes that Adonijah will be elevated to the monarchy, and he tries to dissuade David from anointing him rather than his brother. Solomon prays for wisdom, not for power. He maintains the unity of the tribes by his wise administration of justice. As a result of his faithfulness, not only is the temple built, but in a series of dissolves after Solomon's prayer for wisdom, we see blossoming trees and a city that looks as though it has been through a successful urban renewal program. The narrator intones: "And through the years of peace, Israel grew and prospered. Solomon had fulfilled the sacred pledge to his father." The Deuteronomic formula (a doctrine of earthly rewards for fulfilling the law of Moses) is imposed on the film. Faithfulness to God will bring prosperity, whereas unfaithfulness will destroy the land.

This idea is reemphasized when after Solomon's sacrilege, the voice of God warns that by forsaking God's statutes, God will turn against them, for laying "hold on other gods and worshipping them, and serving them" (II Chronicles 7:19–22). These words are accompanied by a series of shots showing scenes of desolation—the breaking of the symbol of the unity of the Twelve Tribes, parched ground, a dried well, barren trees. God rewards and punishes human actions in his administration of the world.

This portrayal of God presents a problem for viewers who conceive of God in twentieth-century terms. The *Hollywood Reporter* claimed that "it presents a deity who can be haggled with and who can be petulantly unfair."[48] This "unfairness" refers to Solomon's complaint to God that Abishag, who has died while praying for him, was innocent and that the sin was his. It is an ancient argument between the Deuteronomic redactors of the Bible and those with a vision similar to that of the main body of the Book of Job. Evil is not clearly punished, nor are the good necessarily rewarded for their righteousness, but in the main, the God presented in the film is the one who hears prayers, rewards virtue with prosperity, punishes, forgives, and redeems.

Solomon and Adonijah are foils. Adonijah lusts for power; he tries to kill Solomon, and then righteously tells him that he "sought to preserve our country from your contamination." A hypocrite, he makes a deal with the Pharaoh. When Adonijah comes to Jerusalem to become ruler, he sits with a sword across his lap, telling people that he will not waste time with "senseless ritual," such as anointing, and that he will take the kingship with his own hands. Solomon, who did not seek to be king, understands that the unity of Israel is based on peace rather than war. He is anointed because David has a vision; Solomon becomes king of Israel "by the grace of God." In the same scene, David tells Adonijah: "Above all others, the King must respect and obey the Law. In proclaiming yourself, you have violated the law of God and man." This is more an American ideal than a Hebrew one, and reflects the opinion that the rule of law should not be hereditary. According to this point of view, the will of God requires that the most qualified should rule.

The political struggle, however, was not the major interest of the film. *Variety* pointed out that the clash between Solomon and Adonijah "plays second fiddle to the relationship between the Queen and her infatuated target."[49] Eroticism is the dominant theme. Adonijah is a pale villain beside his contemporary, *Ben-Hur*'s Messala, though both are driven by power motives. The theme of unity as a rallying cry, urging the nation not to divide into factions, lest the enemies within and without should bring "the righteous nation" down, settled for second place in *Solomon and Sheba*; the sexuality dominated and probably killed the subgenre.

The biblical spectacular of the 1950s drew on known, but not highly influential stories—the superman Samson, a famous but not paradigmatically significant episode in the life of David, the ministry of John the Baptist, which is usually treated as a part of the Jesus story, and the little-known relationship between Solomon and the queen of Sheba. All have a common thread—the relationship of sexuality to the political survival of the nation.

That relationship is found throughout literature—most notably in *The Iliad* and in Shakespeare's *Antony and Cleopatra*. The idea of opposing work and love is found in many genres of classic and popular literature. Nevertheless, its appearance for a decade in American biblical spectaculars is significant.

Biologically, we experience ourselves as separate individual units. Human beings are both isolated units *and* social beings—that is, humans have a subjectivity that separates them from all other creatures, yet they exist in a culture that directs the options they may take. On the one hand, persons experience themselves as individuals, yet because we speak a common language and have histories, we acknowledge the claim of a culture on us.

The sexual program of a society is an important part of all the social arrangements in that society, because humans are always sexually "in season." This requires us to restrain ourselves rationally, because societies have limited amounts of food and resources, but that effort to restrain the sexual impulse feels like a restriction on personal freedom. Thus, society writes codes and enforces them, deciding what is permissible sex. Out of such a conflict come marriage codes.

These codes become sanctions, without rational justification, and they seem to be part of reality itself.[50] It is ascribed to "human nature," and that threatens the fundamental order of the universe. To deny this order is to deny one's own being in this order.[51]

The nation must believe that there is a proper way to act, that certain institutions are divinely ordained, and that to go outside that order is to tempt chaos—to be outside the very bounds of meaning.

Both law and church polity make clear that one type of sexual behavior has community approval. In the spectacular films of the 1950s, marriage is normative, and any other kind of sexuality is socially destructive. That much did not change with the attack on the Production Code.

The social order is built on laws that are based on divinely given morality, and any challenge to morality threatens the entire social order. Molly Haskell noted that the Production Code "expressed, and reinforced, the instincts latent in the American psyche at its most romantic, puritanical, immature, energetic, and self-deluding," and that the emotion involved in defending marriage was "the fear that without such restraints the precarious edifice of civilization would collapse."[52]

The changing role of women is noticeable in the decade, but though the spectaculars challenged the Production Code, they also indicated that the "proper" function of Delilah, Bathsheba, Salome, and the queen of Sheba was that of wife. All are victims of either personal situations (such as Samson's rejection) or social situations (Bathsheba's forced marriage, Salome's rejection by Rome, Sheba's role as queen).

Michael Wood has argued that in the movies, women metaphorically represent the social order. This seems a natural assumption, given the social location of women in our culture for most of our history. Women have been assigned to domestic work, the socialization of children, and the maintenance of the family. Since they give birth to children and must in the early part of a child's life nourish them, this nurturing role has been prolonged through social arrangements to become a lifelong task. The extension of this pattern to the popular arts is understandable.

World War II created another set of images. Women were called upon to emulate "Rosie the Riveter" as well as to keep the social order at home. When the war ended, many women were forced to relinquish the autonomy of self-support, and their jobs were given to men. The technology of the war, however, when converted to the manufacture of consumer products, produced a plethora of items that had not been available to the average working-class family before. In the decade following the war, many people bought their first cars, first homes, first washing machines, and first TV sets. The expansion of the consumer economy led many women to work outside the home once again. As more autonomous persons, they were freer to express their individuality.

When those who have functioned as metaphors for civilization and socialization assume new roles, however, the whole sexual program of the society—and especially the family—is thrown into chaos unless adjustments are made. When coupled with the threat from without, such as the worldwide communist challenge, subliminal links are set up. In these films, sexuality is related to luxury—to the ownership of material possessions—and the pursuit of luxury conflicts with the woman's spiritual duty to preserve the nation. If passion is allowed to rule over reason and if the pleasure principle, joined with materialism, is allowed free expression, then the entire political and social order may be thrown into chaos.

The solution, therefore, is to make the pleasure principle (sexuality) subject to the appropriate and officially sanctioned social institutions (marriage). Not only does the social order seem to depend on this submission, but so does the cosmic order as well. To transgress is to invite the displeasure of Yahweh and to bring destruction to the nation. The king, judge, or ruler therefore becomes an official surrogate for the people, and it is for his transgression that punishment is meted out to the nation.

The tension of the individual in a collective society suggests that the highest achievement of the individual is to pursue one's natural duty. The man's duty is to serve the nation; the woman's is to serve the foundation of the nation—the family. Under the impact of increasing urbanization and the emergence of technocracy, the sexual images and roles found themselves in an oxymoronic situation. They were given the symbolic task of holding the culture together, while at the same time celebrating the new freedom from the codes that no longer spoke for American life.

NOTES

1. *Variety*, October 19, 1949, p. 13.
2. Robert H. Pfeiffer, *Introduction to the Old Testament* (New York: Harper and Brothers, 1948), p. 320.
3. *The Christian Advocate* 125 (January 19, 1950): 30.
4. Program notes, *Samson and Delilah* (Los Angeles, University of Southern California Film Library, 1949).
5. *New York Herald Tribune*, December 22, 1949, p. 15.
6. *Boxoffice*, October 19, 1949, p. 6.
7. Phil Koury, *Yes, Mr. DeMille* (New York: G. P. Putnam's Sons, 1959), p. 206.
8. DeMille, *Autobiography*, p. 308.
9. Koury, *Yes, Mr. DeMille*, p. 214.
10. George Barbarow, "DeMille's Folk Epic," *Hudson Review* 2 (Winter, 1950): 548.
11. *New York Times*, January 8, 1950, Sec. 2, p. 1.
12. *New York Times*, October 21, 1948, Sec. 2, p. 5.
13. *New York Herald Tribune*, October 23, 1949, Sec. 2, p. 1.
14. Rabbi Max Nussbaum to Cecil B. DeMille, October 17, 1949. DeMille's personal files. DeMille Estate, Los Angeles, California.
15. *Christian Herald* 72 (December, 1949): 80.
16. Ruth Inglis, *Freedom of the Movies* (New York: Da Capo Press, 1974), pp. 206, 216–17.
17. Ibid., p. 212.
18. Martin Quigley, *Decency in Motion Pictures* (New York: Macmillan Co., 1937), p. 49.
19. Gilbert Seldes, *The Great Audience* (New York: Viking Press, 1950), p. 78.
20. Andrew Dowdy, *Movies Are Better than Ever* (New York: William Morrow & Co., 1973), p. 82.
21. Ibid.
22. Cf. Gordon Gow, *Hollywood in the Fifties* (New York: A. S. Barnes & Co., 1971), p. 90.
23. *Time* 58 (August 20, 1951):86.
24. Henry King, interview in his office, July 3, 1975.
25. Dunne, tapes. USC Library.
26. *The Catholic World* 174 (October 1951): 69.
27. *Los Angeles Daily News*, December 16, 1950, p. 54.
28. Seldes, *Great Audience*, p. 74.
29. Dunne, tapes.
30. In the first draft of the script, the curse on the land contains no reference to the war at Rabbah. One month after the Chinese volunteers were sighted in

Korea and the United Nations forces began to suffer reversals, Dunne revised the script to include a reference to reversals in the war at Rabbah. When I questioned Henry King about this change, he told me that he did not recall the reason for the inclusion, but that it was not out of character with Dunne's writing to refer to current events.

31. Dunne, tapes.

32. *The Christian Herald* argued that this was inauthentic since Levitical procedures prohibited any but priests from entering. *Christian Herald* 74 (October, 1951):102.

33. *Extension* 46 (November, 1951): 2. It is interesting that Henry King is criticized in this connection. In my interview with him, he told me he had been a practicing Catholic since 1922. His most famous film, *The Song of Bernadette*, was noted for its pro-Catholic bias.

34. Dunne, tapes.

35. Ibid.

36. *New York Times*, August 19, 1951, Sec. 2, p. 1.

37. *Variety*, March 3, 1953, p. 3.

38. Wood, *America in the Movies*, p. 61.

39. *New York Times*, March 22, 1953, Sec. 2, p. 5.

40. *America* 88 (March 28, 1953):718.

41. *Hollywood Reporter*, March 13, 1953, p. 3.

42. *Dallas Morning News*, December 25, 1959, Sec. 2, p. 14.

43. Marjorie Rosen, *Popcorn Venus* (New York: Coward, McLain & Geoghagen, 1973), pp. 268–9.

44. Ibid., p. 268.

45. Ibid. p. 280.

46. Martha Wolfenstein and Nathan Leites, *Movies: A Psychological Study* (New York: Atheneum Press, 1970) pp. 25–26.

47. Harvey Greenberg, M.D., *The Movies on Your Mind* (New York: E. P. Dutton, 1975), p. 59.

48. *Hollywood Reporter*, December 28, 1959, p. 3.

49. *Variety*, November 4, 1959, p. 6.

50. For a fuller discussion, see Rene Guyon, *The Ethics of Sexual Acts* (New York: A. A. Knopf Pub., 1948), p. 14.

51. Peter Berger, *The Sacred Canopy* (Garden City, N.Y.: Doubleday & Co., 1969), p. 13.

52. Molly Haskell, *From Reverence to Rape* (New York: Holt, Rinehart, and Winston, 1973), p. 21.

6

The Jesus Cycle

In 1954, encouraged by new scholarship on the life of Jesus and the rising tide of church membership and attendance, the Episcopal Church helped finance a film on the life of Jesus, *The Day of Triumph*. Biblical scholars were reticent to lay the death of Jesus on the Jews in the light of the anti-Semitism of Nazi Germany, and responsibility had been shifted to the Romans. Also, new theories regarding Judas' betrayal of Jesus were advanced. One best-selling biblical commentary wondered:

Was Judas disappointed because Jesus refused to be king of Israel and lead a revolt against the Romans? Did he think that in this way he could force Jesus to defend himself and assert his kingship? Or did he hope to protect him from assassination by putting him under arrest? No one can say.[1]

The Day of Triumph was a small-scale production, without name players, or the resources of a major studio to book it or publicize it, but it pictured Jesus full-face for the first time since DeMille's *The King of Kings* (1927). *Day* portrayed Judas as a Zealot and linked him to Barabbas. Judas hoped to force Jesus into the ranks of the Zealots—a theme echoed in contemporaneous biblical theories about the political character of the Kingdom of God. *The Day of Triumph* broke important ground, for it was the first film in which the face and voice of Jesus were depicted in a film.[2]

Three years later, Jules Dassin's *He Who Must Die*, made in Greece from a novel of Nikos Kazantzakis, presented a modern passion play in which the characters' roles eventually become their reality, culminating in the death of the Jesus character. The film, set in the context of the enmity between the Cypriot Turks and Greeks, toured the "art house" circuit. Churches organized groups to see the film whose political overtones had little meaning for American audiences. The groundwork for the cycle of Jesus films was laid in these two films, whereas interest in religious spectaculars faded following *Ben-Hur*.

Five commercial films about Christ were made in the next 13 years. Those with wide commercial release were *King of Kings* (1961), *The Greatest Story Ever Told* (1965), and *Jesus Christ Superstar* (1975). Gaining more critical acclaim were the Italian-made *Gospel According to St. Matthew* (1963) and *Godspell* (1973). Neither of these was produced in the spectacular style, and neither had wide circulation in the United States.[3]

Turning the gospel accounts into spectacular big-budget melodramas was by no means a commercially "sure" investment. George Stevens is estimated to have lost a fortune on *The Greatest Story Ever Told*. To be sure of the investment, several problems had to be faced in preparing the scripts.

Marketing had to be considered. The scripts had to have both authenticity and wide commercial appeal. Movies were no longer the fundamental mass form of entertainment, and churches disagreed in their interpretation of Scripture. The problem was to find a suitable treatment that would unite rather than differentiate groups. DeMille had found the formula with Moses, but Jesus presented quite a different problem because he was the *object* of faith.

Some thought that the life of Jesus had intrinsic dramatic excitement. One such summary pointed out:

Jesus' early survival was a . . . case of escape from infant mass murder ordered by a superstitious tyrant. His short life and mission covered a very small and in that time out of the way portion of the earth's surface. His contacts were relatively small in number, his hardcore working force consisted of 12 men—one of whom was a traitor. His death was most agonizing and humiliating. It would be hard to conceive of a leader's death more shameful and bitterly painful. Immediately prior to it, he was denounced three times by a disciple who later became a cornerstone for the faith Jesus preached. Believe or disbelieve the story of the Resurrection, the fact remains that the ignominious death of this man of relatively little contemporary influence against the crushing might of ancient Rome—this death is about the livest thing that has happened in historic terms of worldwide influence on ways of thought and manners of living.[4]

The assumption is faulty. The story's details were well-known, and existed in four different versions. Both Leo Tolstoy and Thomas Jefferson had at one time sought to present "the" gospel as a single unified story, but their efforts were not widely appreciated. The film makers, men of considerably less stature, had to find an acceptable mode for telling the story, yet keep the scale in "the grand style." This task proved difficult.

Judith Crist questioned whether the story could be told at all. Whether to make the character of Jesus a known actor, or how to blend biblical and fictional dialogue are just two of the problems facing the film maker. The scale itself presented a problem, raising the question of the literalism of the image itself.

How to personify the mystery and divinity and, once personified, how to make the figure move among men? . . . The great big screen and the great big names are too much for the survival of matters of the spirit. So many aspects of big movie-making intervene that the Passion cannot predominate.[5]

There are other problems. The miracles of Christ must not appear to be optical illusions or cinematic tricks. The question of which miracles to portray and how to photograph them reveals the concerns of the film makers. The way in which the film maker handles the miracles gives us what he thinks the audience's vision is of the relationship between the natural and the supernatural—between a scientific world view and a religious one.

The Resurrection cannot be omitted, for it is the evidence of the divinity of Christ. Yet if people function on the basis of empirical thought, an audience is required either to acknowledge that its world view does not encompass things of the spirit or that there is some other explanation that is not portrayed. This forces the film maker to redefine salvation and atonement, changing "ransom" and "substitutionary" theories for variations on the "moral influence" theories.[6]

The reason for the Crucifixion is not well-established in the modern world. The Scriptures suggest a God whose plan is to have his son murdered. The theological assumptions behind that interpretation presume a world order determined by a Divine Intelligence in a most personal manner. Such a world view conflicts with modern thinking, which conceives of determinism as an impersonal force. According to the gospel accounts, Judas caused the Crucifixion because that was his role in the divine plan, but in the modern world view where there are no supernatural interventions into the natural order, it is difficult to make sense of Judas' motives.

"Why did Judas betray Jesus?" is complicated by another consideration: Was it possible that the infallible Christ made a mistake in choosing Judas as a disciple, or given the divine foreknowledge of his fate, did Jesus seek self-destruction? Various interpretations of Judas' role seek to resolve those conflicts in the modern consciousness.

The problem of portraying Jesus is also troublesome. Many perceptions about the life of Christ are formed by art—especially by popular art, such as that of Werner Sallman, whose head of Jesus seems to be the most widely recognized piece of religious art in America other than Leonardo da Vinci's *The Last Supper*. The question of whether to allow a recognizable actor to play Jesus plagued the Hollywood community. Even more perplexing was *how* to portray the Christ. For example, Ivan Butler noted the difference between the strength of Max von Sydow of *Greatest Story* and the gentleness of H. B. Warner of DeMille's silent *The King of Kings*. "Warner, for all the beauty, tenderness, and dignity of his portrayal, or perhaps because of these very virtues, never quite convinced as the Son of Man as well as the son of God . . . a 'gentle Jesus' of the child's bedside," whereas von Sydow has "the physical strength to undergo the strains imposed on Christ."[7]

The problem is to present a plausible Christ who fits the intentions of the director and simultaneously suggests both spirituality and humanity. Most critics concluded that one or the other was missing in each of the films, leaving audiences to wonder what was so compelling about Christ that he became the foundation for the massive institution that bears his name.

The synoptic Gospels and John are agreed on the Sanhedrin's culpability for the Crucifixion. The United States, however, has a large Jewish community, numerous influential Jewish organizations, and a solid commitment to the existence of Israel—which in the popular imagination has somehow been metaphorically linked with the beginnings of our own nation, and with earlier ideals of freedom and independence. Moreover, a sizeable portion of the film community was Jewish. The shocking anti-Semitism of Nazi Germany that resulted in the genocide of over 6 million Jews made the perception that Jews had been "Christ-killers" reprehensible in the eyes of most Americans.

The film makers were aided by the twentieth-century reexamination of the question by biblical scholars. There were numerous points made to counteract the doctrine of Jewish culpability—the competence of the Sanhedrin to punish blasphemy, the breaking of tradition in holding a meeting of the Sanhedrin during the Passover, the fact that the punishment was Roman (crucifixion) rather than Jewish (stoning), the conflicts between the Synoptics and John.

These ideas were what a screenwriter researching the life of Christ might find being taught in any major mainline Protestant seminary in 1960. Indeed, any other approach might alienate much of the Jewish community.

In the final analysis, the central problem was that of dealing with a sacred story in a technological and pluralistic society. Since the United States was at least nominally Christian, and since Christian doctrine had supplied the imaginative resources for much of America's finest literature, it was understandable that artists would want to present the story of Christ in the most technologically advanced medium available.

Since the story was so fundamental to the society, the spectacular form seemed the proper genre. The spectacular form, however, no matter how it was manipulated, seemed to demand a melodramatic archetype, and a melodrama fashioned from the sacred story of Christ worked against itself, creating a "moral fantasy" out of what had been considered the supernatural norm of ethical behavior.

I have argued that the biblical spectacular of the 1950s was a vehicle to examine the moral dilemma posed by the relationship between nationhood and sexuality, metaphorically exploring the need to place duty over pleasure. In these films, since Jesus Christ was the model for moral behavior, the film makers began to look at power and morality more carefully.

In *Kings of Kings*, the moral questions are associated within the politics of social change, a dominant concern of the decade. *The Greatest Story Ever Told* seems to be a meditation on the foundation of ethical behavior in a society that is technological and secular, and whose collective consciousness stands in opposition to a supernatural world. *Jesus Christ Superstar* reversed the imagery of the "righteous nation" to show how moral values based on the Christ-model were doomed to failure.

As the first of the Jesus films, *King of Kings* (1961) met with a great deal of hostility from both the secular and religious press. The Catholic newsweekly, *Our Sunday Visitor*, treated it as a "Judean hoss opera that might well be titled 'The Legend of White Robe.' "[8] *Commonweal* commented that:

The battle scenes, with the blood and gore, add excitement and realism . . . Battle scenes? You may well wonder just how battle scenes figure in the story of the Prince of Peace. But there's the rub. Unable to find enough drama in the greatest story ever told, in the beautifully written Gospels themselves, *King of Kings* has added and padded until it has become not the Life of Christ but a fictional version— with the historical facts adjusted and changed to make them fit a dramatic panorama of the times.[9]

Setting Jesus in a historical framework irked the Christian critics, who sensed that the depiction of Jesus was neither spiritually profound nor dynamically earthy.

Samuel Bronston, Philip Yordan, and Nicholas Ray fashioned their story in counterpoint, counterbalancing the scriptural passages with the fictional political savagery of ongoing wars between Romans and Jews. Pompey's Romans defile the temple and kill the priests. There follows a montage of Jews as slaves, mixed with shots of Herod carried on a red carriage through row upon row of crosses. This juxtaposition forms the framework of the film, where crucified bodies being tossed into open graves are set against Caesar's proclamation calling for a census. This sequence is followed by scenes of the Nativity.

In depicting the biblical scenes, *King of Kings* adheres rather closely to the synoptic Gospels.[10] Some accounts have been changed for dramatic purposes; for example, Mary Magdalene is identified with the adulteress saved from stoning, and Jesus goes to see John in his cell to confirm his messianic character to the doomed Baptist.

Two subthemes are also developed: Jewish oppression by the jaded court of Herod and Pilate, and their confrontation with Barabbas, who as a Zealot first wants the Baptist and then Jesus to join his political rebellion. Woven throughout is the story of Jesus as God's emissary of universal peace and goodwill. A third story—the salvation of the Roman centurion, Lucius, and Pilate's wife by their gradual and reluctant conversion to Christianity—represents the victory of Christ's way over Barabbas, who is treated as the Jewish counterpart of the Romans.

In the latter half of the film, the story lines are merged. Jesus' entry into Jerusalem on Palm Sunday coincides with the insurrection led by Barabbas. Skilfully crosscut are shots of the crowd waving palm branches and the cruel entrapment of Barabbas' forces as the Romans force the insurrectionists into the closed gate and then walk over the bloody bodies beneath their iron phalanx, mowing down the Zealots like wheat before the reaper. Judas is a Zealot who has been trying to mediate between Barabbas and Jesus. He believes that Jesus, "when he feels a Roman sword at his throat, will smite them down with the wave of one arm." Thus, he delivers him into the hands of the Romans.

The underlying principle of selection was to avoid an abstract mythic Jesus figure and set him amid the turmoil of times presumed to be not greatly different from 1961. The program for the film opened with the prologue, "*As it is today*, so it was in the turbulent times before Christ, that the menace of pagan tyranny shadowed the hearts of men who would be free. . . . Into this troubled world came Jesus of Nazareth, who feared none, nor even death, to bring forth enlightenment and triumph."[11]

Jesus becomes little more than a pawn of contending social forces. Political obedience forces Lucius to kill little children and to crucify Jews, and Barabbas to justify his anger by spending the lives of his patriots and to use decent men (like Jesus) for purposes they do not consent to.

Barabbas, in assessing the Sermon on the Mount, tells Judas "I am fire, he is water," bringing to mind the Irgun, the terrorist faction that operated in Palestine before the creation of the Israeli state in 1948. He is clearly the most interesting person in the film.

Church people, expecting a film about Christ, found instead a melodrama that explored a character mentioned in connection with only one event in the New Testament. The plot line hinged on the gospel description of Barabbas as "a man who had been thrown into prison for an insurrection started in the city, and for murder" (Luke 23:19). His revolutionary character is conjecture; the Scriptures indicate only that he started a riot in the city. In a perceptive analysis, one review noted that "in the life and times of Jesus, 'the times got the upper hand,'" and that by focusing on Barabbas, producer Bronston created two stories." As the screenplay relates the actions of Barabbas to Christ, "the actions of Jesus become strangely confused in an almost impersonal manner, leaving the film without a living personality for him."[12]

In all likelihood, Bronston, Yordan, and Ray believed that they were expressing the mood of the new America. John Kennedy's inaugural address had warned that those who make freedom impossible made revolution inevitable, that "a society unable to help the many who are poor could not save the few who are rich." Kennedy had suggested that Americans should "ask not what your country can do for you; ask what you can do for your country." Barabbas, representing the violent side of social change, called attention to these same fears.

Jesus, however, does get lost in the process. Trying to pin down precisely what had gone wrong was more difficult. Artists had portrayed Christ in all kinds of settings, but the choice of Jeffrey Hunter seemed to enrage a large part of the critical community. He was described as "a fan-mag baby-blue eyes with barely enough histrionic ability to play a Hollywood marine." The definitive criticism of Bronston's Christ, and indeed of his entire film, is expressed in the snide subtitle by which it was known in the trade: *I Was A Teenage Jesus.*[13]

A Catholic magazine argued that there is no "dramatic engagement between Him and the audience."[14] The picture of Jesus was not personal enough to counter Barabbas or socially aware enough to offer a peaceful alternative to the revolutionaries. Christ was not presented as *the* Son of God whose actions represented a clear alternative to the Roman Empire and Barabbas.

Christ as the object of faith had been neutralized, because pluralism demanded the film give the least possible offense to the religious sensibilities of all shades of believers and unbelievers in the audience. When placed alongside a real revolutionary, the figure of Christ becomes an anachronism. "The problem was not the quality of the acting nor the actor's makeup but the film's inability to unlock the mystery behind the figure."[15] *The Sign* concluded, "He is no Messiah in this presentation. He is nothing more than a young man dedicated to a racial or political purpose."[16] Given the Christ portrayed on the screen, it is difficult to understand why anyone would follow him.

Although Barabbas is hard and fiery, and Lucius is confused and yet attracted to Jesus, the film tries to portray Jesus as warm and human. Bronston chose Hunter for his eyes. "In costume as Jesus, His pale blue eyes leap out at you from a bearded sunburned face."[17]

This personalization accounts for the deviation from Scripture when Jesus goes to see John in prison. Repeatedly the screen is filled with Jesus' eyes in extreme close-up as Ray cuts back and forth from Jesus' outstretched hand to John's agonizing climb up the side of the dungeon wall. The Jesus of this scene seems quite charitable when placed alongside the

Jesus of the scriptural account who tells John's messengers to go back and tell him what they have seen, rather than going to meet the imprisoned man himself (Matthew 11:2–6; Luke 4:17–21).

To keep Jesus's humanity dominant, the film undercuts the miracles. The miracles can be explained naturalistically. The major miracles, raising Lazarus, the cleansing of the lepers, and feeding the 5,000 are not depicted, and those that are give "natural" causes, as when Christ "calms" a possessed man by grasping his hands and looking into his eyes.[18]

The script says that when the shadow of Jesus passes over the paralyzed young man, "energy seems to flow into the immobilized limbs." When Pilate sends Lucius out to spy on Jesus, he comes back to report that though he has seen no miracles, there are those who tell of healings, the feeding of the 5,000 people, and Jesus walking on the Sea of Galilee. Pilate mutters with exasperation that thousands of such healings are reported.

The film's effort to rationalize or obfuscate miracles is centered in the American acceptance of experience as the only reliable way of knowing. Seeing is believing. In the nineteenth- and twentieth-century scholarship, the suggestion that there were other causes for the miracles became prominent and popular. For example, people may have shared their lunches with others at the feeding of the 5,000. With the advent of psychology as a "social science," however, explanation of miracles began to swing toward it. Most of the healings could be explained psychosomatically, thereby maintaining the "truth" of the Bible record, while at the same time providing empirical verification. That such constructs as the ego, the id, and the superego were imaginative interpretations did not seem to matter a great deal.

This did not go unnoticed. Dwight Macdonald concluded that "they were omitted because it was felt they wouldn't go down with a modern audience. Probably not, but that merely shows we aren't a religious people." Moreover, they could not avoid the Resurrection, but they "suggest it might have been an hallucination." In the end, they "yield to no one in their respect for religion, but they don't want to make fools of themselves."[19]

Macdonald equates belief in miracles with being religious—something many Protestants would never agree with, since the mainstreams of Protestant theology from Schleiermacher in the nineteenth century on has struggled with questions of adjusting to changing metaphysical conceptions of scientific rationalism. On the other side, the evangelicals and fundamentalists perceived that such adjustments and modifications to science would erode the authority of Christianity, confirmed in the divinity of Christ, and have been unwilling to make such concessions to modernism.

The problem of the Resurrection, however, cannot be avoided. When the audience is shown several possibilities through the use of quick cutting and long shots, the moviegoers find it difficult to know what they have actually seen. The film seems to suggest that the audience fill in its own beliefs at that point—what we believe determines what we see. The cumulative effect of this approach is to emphasize the humanity of Jesus while leaving the divinity in doubt. The *Boston Globe* commented that "His chief godlike attribute is the *eloquence of virtue.*"[20] The nondenominational Jesus of pluralistic America is reduced to human virtues, and his divinity rests in "the eloquence of virtue"—a shift from theological values to human ones.

"The grand style" imposed limitations. The central spectacles were the battle scenes and the Sermon on the Mount. The pairing of these two is crucial, because they represent the polarities of thought and action. Barabbas witnesses the Sermon; disgusted, he says to Judas, "Words!" On the other hand, he sits helplessly wounded as the soldiers kill the Zealots trapped in the city.

Director Ray tried to break the static recounting of Jesus' teachings (the collection of sayings in Matthew known as the Sermon on the Mount and in Luke as the Sermon on the Plain) by having Jesus move among groups standing on the hillside teaching, exhorting, and answering questions. A great deal of money was expended on this scene. A long dolly shot required more than 160 feet of track on a 58 degree mountain slope, with complicated counterweights for the camera truck. More than a month was spent preparing and filming the scene, with 81 separate setups and 21 days of shooting.[21]

All the characters of the story are assembled—Pilate's wife and Lucius, Barabbas and Judas, Nicodemus and Caiaphas, the disciples and Jesus' mother, the adulteress and Mary Magdalene. Starting with the Beatitudes at sunrise, Jesus talks to camel drivers, the rich young ruler, elderly people, cynics, merchants, members of the Sanhedrin, students, and children. Not only is much of the Sermon on the Mount covered, but also several interpretations of parables and material from the "I am . . . " sayings of the Gospel of John. The scene is both personal and intimate, consistent with Ray's vision of Jesus.

These quotations from the gospels offer an alternative to Barabbas and Rome. Barabbas is right—they are words—ideals that must be demonstrated within the context of the film's dramatic action. On the one hand, the story of Christ demands spectacular treatment; at the same time, it defeats such treatment because one must adhere to the biblical record, whose ideas are not easily rendered on the large screen.

Setting the film in a political context virtually demanded that there be a political solution to the problem of Judas. Ray said that Judas misunderstood Jesus. "He was one who served and found it impossible to perform miracles. He tried and couldn't because his faith wasn't great enough." They chose this over the greed (30 pieces of silver) and had Judas hang himself with the strap of his coin purse.[22]

Since Judas believes more strongly in Jesus' temporal power than do the other disciples, he is partially redeemed for us. His faith serves two functions—to show that Christ was not wrong to choose the disciple who later would betray him (thereby keeping intact his deity), and to allow the audience to identify Judas as one who believed, and therefore was worthy of eventual salvation—the popular American conviction that everyone will finally be saved. Judas' deeds have tragic consequences despite his good intentions. Also, dramatically the film does what the Bible has never done—provides a human reason for Judas' act of betrayal, wrapping the motivations up in a plausible package.

In *Kings of Kings*, the Jews are not culpable. The Sanhedrin does not even appear in the film. The trials are before Pilate (a Roman) and Herod Antipas (described as being of Arabian heritage). Herod says of John the Baptist's death: "Why did I do it? I am not an evil man." and Pilate replies: "Your mistake was not to do it the first day." When Jesus comes to him, Herod mocks Jesus, and has him flogged and sent back to Pilate for final judgment. *Films in Review* commented that the film made it seem as if no one was anxious to put Christ to death. "The implication is that Christ died by default, and that not a single Scribe, Pharisee, Sadducee, priest or high priest had anything to do with it."[23] The script suggests a fervent effort to absolve the Jews of any suggestion that Jews were "Christ-killers."

The volatility of the issue was perceived by Dwight Macdonald. Of *Ben-Hur*, Macdonald had written, "In this film we see merely Pilate washing his hands and delivering Christ over to the brutal soldiery; ain't nobody here but just us Romans. . . . But there are no ancient Romans around and there are many Jews and $15,000,000 is $15,000,000."[24]

For his criticism, Macdonald reported that he had been called a bigot in print and reported that "Israel is now as much 'a secular cow' as Soviet Russia was in the thirties."

When I made my gaffe two years ago, I took it for granted as a WASP by upbringing that the biblical account of the trial and crucifixion of Jesus was correct. Since then, I've learned that a good case can be made out that the Gospel writers, for propagandist reasons, played down the part of the Romans in the tragedy and played up that of the Jews.

Macdonald admits that he might have erred on matters of biblical scholarship and historical fact. What he would have none of is the argument that he is racially prejudiced. He noted that certain racial groups have become sacrosanct, "so that when one states, depending on the New Testament, that certain Jews two thousand years ago wanted Jesus killed, one is accused of denouncing all Jews today as 'Christ-killers.' "[25]

Macdonald's comments exposed two important changes in American culture: (1) the Bible was no longer sacrosanct and now needed to be synchronized with certain contemporary American values, and (2) the "melting pot" theory was incapable of working its magic on the persistent American problem of anti-Semitism.

The first of these shifts is obvious. Biblical scholarship had suggested alternatives to Jewish culpability, and even those most committed to biblical inerrancy found themselves unable to discuss the issues. Most fundamentalists and evangelicals were still staying away from films in the early 1960s, so there is little discussion from their point of view, since movies in themselves were an evil to be avoided. Catholic criticism, however, noted the issue but then avoided discussion of it, and the Protestant Motion Picture Council did not even mention the matter. To choose any interpretation other than one that mitigated the scriptural contention of Jewish culpability was to risk being labeled a bigot. The Bible could be "propaganda," and if that were so, the authority of the churches was on shaky ground.

The melting pot theory of American society suggests that along with the process of urbanization, a concurrent process of homogenization takes place, so that differences in character traits eventually disappear. Martin Marty noted that Will Herberg had shown there were three "melting pots" (Protestant, Catholic, and Jew), and that subsequently black Protestants were added. "The process of national amalgamation had not been smooth, but ethnic, racial and religious groups seemed all to have been on a course toward the development of the process—until the late 1960s."[26]

Jews have a long history of being scapegoats and written into their rituals are references to the need for constant vigilance, because another tyrant arises in every generation with the intent to wipe them out. Those who would legitimate such action against Jews have often used "Christ-killer" to excuse their own action, especially in Christian nations.

American films were slow to face the problem of anti-Semitism. *Crossfire* and *Gentlemen's Agreement* (1947) were the first films to confront the problem openly. Americans were more inclined to displace the attitudes onto the Nazis than to blame themselves for anti-Semitism. What Macdonald did not seem to understand was that Jews faced anti-Semitism on a regular basis and wanted no reinforcement of those attitudes, even in film criticism. Will Herberg, who in 1955 maintained that "the American Jew was now in a position where he could establish his Jewishness not apart from, nor in spite of, his Americanness, but precisely through and by virtue of it,"[27] had to admit in the revision of his book that perplexity and restlessness had set in. The American way of life had not made it possible for Jews to forget their jeopardy in American culture or for the Christians to understand why Jews were so worried.

The fundamental problem underlying *King of Kings*, however, was the question of the adequacy of the melodramatic archetype as a cultural vehicle for the story of Jesus—the model for Christian ethical behavior.

Many Christians would be offended by the suggestion that their faith was based on a melodrama. The melodramatic archetype, although very popular, is not highly prized. In American culture, mimetic forms, such as tragedy, are valued partly because they are imitations of experience and, thus, are "realistic." Moral fantasies, on the other hand, are popular but not highly valued, partly because they are assumed to be renderings of our wishes and thus not anchored in "reality." To treat the story of the Christian faith as a melodrama undercuts its authority, for it asks people to behave as if their fantasies might be fulfilled.[28]

Bronston, Yordan, and Ray were concerned that the audience sense something of America's political situation in their film. Bronston and Yordan collaborated not only on *King of Kings*, but also on *El Cid*, *55 Days at Peking*, and *Fall of the Roman Empire*, all of which explore similar political themes reflecting changing American commitments on the international scene.

King of Kings seemed to suggest that Christ's way was an alternative to the violent means of throwing off oppression. The makers thought of it as a way of approaching the serious moral challenges that the 1960s would bring. The trade papers saw the film in that light. One noted that it "tingles with contemporary meaning," and that the world was "trembling at the prospect of nuclear destruction," whereas another saw the film as offering a ray of hope "in a spiritual salvation which far transcends any power of man to impede." The advertisements billed it as dealing with "good and evil, love and hate, war and peace."[29]

In the final analysis, the apolitical atmosphere in which Christ wanders among the white-hot forces of Rome and Barabbas and the fact that he is not even aware of the insurrection taking place in the city on Palm Sunday while he is receiving accolades suggest that the Christian message is pallid and impractical, because it does not address the issues raging in the colonized world. The interior freedom the film extols does not ensure the victory of good over evil and bears little resemblance to the freedom for which Barabbas is fighting.

Seeming to resolve the tension within a melodramatic framework, the film finally provides little help for the moral dilemmas facing the country. These would be cast in very specific terms—access to public accommodations, education, and voting rights for all; the threat of rising militarism; an unstable communism in Asia. These were material problems, and the Jesus of *King of Kings* is above materialism—indeed, above political considerations. The image that remains is not that of a resurrected Christ with the fisherman standing in his shadow at the end of the film, but Jesus standing in the lonely shadow of Pilate's courtyard, waiting for Pilate to decide his fate.

All the things that could go wrong with a film came together in George Stevens' *The Greatest Story Ever Told*. While it was still in preparation,

King of Kings was released. Twentieth Century Fox, already overcommitted on *Cleopatra*, was forced to back out on its commitment to Stevens. Stevens, deciding that he did not really want to make a formulaic spectacular, cast the main parts with relative unknowns; then, to obtain financing, he put together dozens of "cameo" parts with name actors coming in to work for a day. The cost of shooting and sets went well over budget, boosting the total cost of the film from an estimated $10 million to an actual $25 million.

Wanting a fresh look at Jesus, Stevens worked with a series of scriptwriters and consultants (most notable of whom was Carl Sandburg) who developed a long, arduous script using some of the elements of biblical spectaculars, but substituting a different archetype. His cast grumbled at the leisurely pace, and snow shut down the production on the sets in Utah and Nevada for nearly three months. The film as released was 225 minutes long; it was cut to 197 for the London release and for screening in many of the larger American cities, and finally went into the neighborhood theaters at 141 minutes, a shell of Stevens' intentions.

A few critics tried to say good things about the film. All were impressed with Stevens' previous work—his credits included *Alice Adams*, *A Place in the Sun*, *The Diary of Anne Frank*—and he considered *Greatest Story* his most important work. The film was a spectacular failure, however, and the critics' reactions reflected it.

In *Life*, Shana Alexander complained that despite the "beautifully photographed, relentless good taste," the total effect eventually was "sets by Hallmark, panorama by Grand Canyon Postcards, Inc. and a script by an ecumenical committee," and that made her angry.[30]

In other reviews, certain phrases recur—the "Hallmark postcard" metaphor; the lack of spectacular effects; complaints of the "inoffensiveness" of the script to Protestants, Catholics, or Jews. As they praised the photography and lack of cliches, the critics also seemed to miss them. Alexander talks about "a couple of dozen film biographies of Christ" when, in fact, *Greatest Story* was only the sixth—one of these had not played commercially in the United States, and two were silent films. One has to suspect that the spectacular form had made a deeper impression on film critics than their frequent condemnations acknowledged.

The first half of the film alternates between pastoral scenes and conflicts. Herod's Slaughter of the Innocents, the temptation, the gathering storm around John the Baptist—all are presented in high relief. Interspersed is the ministry of Jesus. The key scene in the first half is the resurrection of Lazarus, used to foretell Jesus' own Resurrection.

The second half details the consequences of Jesus' ministry and the raising of Lazarus. After Jesus cleanses the temple, Herod and Caiaphas plan to arrest him in the temple as he teaches. Judas' betrayal, the capture of Jesus in Gethsemane, and the trials before the Sanhedrin and Pilate are followed by long scenes of the Via Dolorosa and the Crucifixion. The Resurrection is preceded by the Matthean account of Caiaphas having Roman guards placed around the tomb, and the Resurrection itself is a combination of the Lucan and Johannine accounts.

Stevens freely borrows from one gospel account to another, telling the story in its most familiar form. Unlike *King of Kings*, Stevens steers away from fictional events, providing only as many as are necessary to hold the story together. His dramatic cohesion comes by positioning the events he chooses.

He makes his characters into symbols in order to present a universal Christ. Some of the missing parts (the boyhood reading of the Scriptures, the marriage feast at Cana) would have set Christ in the midst of the Jewish community. Even his family is played as a symbol.[31] He decides to present the Christ of faith rather than the Jesus of history; yet at the same time Stevens seems to be trying to set him within a scientific world view. Of the Jesus films in the sound era, *Greatest Story* was least interested in "humanizing" the character of Jesus. The focus on Christ and his teachings is aimed at the churches rather than at the general public.

This intention is often undercut by the emendations. Dwight Macdonald acerbically points out the effects of such interpretations: " 'Do you consider wealth a crime?' the rich Lazarus asks. 'Not at all,' smoothly replies Max von Norman Vincent Peale, 'but it may become a burden.' One of the many things I admire about Jesus is his prejudice against the rich."[32]

In the temple, Stevens places Paul's passage about love (I Corinthians 13) in the mouth of Jesus, as he cuts back and forth between Jesus and Romans invading the temple. The effect jars those familiar with the Scriptures.

Something of Stevens' strategy peeks through here. He knew that the majority of church members were biblically illiterate and saw the New Testament as a seamless whole rather than as disparate accounts. By placing the words of I Corinthians 13 in Jesus' mouth, Stevens dramatically suits his own purposes—he creates tension between the sayings of Jesus and the deeds of the Romans—and at the same time dramatizes a familiar and beloved passage that many people have mistakenly thought of as the words of Jesus.[33]

Yet Stevens was forced more and more into repeating the familiar. At one point, he had indicated that he did not want to do scenes from the Old Masters, saying, "We're not going to thank Mr. DaVinci for his arrangement of the Last Supper. When the scene comes, we hope audiences will feel that it happened this way." When the time came for the scene, however, Stevens found himself building it on the classics of religious art.[34]

Stevens' conception of the film changed between the time he uttered the earlier statement and the completion of the project. In the beginning, Stevens did not want to do a spectacular, but with the pressures of money, time and his inability to project a clear and fresh picture of Jesus without adding a great deal of fictional material, he was drawn more to the juxtaposition of the spectacular sweep of his landscape with a presentation of events as people had come to think about them. He hoped to create a visual tension that was lacking in the story line and to give a new perspective to the mysterious man of faith that he was portraying.

A fundamental problem in doing the life of Jesus is that the story is so well-known. Bronston, Yordan, Ray, and company had sought to play it within the framework of a fictional story, using it to evoke their interpretation. Since Stevens would not use fictional episodes, the problem was how to make a dramatic structure for the screen.

Dialogue becomes a problem here. Does the film maker write dialogue for Jesus, make small talk to suggest an everyday human, and establish motives where they are unclear? How does one establish the world and culture in which he is set, aside from set design? How do you provide continuity for such moments as the centurion's conversion or the thief's confession on the cross?[35]

Stevens' major change was adding a character called "the Dark Hermit." In the scenes of the temptation, the Dark Hermit speaks colloquially to Jesus, while Jesus answers with Scripture. The script explains that the Hermit is the voice of Jesus' consciousness. When Jesus is about to heal the blind Aram, the voice of the "Dark One" is heard offscreen: "If you are not a faker, show us a miracle," and when the crowd cries out for Jesus' Crucifixion, the Dark Hermit is among them. There are visual suggestions that the Dark Hermit is responsible for the Slaughter of the Innocents, for Judas' betrayal, and for Peter's denial. The role became progressively smaller as the film was edited and reedited; in the 141-minute version, the whole character was excised, making such actions as those mentioned all the more ambiguous, and providing a special problem for the interpretation of Judas' betrayal.

Stevens wanted the Christ to be believable to the modern mind; yet he wanted to be faithful to the New Testament. The Gospels blame Satan for much of what happened in the New Testament; for example, in both Luke and John, we are told that Judas betrayed Christ because Satan entered into him. The popular conception of Satan with tail and horns, however, would not fit such a conception. The costume maker pointed out that the real devil would hardly be found in uniform.[36] The Dark Hermit is the answer to the problem.

The Dark Hermit represents Satan as an aspect of Jesus' consciousness (as when he tempts Jesus to cure Aram to show his power and to gather fame) or as an evil manifestation of the imagination (as in the crowd). It was a figure that fulfilled requirements for both biblical fidelity and plausibility in a way that so many of the other innovations that Stevens tried did not.

The critics wanted very much to like Max von Sydow as Jesus. They wrote such things as "Stevens felt it would be difficult for audiences to accept as the Lord an actor who might have appeared on the screen as a quick-draw sheriff or a two-fisted business tycoon."[37] Others heralded von Sydow for the virility he brought to the figure of Christ, and spoke of his compassion and his ability to utter the words of Christ firmly and emphatically. Bosley Crowther exposed the enigma, saying that von Sydow's performance was of "an inspired, devout, benevolent man. But . . . one senses Mr. Stevens may be working toward a presentation of the historical Jesus rather than the divine Jesus, until the episode of raising Lazarus from the dead."[38] Crowther's description is not of a "historical Jesus," but of a "divine Jesus." It is the ability to mingle with people, the accessibility, and the outwardness that is humanly appealing. The Christ of faith is an object of adoration, somewhat removed from the normal human qualities and benevolent because of a deeper understanding of human nature. Crowther describes the Christ of faith but does not recognize that he does so.

The medium of film itself, well-suited to the portrayal of surfaces and action, offers the illusion of reality, but works against the divine presentation of Christ that Stevens has chosen. Thus, the figure of Christ becomes more enigmatic. "Surely, Christ was not the cold, humorless fish von Sydow makes Him in . . . his godly, solid, almost stolid portrayal."[39]

Von Sydow's presentation was too distant, too foreign, and moved toward an emphasis on the Christ of faith and away from the humanity of Jesus. Stevens wanted the Christ of faith, but to make Christ believable required solid human qualities, especially those missing in the film: humor and joy.

Stevens attempted to add to the film's plausibility in his treatment of the miraculous. One is never clear how, why, or even *if* Jesus granted sight to old Aram, since the moment occurs privately, with Aram looking up and saying, "You are quite tall now." Jesus, however, is no longer there, and the camera shows nothing but the empty sky. When he heals the crippled Uriah, Jesus tells him that his faith is weaker than his legs—a suggestion that what is at stake is really a struggle of the will—and when Uriah walks, Jesus informs him that his faith has made him well. By relegating miracles to the realm of the knowable, Stevens strips much of the mystery from the character of Jesus.

The key scene of the film, the resurrection of Lazarus, becomes the crucial moment. The scene puzzled many critics. *Time*, in noting that Stevens avoids the less credible miracles, argues that here he does a reversal, letting "his whole drama turn on the raising of Lazarus."[40]

The sequence starts in Nazareth, with Lazarus coming to Mary's house to warn Jesus about the Romans. After curing Aram's blindness, Jesus and his disciples leave Nazareth; outside the village they hear that Lazarus is sick and dying. Jesus says that Lazarus' sickness is for the glory of God.

On their journey to Bethany, they stop at the pool where John baptized Jesus. The disciples are tired and dispirited, and James the Less says that the place is not the same without John. After Jesus teaches them the Lord's Prayer, they learn of Lazarus' death. The disciples are more despondent than ever: though Jesus had cured many people, he did not help his friend. The scene is lit darkly and played as an elegy, as if the faith of all had been lost.

As they enter Bethany, the camera pans down to Lazarus' house, where Mary and Martha are mourning. Martha accosts Jesus, demanding: "Was it too much to keep my brother from dying?" Jesus replies: "I am the Resurrection and the Life." He asks her if she believes those words, and she tells him that if he had been there, her brother would not have died.

Jesus mounts the hill toward the tomb of Lazarus, making his way through barriers and through crowds of people. The skeptic Bar Amand is introduced. Christ stands in front of the tomb, his figure in darkness with a bright sky about him—the lighting effects suggesting the interplay of death and life. Praying, "You wound and you heal, you kill and you make alive," Jesus opens the seal of the tomb and whispers: "Lazarus." A series of reaction shots are intercut at this point. Then in a long shot, he shouts for Lazarus to come forth, the words echoing in the tomb. Again there are a series of reaction shots, especially featuring Bar Amand, who seems to be retreating from the crowd, the counterreaction to Jesus' move into it as he went to the tomb. Lazarus is seen first from behind and then in an extreme long shot. The three men—the healed cripple Uriah, the previously blind Aram, and the skeptic Bar Amand—rush toward the gates of Jerusalem as the soundtrack fills with the "Hallelujah Chorus" from Handel's *Messiah*.

The important element of the scene is not the raising of Lazarus, but the restoration of faith to the community in the midst of doubt. The lengthy sequences with John the Baptist show him as a possible rival to Christ, but this sequence clearly establishes that Jesus is the Divine One. John is earthy, angry, and righteous. On the other hand, Christ is never out of control, and does not respond to political violations or ephemeral matters, but concerns himself with bringing humanity and the natural order, including the miraculous interventions into nature, into harmony. The disciples and others must learn what his mission is. Thus, when he brings Lazarus back from the dead, Stevens eclipses our assurance by shooting Lazarus from behind and in an extremely long shot. The three men—the blind, the halt, and the unbelieving—race toward Jerusalem to proclaim that Christ is indeed what he claims for himself.

Bar Amand: The Messiah has come! A man was dead and now he lives!

Aram: I was blind . . . and now I see!

Uriah: I was crippled . . . and I walk!

Soldier: Who has done this?

Aram: The man called Jesus.

The word is spread of the miracle of resurrection.

This scene allows Stevens later to avoid much of the controversy surrounding the Resurrection of Jesus. The Resurrection is introduced at the pool of the River Jordan, recalling John the Baptist. A stone is thrown in, and the circles in the water grow wider and wider. Then the trumpets sound from the parapets as the sun comes up over the empty cross. When they find the stone rolled back, the centurion and the legionnaires are shocked, the women are bewildered, Thomas doubts—but Mary Magdalene, photographed in the fulness of the sunlight, believes. Caiaphas later says the whole thing will be forgotten in a week, but the film cuts immediately to Jesus' face in the clouds, and the camera tracks down to the assembled disciples—now including the women as well as Joseph of Arimathea and Nicodemus. The clouds come as the voice of Jesus announces that "today's troubles are enough." Stevens follows this with a long lap dissolve superimposing the picture of Christ over the scene.

Normally, spectacular scenes were conceived of as employing elaborate sets and costuming, battles and other action devices, and masses of people. Stevens challenged that conception. A 1962 "Progress Report" sent out by his studio's publicity department noted: "It is his intention to leave unchallenged the astronomical figures set by previous films, either in the number of extras used in a single scene, the elaborateness of the costumes or sets, or even in total monies expended."

He decided against shooting in the Holy Land, because it no longer had the rich forests and fertile farm land. "Now it is barren and burned out— invasions and wars account for transforming the countryside. The centuries of human erosion have smoothed out the land." He wanted to create a visually exciting environment.[41]

It was a choice undoubtedly influenced by the visual power and scope that had given Stevens' *Shane* its mythic power. Stevens sets Jesus and his ministry in the midst of a spectacular natural world. Stevens had said that he wanted to film a definitive biography, developing its excitement in Christ's ideas rather than in spectacles, sword fights, or bacchanals.

Unlike *Shane*, however, *Greatest Story* had no powerful dramatic tension within its script. The film put Jesus in a natural, but timeless frame. The spectacle worked to emphasize this sense of timelessness, but it also worked against dealing with the historical moment. The suspension of disbelief was made more difficult because Jesus was so obviously displaced into myth. This disparity is even more evident in the scenes of John the Baptist and Herod, who seem very real because they are disputing specific issues of the relationship between religion and politics. His antagonists—Herod

Antipas, Pilate, Caiaphas—the state and the established church—are more vivid than his followers.[42]

Stevens may have been aware of the problem. He said that the landscapes were extraordinary and wanted a visual equivalent for the ideas. "If I can show through imagery the beauty of the ideas, and if it has strength and moments which are at the heart of the matter, then we have done our work well."[43]

Gambling on the majesty of the pictorial presentation to lead people to reflect on the ideas he presented, Stevens forgot that the ideas themselves were very familiar to the audience, and that changing the ideas film patrons brought into the theater would require intense dramatic conflict. His failure to provide that conflict opened him to some vituperative comment.

As they camp by a broad river at the bottom of what looks like the Grand Canyon dramatically silhouetted against the sunset, with great black cliffs beetling over him and the wide river rolling turbulently as it catches the evening light, Jesus delivers the Lord's Prayer complete. The setting is impressive, a little too impressive. Custer's Last Stand or the battle of the Alamo might successfully compete with such natural grandeur. The Lord's prayer gets lost in the scenery.[44]

Moreover, the spectacle seemed to include what was described as a game of "name-the-star." The many cameo appearances provided a jarring note, especially since Jesus and the disciples were being played by relatively unknown actors. For John Wayne to appear as the centurion who proclaims Christ as the son of God, Shelley Winters as the leprous woman, or Pat Boone as the young man at the tomb distracted the audience's attention from the ideas Stevens was seeking to convey.

Probably the most puzzling aspect of the film is the motivation of Judas. *Variety* commented "that Judas stands in need, for modern psychology, of some explication."[45] Stevens plants reaction shots to suggest Judas' doubt. There is one scene to suggest his penury. In choosing David McCallum, he had decided on a wholesome, almost boyish face.

In 1968, Stevens had planned to make Judas ruled by expedience and self-centeredness.[46] Nino Novarese, the costumer, conceived of Judas as a man from a middle-class family with "a sort of cruelty toward himself." He goes barefoot throughout the film and is baptized by John in the Jordan. Novarese said, "He is not a nationalist, it is something in his person that is wrong."[47] It is not in Judas' politics (as in *King of Kings*), but in his character that things go awry. He is dressed simply, without frills; he is given a black cape by the Sanhedrin to wear over his white robe, suggesting a split personality. When he turns Jesus over to the Sanhedrin, he makes the members of that body promise that they will not hurt him, and to their queries, he replies:

Jesus is the purest and kindest man I have ever known. I have never seen him do anything but good. His heart . . . his heart is so gentle I have seen him cry over little things that would go unnoticed by other men. He has the soul of a small bird, but at the same time, he has the soul of an eagle. He sees beauty in the most wretched flower, and hope in the most evil of men. To him ugliness is not a thing of itself, but merely the means to a great beauty. Old people worship him, children adore him. I love him.

The speech shows Stevens' original intent to locate Judas' flaw in his character.

Throughout the film, evildoers are characterized by atheism or pragmatism. Herod the Great's edict for the Slaughter of the Innocents is set in a dialogue in which he asks: "Where is God except in a man's most dangerous imagination?" Pilate tells Herod Antipas that he cares nothing for "your superstitions or your God." Caiaphas is "corrupted by Roman realism." Thus, when the Dark Hermit is seen in the vicinity of Judas, it is unbelief that challenges him. Judas dies not by hanging, but by shedding his coat and falling into the fiery pit in the temple. It is a more Buddhist-like act than the defilement that the gospel writers suggested—though there are two different means of self-inflicted death recounted in the New Testament—where Judas either hangs himself or flings himself off a cliff. The Buddhist style of death suggests the depth of his alienation from Jesus' message. Judas is presented as a do-gooder without the crucial element of belief.

To resolve the question of the culpability of the Jews for Christ's Crucifixion, Stevens split the Sanhedrin. Nicodemus tells the Sanhedrin that he has a fondness for children's stories, because he has "never heard a story for children which did not appeal to a child's sublime and unalterable faith in the impossible." Caiaphas thinks Nicodemus and Joseph of Arimathea are softheaded, but another Sanhedrin member, Sheymaya, argues: "Goodness is not weakness . . . and the difference is in those who have not been corrupted by Roman realism."

Pilate is depicted as a strong-willed man; Herod Antipas dresses in purple to remind himself that he is king. Pilate makes the decision to execute Jesus, and the people in the courtyard are divided, with the voices of those shouting for Barabbas prevailing, but several shots show the people's grief.

By these devices, Stevens argues that responsibility for Christ's death was an individual decision rather than a collective responsibility. By leaving an ambiguous impression, Stevens suggests that Jesus' main offense was that he was the Messiah and that it was the unbelievers who put him to death.

In a 1962 interview, Stevens said that "there's never been a picture made about religion," and that his film was dealing with the ideas. "The story of Jesus is strong stuff without that. The other films had vigor in surroundings and ideas without vitality. Our film has vigor in the ideas."[48]

No other director seems to have taken such an intrinsic interest in the theological dimension. Stevens wanted to get at the basis for ethics that Christians lived by; in order to do this, it was necessary for him to go to the sacred story itself. Stevens believed that he was doing nothing that painters, sculptors, and dramatists of their time had not done, using the conventions of his medium and culture to depict Christ. He believed that he could get at the ideas themselves.

He did not reckon, however, with the intractability of the gospels. People know them by bits and pieces—a favorite verse here and there—with events and parables transposed from one gospel to another, the assumption being that they are all alike. All are considered sacred and putting them together requires some kind of form.

Deciding against a formulaic pattern, he chose not to dramatize good and evil in stark terms. He devised a structure that most viewers could not decipher, a form combining elements of biography and peripatetic saga that has not had a great deal of success in film. Stevens moves Jesus around a great deal, gives him stories to tell, and shows the conflict among Rome, its puppets, and the conquered Judeans, but never in the stark dimensions that would necessitate the Crucifixion. Jesus is too ethereal to pose a threat to anyone—too much the object of faith. *King of Kings* had solved the problem by making Jesus a ploy in the hands of the revolutionaries, who were a real threat to the Roman order, but in *Greatest Story*, Jesus is not perceived as a real threat to anyone, because in von Sydow's portrayal, he is so emotionally removed.

The world had changed between the conception of the film and the execution. Stevens began his planning at the end of the 1950s, just at the changing of the guard. With John F. Kennedy as president, a new wind was sweeping America—just as under the leadership of Pope John XXIII, new winds were blowing in the Roman Catholic Church, and in the Protestant Church, changes were afoot in the form of the burgeoning ecumenical movement. There was, however, racial conflict, youth were turning to countercultural movements, and technocratic control increased, fueled by scientific discoveries in the space program and the military-industrial complex. These were reshaping American perceptions of ethics and religion.

Dietrich Bonhoeffer's "religionless Christianity" had spawned new studies about secularity, and Harvey Cox's *The Secular City* hit harried clerics like the Declaration of Independence. The death-of-God movement was toward a more earthly Jesus—toward a period in which the old sacred assumptions were being challenged and secularity affirmed.

Stevens had rationalized the miracles by cloaking them in ambiguity; he had tried to be responsible to the growing ecumenical dialogue; he had focused on the individual of Jesus and aimed his film to the people in the pews of the broad mainstream churches. He wanted to be relevant to his time. The attempt to occupy the middle ground and to find that which bound people together came at a time when the social order was being rent by factions based on wide divisions of ethical opinion. A month after the film opened, the first teach-in against the war in Vietnam took place at the University of Michigan. Two-and-a-half weeks before, the nation had witnessed on its television screens the beating of blacks trying to cross the Edmund Pettus bridge in Selma, Alabama to demonstrate for their voting rights. In the midst of such a superheated context, the possibility of leisurely contemplation of the basis of the moral order was manifestly impossible.

Stevens had tried to bring a plausible gospel to reasonable men and women, but people saw things starkly in terms of good and evil. Stevens had presented a meditation on the basis of Christian ethics, but Americans were being torn apart by a world that made no sense to them—by burning cities and expanding crime, by a radical alteration of social arrangements between blacks and whites, between the young and the middle-aged. For the young, the fundamental mode of ethical discussion was action first and rationalization after. In the end, it was the wrong film for the wrong time.

Three films about Jesus were issued commercially in 1973. *Godspell* concerns a group of hippies in clown dress roaming about New York, baptizing in fountains, and using New York's familiar landscape for their interpretation of the Gospel According to St. Matthew. *Gospel Road*, by country-and-western singer Johnny Cash, was shot in Israel; it features a country music background for the story. Neither of the films returned $1 million domestically in rentals, and thus did not make the *Variety* charts that year. On the other hand, *Jesus Christ Superstar*, with $12.6 million in rentals became the largest-grossing film about Jesus made in the sound era.

If Catholic critics were bothered by *King of Kings*, and the professional critics found *Greatest Story* dull, one would suspect that the whole Christian community might have trouble with *Jesus Christ Superstar*, a film that took great liberties with its protagonist. *Superstar*, however, seemed to appeal both to the Christian press and in the main to the secular press, though large national magazines treated it somewhat more disdainfully than local newspapers.

However, organizations reflecting the concerns of the Jewish community denounced the film, and surprisingly *Playboy* and *Rolling Stone*, the scions of sex and rock music, came down hard on it. In a letter to *Playboy*, film historian Arthur Knight wrote: "I can anticipate howls of indignation from B'nai B'rith and fundamentalists, but I didn't expect it from *Playboy*."[49]

The article he referred to was published before the film's release, and was illustrated with a photograph of a wildly bearded and frizzy-haired young man wearing a white silk smoking jacket, fringed belt, dark glasses, and a crown of thorns, and smoking a cigarette in a long holder. He is sitting in a director's chair marked "J.C.," with a star above it. The article was titled, "Jesus Christ Superham."

Nik Cohn, author of the piece, noted that the record and play had by that time grossed between $50 and $80 million. The article ridiculed the film, its makers, and players. Cohn mocked the piety of the production, the company's division into the "Jesus group" and the "Judas group," and especially the character of director Norman Jewison, calling him "addicted to profundity."

Cohn was bothered by what he envisioned as the nature of *Superstar*'s appeal, which he described as a halfway house for the middle majority, integrating pop into mainstream culture. "Electric guitars no longer meant, orgy, anarchy, imminent holocaust—in *Superstar*, din was mere high spirits, anger only a gesture." His article follows the radicals' suspicion of the liberal establishment, siphoning off revolution by humanitarian values, affirming ethnicity and feminism, antiwar, a "massed liberal *bourgeoisie*, oozing with cash and changed aspirations."[50]

The film responded to the new emphasis on pluralism and society's ability to co-opt the *avant-garde*. The Port Huron Statement, the establishing document of the leftist 1960s group, Students for a Democratic Society, describes how distrust of the previous generation manifests itself in attempting to abolish poverty, racism, militarism, and so forth. Sexual practice had become less private, and sexuality became a topic for public discussion and a symbolic weapon against the older generation's values. "Hard rock" and "acid rock" became metaphors for this attack. Cohn's article used all the code words for these altered presumptions.[51]

The film is framed by the device of introducing a troupe of young actors and actresses who are giving a definitive performance of *Jesus Christ Superstar*, "both for themselves and for the movie audience." It centers on the conflict between Judas and Jesus. Judas worries about the consequences of Jesus beginning to believe that he is the Messiah.

The Bible is altered to fit the needs of the dramatic tale. When Judas complains of Mary Magdalene's attempts to reduce Jesus' tensions and wonders aloud why Jesus would waste time with "women of her kind," Jesus becomes irate and tells him: "If your slate is clean—then you can throw stones." Later, after cleansing the temple, Jesus goes to the valley of Lepers; in a surrealistic scene, he is urged to perform the healing miracles and fails to do so. Even some of the temptation is put in Herod's mouth: "Feed my household with this bread/ You can do it on your head."

The Last Supper becomes a picnic in which, at one point, the disciples take the pose of Leonardo's painting. Mary the mother of Jesus is absent, as are a majority of the adult figures. The film ends with the Crucifixion and with the troupe leaving without Ted Neely (Jesus); the sun sets over Golgotha; an empty cross, a shepherd, and sheep can be faintly seen below the horizon.

The film can hardly be called biblical in any strict sense. Paraphrase replaces the language of the gospel writers. Biblical scholarship and research were not employed to authenticate the film. In previous films, producers of biblical spectaculars had spent large sums on research, but Andrew Lloyd Webber (the composer) and Tim Rice (the lyricist) never intended for their opera to be biblical scholarship, historical realism, or official doctrine. They wanted it to be their personal statement and interpretation. Tim Rice said they found both Christ and Judas fascinating. Then with the ethical relativism characteristic of the time, he indicated, "I feel I've got no right to impose my views on other people. I have the right—everybody does—to say what my ideas are."[52] By not trying to be normative, they could tell the story the way they wanted.

By 1973, all norms were being challenged, including the Bible. "Secularity" made all things, including morality, relative. Following the lead of Dietrich Bonhoeffer, who died in a Nazi concentration camp, Harvey Cox argued that Christian ethics needed to be "unreservedly contextual," responding to the particularity of each situation. Gibson Winter had defined the secular as the "sphere of work in the world" and said that "secularization means a shift of responsibility from religious authority to worldly authority."[53] Both Winter and Cox affirmed secularity.

For many Americans, a dualistic metaphysics, suggesting one realm as that of God and another as that of experience, was becoming increasingly difficult to maintain. Also, without supernatural underpinnings, ethics became wholly relative.

By the 1970s, the iconoclasm of old ideologies had filtered deeply into popular consciousness. *Superstar* is written in an ethical atmosphere in which no one can say anything definitive about ethics and have credibility. What *can* be demonstrated is that even in the Jesus story, the interpretation of ethical behavior is less dependent on God-given norms than on the personal decisions and understandings of the characters in the drama. The film depicts multiple views of Jesus, including his own self-image, and no two correspond. *Variety* laid it to reforms in the ecumenical movement and the Vatican Council, noting that the story coincided with reforms designed to "strip away the barnacles of administrative, man-made rubrics which had been obscuring for centuries the root concepts of Western theology." They saw the film as being appealing to the youth who had never known any other way and to people weary of the church rather than the religion, concluding that "*Jesus Christ Superstar* was almost literally, a divine inspiration."[54]

Released during the Senate Watergate hearings, and made in a time when distrust of institutions was a recurrent cultural theme, the film struck a responsive chord in a broad audience.

In one sense, the film is all fiction—that is, the words are all interpretations of biblical acts and sayings. There is little of the Bible's prose, but in some ways, the dialogue is more authentic than the dialogue from the other Jesus films. Most of the New Testament was first received in the colloquial Greek language and had no literary pretensions. In previous films, the Bible was treated reverently, and the archaic tone of the dialogue stultified the creative expression and language of contemporary speech, creating a psychological distance between the audience and the actions on the screen. No small part of the audience's ability to identify with *Superstar* is to be found in the colloquial familiarity of the rock lyrics, which create closeness rather than distance because the idiom is familiar.

Whether by design or accident, the figure of Jesus comes off second best. As *Variety* commented, "In reconstructing the character of Judas in the most plausible fashion, the film makers have not given him an adequate foil in Jesus." The testimony at this point is thunderous. The reviews describe Jesus as a "wishy washy figure with a whine to his singing," "a puny college pacifist," "confused and shapeless," "a plastic icon," "a dead ringer for all those sentimentalized figures one sees in second rate religious art."[55]

Much of the problem must be attributed to authors' intentions—to make a figure who both transcends time and can be seen from many perspectives. They decided that they "were more concerned with the human elements than with Biblical accuracy." Rice avoided reading books and doing scholarly research before they wrote it.[56] Ted Neely (Jesus) said that he was "playing him as a man, with it all coming from within him—all the doubts, the fears."[57] They center on his limitations. The question posed to the audience was: "What if a man with claims to divinity came among us"?[58]

The film makers made several significant interpretations:

1. Jesus reacts in frustration to the disciples' views of him.
2. He has an ambiguous sexual relationship with Mary Magdalene.
3. At various points he is beset by fears and doubts.
4. In the cleansing of the temple, Jesus' anger is translated into contemporary images of rage.
5. He fails to perform any miracles.
6. The Resurrection is at best ambiguous.

Almost from the first, we find Mary Magdalene trying to calm a nervous Jesus, telling him, "Try not to get worried, try not to turn on to/Problems that upset you oh don't you know/ Everything's all right."[59] This song creates a tense situation with Judas, who thinks that Jesus is more concerned with popularity than with his mission. Later, when Simon Zealotes tries to persuade Jesus to politicize his campaign, Jesus becomes angry, saying:

Neither you Simon, nor the fifty thousand
Nor the Romans, nor the Jews nor Judas nor the Twelve
Nor the priests, nor the Scribes
Nor doomed Jerusalem itself
Understand what the power is
Understand what the glory is
Understand at all . . . understand at all.

During this song, the disciples sit in a circle and listen to Jesus "as to a star at a pop concert." (Script).

At the Last Supper, Jesus tells his disciples, "For all you care, this wine could be my blood/For all you care this bread could be my body." This peevishness undercuts any claim to Jesus' superiority "in kind" as in the early church debates over whether Jesus was "wholly God" or "wholly man."

The relationship with Mary Magdalene further humanizes him. The soothing and the stroking in the earlier scene is clearly sexual. Shot in rich brown earth tones with a series of close-ups on the faces of Jesus and Mary Magdalene and kinetic movement by both the camera and the actors, the sequence develops a strong suggestion of sensuality. She tells him to "Sleep and I shall soothe you, calm you and anoint you." Although the stage version was more erotic, Jewison and the scriptwriters did not think that the larger film audience would be ready to accept Jesus as a sexual creature and changed the focus.

Magdalene's ambiguity is summed up in the show's most popular song, "I Don't Know How to Love Him":

He's just a man he's just a man
And I've had so many men before
In very many ways
He's just one more
Should I bring him down, should I scream and shout
Should I speak of love, let my feelings out
I never thought I'd come to this—what's it all about? . . .
Yet if he said he loved me
I'd be lost, I'd be frightened
I just couldn't cope, just couldn't cope
I'd turn my head, I'd back away
I wouldn't want to know
He scares me so
I want him so
I love him so.

Thus, as superstar, Jesus presents for both Mary and the audience an ambiguous image—visions of a rock star with a groupie, mixed with the vision of an untouchable holy man. Many felt the sexuality had to be denied.

Some observers say that *Superstar* suggests a sexual relationship between Jesus and the prostitute Mary Magdalene.... Balderdash! Listen to the lyrics of "I Don't Know How to Love Him." Some rabidly romantic humanists would read such a relationship in the words of the song, seeing it as the final humanizing expanding facet of the portrait. Sorry, the words don't parse that way.[60]

This humanizing is important, yet there is an attempt not to deny Christ's divinity.

At various points, Jesus does not seem to know quite what his mission is. In "What's the Buzz?" he asks his apostles: "Why are you obsessed with fighting times and fates you can't defy?/If you knew the path we're riding you'd understand it less than I." At the Last Supper, he sings regretfully: "I must be mad thinking that I'll be remembered.... My name will mean nothing/Ten minutes after I'm dead."

In the Gethsemane scene, he plays out his doubts at considerable length, much more uncertain than the one who, in the biblical record, wants to avoid the agony that lay before him:

> Take this cup away from me for I don't want to taste its poison
> Feel it burn me, I have changed I'm not as sure
> As when we started
> Then I was inspired
> Now I'm sad and tired
> Listen surely I've exceeded expectations
> Tried for three years seems like thirty
> Could you ask as much from any other man?

As this song is sung, 23 shots of great art masterpieces depict the Crucifixion in 26 seconds. The sequence dissolves into a close-up of Judas' face, making the connection between Jesus' uncertainty and Judas' betrayal.

Traditionally the cleansing of the temple has been a sign of Jesus' humanity. The anger he feels at the turning of religion into commercial enterprise appeals to the righteous rage most people feel on occasion. The forecourt of the temple is set up like a Western image of a Middle East bazaar with drugs, weapons, hookers—a bazaar of human weaknesses. He pushes over stalls of meat and artificial limbs, slamming a rifle against a military display, dashing crystals and mirrors, destroys the stalls, and clears the temple.

The biblical account rages against changing Roman coin into temple coin and selling animals for sacrifice within the temple. *Superstar* displays a catalogue of secular vices. Jesus' rage is directed against the abuses of modernity. John Simon suggested the scene lashed out at consumer goods rather than people "to placate peace-loving but possession-lacking flower children."[61] Although there is some suggestion of that motive, the anger is directed toward the symbols of "human weaknesses." The artificial limbs, guns, and military display conjured up images of the Vietnam War. This is a Jesus less concerned with religious abuse than with a broader range of evils. It makes Jesus a more humanistic leader than the religious leader of the Gospels—a view that undercuts the theological legitimacy of the claims of his divinity.

Immediately following, Jesus seeks solitude in a deep canyon wadi. The scene opens with a shot of a circling vulture. The camera then pans down to a long framing shot of Jesus in the wilderness. As he moves, high angle shots emphasize his weakness, and people stream toward him. The people, dressed in black, claw at him, demanding that he heal them.

> See my eyes I can hardly see
> See me stand I can hardly walk
> I believe you can make me whole
> See my tongue I can hardly talk
> See my skin I'm a mass of blood
> See my legs I can hardly stand
> I believe you can make me well
> See my purse I'm a poor poor man
> Will you touch will you mend me Christ
> Won't you touch will you heal me Christ
> Won't you kiss won't you pay me Christ.

At this point, the demands are accentuated by the strong and insistent rhythms of the music, and the tempo and dissonances build toward a frenetic edge.

The script indicates that "JC is rendered impotent by the multiplicity of the demands made upon him." Finally, in anguish he cries out, "There's too many of you—don't push me/There's too little of me—don't crowd me/Leave me alone!" Such words astonish those who hold traditional concepts of Jesus, the "Man for Others." The script says that he "is unable to exert his authority by his kindness." The translation of miracles into "kindness" humanizes the character almost to the exclusion of divinity.

The significant departure from the Gospels was the film makers' decision to conclude the biblical account with the Crucifixion. In a short scene, Jesus speaks only three of the seven last utterances from the cross—"Father forgive them—they don't know what they are doing," "My God, My God, why have you forsaken me?" and "Father, into your hands I commend my spirit." As he says these last words, the sun comes up and forms a corona around the cross, the thorns, and his head outlining the figure on the cross in silhouette. Then the soundtrack abruptly ends, and the figure disappears into myth and art.

In the last sequence where the troupe of actors reappears, Ted Neely as Jesus does not board the bus, but on the screen a shepherd is dimly seen beneath the hill in a soft-focus haze, leading his sheep up the hill toward the empty cross still silhouetted against the orange sun. The effect, like that of the rest of the film, is ambiguous. Of this, Jewison has said: "Some will feel the scene gives the idea of a resurrection. Others will assume Ted Neely just got on the bus earlier. Religion is very personal, and I'm glad the scene can be interpreted in different ways."[62] The scene leaves the question of resurrection open. Having refused to violate its naturalistic point of view up to that point, the film appropriately maintains ambiguity to the end, thus salvaging *Superstar* from the problems encountered by other Jesus films whose directors felt they had to include the Resurrection. Jewison said: "I feel there is an aura of mystery in all religion and this feeling should prevail at the end of the film."[63]

Jewison confuses ambiguity with mystery—an understandable mistake from a secular point of view. Mystery, according to Paul Tillich, "cannot lose its mysteriousness even when it is revealed."[64] If we were to learn that Neely had boarded the bus or that he was the shepherd on the hill, the ambiguity would vanish. On the other hand, to affirm the Resurrection is an affront to the world view many people operate from, a perspective that does not allow for interruptions in nature.

Taken all together, the crucial six decisions made by the film makers combine to humanize Jesus thoroughly and to deny that Jesus was the Christ. Humanity is emphasized at the expense of divinity, and it becomes difficult to imagine this Jesus as any sort of paradigm for ethical behavior. Dramatically, the character of Jesus becomes weaker in appeal, because very little charismatic power comes across on the screen.

James Wall found this aspect of the film appealing. He said that the performers, having given their definitive version, gave their own view of Jesus and "in the process have raised the same questions that have always been raised about him: Who is he and what is this strange power that drives him?"[65] Although Wall is correct in his contention that the most basic questions are raised, in its treatment of Judas, the film gives a clear answer to the question of who can follow Jesus.

Carl Anderson (Judas) contended that the timing was right, and that "at that moment youth needed another look at religion and when *Superstar* came along, everybody jumped on the coattails because it gave that look."[66] The story is told through the eyes of Judas. Rice and Webber "do not present Judas as the archetype of evil that he has become in Christian mythology, but as questioning friend of Christ's."

The time was right, because there was a need to look at ethics in an atmosphere where moral absolutism had become an anachronism. "Everyone doing his own thing"—that is, the collapse of ethics into a solipsism—had significant drawbacks. Looking at the figure of Judas allowed people puzzled by the changes in American life to try to understand the moral situation in which the country found itself. The children who had grown up during the racial strife in which conscience was elevated to the stature of law, and the parents, who were influenced by this persistent theme in American history (Jefferson, Thoreau, Debs, King, et al.), needed to look at the moral complexities it brought with it. The film presented one opportunity to do so.

Judas, presented as a hero who was "mistaken" rather than "evil," helped a segment of the public to appropriate emotionally the contradictions in the culture. Although it is difficult to tell who went to see the film, *Superstar* seems to be targeted for the minority of Americans who had voted for George McGovern and Eugene McCarthy—those who were slightly left of the American middle politically and somewhat troubled, yet who did not regard America's problems as so intractable that revolution was necessary.

Judas is not really a foil for Jesus, as some have claimed and as appears to be the case at the film's conclusion when he descends in gleaming white fringed rock star clothes to taunt Jesus with the song "Superstar." Judas does not believe that Jesus is the Christ. In "Heaven on Their Minds," which opens the performance, Judas is seen in a rocky desert. The shots crosscut between Judas and Jesus, who is conversing with his disciples. Judas, in isolation, is concerned because Jesus "has started to believe the things they say of you."

> I remember when this whole thing began
> No talk of God then—we called you a man
> And believe me—my admiration for you hasn't died
> But every word you say today
> Gets twisted around the other way. . . .
> Listen Jesus do you care for your race?
> Don't you see we must keep in our place?
> We are occupied—have you forgotten how put down we are?
> I am frightened by the crowd
> For we are getting much too loud
> And they'll crush us if we go too far. . . .
> But it's sad to see our chances weakening with every hour
> And your followers are blind
> Too much heaven on their minds
> It was beautiful but now it's sour.

The choice of a black man for the role of Judas could have been avoided, but Jewison believed he was on safe ground. The audience was not likely to identify Judas solely with his blackness. Judas here is insufficiently revolutionary, unclear about what he wants, torn by his love for Jesus, and bothered by the superstar image that Jesus is tending toward.

Judas' foil, also played by a black, is Simon Zealotes, who tried to develop a political revolution, telling Jesus that "you're easily as strong/As the filth from Rome who rape our country/And who've terrorized our people so long." *King of Kings*'s Barabbas has become one of the disciples. Zealotes wants Jesus to create a political revolution by telling the people to "keep them yelling their devotion/But add a touch of hate at Rome." These are two perceptions of the black freedom movement: One moves deliberately; the other demands a premature revolution. Neither Judas nor Simon Zealotes has an adequate framework for understanding Jesus' mission.

Two controversies surrounded the opening of the film. The American Jewish Committee thought the film was anti-Semitic, and a group of black Baptist ministers complained to Universal that the film was racist because of a black's portrayal of Judas. James Wall argued that "Judas is presented as the only real friend Jesus has, struggling desperately to make him follow a reasonable course of action which will avoid bringing down the wrath of the establishment upon the whole lot of them." In this version, Judas becomes an "everyman . . . drawn to Jesus and yet unable to comprehend the strange demands he makes both on himself and his followers."[67]

Judas' character stands out beyond its "blackness." It is because Judas is so conservative that he has trouble; his stance parallels the position of many Americans who delayed moral judgment and felt guilty about their late entry into activism on the issues of race and the war in Southeast Asia.

The reason Judas turns Jesus in to the authorities is that Jesus "let the things you did get out of hand." He rationalizes that he is not betraying Jesus, but rather that Jesus has betrayed the shared vision—"our ideals die around us all because of you." In "Damned for All Time," Judas is found on the desert, isolated as he has been during most of the film. Tanks appear up over a ridge and move through the sand in silhouette. They serve to resolve his torment into action. This hallucinatory vision suggests the power to destroy any visionary. Judas tells Annas and Caiaphas, "I have no thought at all about my own reward/I really didn't come here of my own accord/Just don't say/I'm damned for all time." He feels free to make the choice and to take the historical consequences, but also is not acting of his own free will. This conflict is repeated when, at the Last Supper, Jesus provokes Judas to do the deed.

Judas is the dreamer. He is in anguish when he finds Jesus tortured. Still torn between his own self-image and his empathy with Jesus, he sings that he "only did what you wanted me to. . . . I have been spattered with innocent blood/I shall be dragged through the slime and the mud." Then, however, he picks up a reprise of Mary Magdalene's "I Don't Know How to Love Him."

The writers have given Judas unclear motivation. In the absence of a clear moral perspective, anyone might become a Judas. As Jesus is being led to the cross, the pathetic dilemma of Judas reemerges in a fantasy. Judas descends from heaven with all the glory of a superstar. He is garbed in white with tassels and accompanied by a wildly shimmying cast of black women and dancers, but he still asks the fundamental questions that he could not answer during Jesus' life: "Jesus Christ Superstar/Do you think you're what they say you are?" To this he adds the pathetic disclaimer, "Jesus! I only want to know/Tell me tell me tell me/Tell me don't you get me wrong/I only want to know." Our final glimpse of Judas is of a character who does not understand what he has set in motion; although numerous motives are ascribed to him, he finds himself unable to understand his own actions.

If Judas is not responsible for his actions, then who is? The biblical answer is fairly clear. Pilate and Herod are depicted as weak characters, whereas the Sanhedrin seems relatively sophisticated and strong. Christ offends them with his claims to be the Messiah and with his taking of authority to cleanse the temple, overthrowing religious practices. Only later does the Christian faith become a threat to Rome in the New Testament. Although historical scholarship suggests other alternatives, the literal record assigns collective responsibility to the elders of Israel—the Sanhedrin.

Earlier film makers went out of their way to give another interpretation, exculpating the Jews from responsibility. The alternative explanations were often based on research, but Webber and Rice did not research. They chose to stick roughly to the story as recorded in the Gospels. The American Jewish Committee saw in the film another anti-Semitic Passion play. Marc Tanenbaum compared it to medieval morality plays, "constructed on the Manichaean dualism which arraigns good versus evil, the divine versus the demonic, Christ versus the antichrist." In such dramas "the Jewish people have been type-cast as villains, the Jewishness and Judaism have been equated with the Satanic and perfidy."[68]

Rabbi Tanenbaum's charges are based on several points in the film. Pilate and Herod are portrayed as weak men; they do not appear as strong enough characters to be the incarnation of evil that would replace Judas as the archetypal villain.

We see Pilate watching the walls of the city as the crowd carries Jesus through the streets. There is a suggestion that Pilate's power is based on fear and superstition. He tries to transfer his responsibility to Herod: "Since you come from Galilee then you need not come to me/You're Herod's race! You're Herod's case!"

Pilate is a weakling; Herod is a pampered child, a modern spin-off of the Laughton-Ustinov Nero. Aboard a yacht, surrounded by transvestites, prostitutes, and homosexuals in gaudy clothing, Herod himself wears white Bermuda shorts and yellow sunglasses. He plays the devil, urging Jesus to perform miracles for him:

Prove to me that you're divine—change my water into wine. . . .
Prove to me that you're no fool—walk across my swimming pool. . . .
Feed my household with this bread—you can do it on your head.

Since these taunts fail to achieve their purpose, Herod falls into a tirade of disgust and fury, calling Jesus a fraud and sending him back to Pilate. This injection of a comic number into a tragic theme distances Herod from the horrifying circumstances. His authority is secular, not religious. The comic treatment and the image of the malicious Herod as a kind of harmless pervert make it difficult to accept him as archetypally evil.

The Jews are the only candidates left to blame. It is not just the Sanhedrin that is faulted, but the Jewish community.

Some of the secular press agreed, arguing that the Pharisees decide to murder Jesus "because the Romans would never accept Him as their leader," absolving Judas and Pilate of principal responsibility, making them culpable only as accessories to the crime.[69]

If, however, there were daily papers that sided with the American Jewish Committee, there were also Jewish critics who sided with those who did not sense any anti-Semitism. Stanley Kauffman, in a generally unfavorable review, said that though he accepted the committee's unfavorable analysis, "as a Jewish member of the audience . . . I got no anti-Semitic emphases. Probably this is because I felt that Caiaphas and the others were no more distorted than Jesus."[70] Jewison was horrified: "We were not trying to make a theological statement. . . . It's unlikely that the Universal office thought the picture was anti-Semitic. Otherwise they would have shot it differently."[71]

The film does suggest the collective guilt of the Jews. Our first sight of the Sanhedrin is on a scaffold, where they appear like giant vultures roosting on the branches of a tree. They were wearing black hats and robes, suggesting Hell's Angels playing the Sanhedrin. In the song "This Jesus Must Die," Caiaphas outlines his reasons for wanting Jesus' death:

I see bad things arising—the crowd crown him king
Which the Romans would ban
I see blood and destruction, our elimination
Because of one man. . . .
We must crush him completely
So like John before him, this Jesus must die.
For the sake of the nation this Jesus must die.

Later, Caiaphas tells Judas, "What you have done will be the saving of everyone." Judas has made "pretty good wages for one little kiss." The crowd is bloodthirsty in its desire for Jesus' blood, cheering his lashing and screaming for Pilate to crucify him. Given this evidence without any mitigation, Tanenbaum's charges seem justified.

The issue became national in scope. Rabbi Tanenbaum and James Wall were called as adversaries to the NBC "Today" show. There they argued about what they had already written. Wall had argued that their Jewishness is not well-established—that indeed they are the Establishment. "The Pharisees represent the same kind of ominous power that Sergei Eisenstein gave his elaborately costumed and hooded German soldiers as they fought across the ice against the Russian troops in his classic film *Alexander Nevsky*." The charge of anti-Semitism is based on "feelings generated by earlier portrayals of Jews as "Christ-killers," rather than on the film itself.[72]

Both Tanenbaum and Wall had put their finger on important insights. Protestant, Catholics, and the general public were very unlikely to make the transpositions from the villains of *Superstar* to American Jews, who had for the most part become invisible in the culture. The more plausible target in 1973 was "the Establishment," which seemed to be acting like vultures. On the other hand, Tanenbaum sensed that there was a growing residue of anti-Jewish feeling, directed at the Middle East, where our military and financial commitments were considerable but generally not well-understood. Since the U.S. government seemed untrustworthy and these commitments had been accepted on the basis of trust in our government, there were fears that we might become entangled in another war. As the American Jewish community became religiously more committed to the state of Israel, they regarded the film as a slur on their character. Tanenbaum covertly acknowledged this viewpoint in his *Christian Century* article. "Both Soviet and Arab propagandists persist in manipulating Christian images and rhetoric of anti-Jewish content in their politically motivated campaigns against Jews and the state of Israel."[73]

Superstar's spectacle is almost all naturalistic. Unlike *King of Kings*, this film has no battle scenes and no long tracks laid for a scene like the Sermon on the Mount. Nor is there one peak emotional experience, such as the raising of Lazarus in *Greatest Story*.

In spectacular terms, what is memorable is not the play's action, but the environment in which it is set. "There was," said Jewison, "an attempt to give the film a timeless feeling. I didn't want to do a *Ten Commandments*."[74] Some reviewers believed this decision worked against the film: "Seeking an effect of timelessness, the director mixes ancient amphitheaters, modern tanks, Biblical costuming, a tourist bazaar and a traditional Crucifixion in a melange that isn't so much timeless as mindless."[75]

Others were impressed with the beauty of the settings, even when they did not like the film, suggesting that the territories on the west bank of the Jordan were perfect places to photograph such action. "When matched with the solitary dark figure running across the raw desert there is no denying that [the music] has a legitimate power beyond its considerable volume."[76]

The film is not a spectacular in the formulaic sense defined earlier. *Godspell*, a film that the national critics liked considerably more than *Superstar*, could not find a wide audience. In some ways, it tried to do with New York's skyline what *Superstar* does with the Israeli desert. The significant difference is that its roots were in the musical comedy, whereas *Superstar* was similar to the spectaculars. The theme of Christ as the ethical paradigm still had considerable potency, and although this theme required alterations of historical perspective and dramatic form, the film nonetheless had to suggest the "grand style" to present the most potent myth in the Western world.

The steel structures on which Caiaphas and Annas are often seen serve as symbols of the empty forms of institutions served by the high priests of the social order. Those institutions are pitted against the struggle for community in the desert wilderness—the wilderness being a metaphor for the moral chaos in which humans are called to survive. The melodramatic emphasis of the clash between good and evil is dissipated by the lack of a strong villain, by ambiguous motives, and by the humanization of Jesus. No longer does evil seem so potent and so clear, but among and around us. Simon Zealotes, Judas, and Mary Magdalene are on the same side as Jesus, yet there is no sense that they are natural protagonists with heroic virtues. Pilate, Herod, and the priests are too weak to function dramatically as "incarnate evil," and without a clear direction, the film undercuts the possibility of a Divine Providence working itself out in history.

Much of the film's power comes from this refashioning of the melodramatic archetype. Jesus seems more vulnerable because he is more human. He is not rendered as a mythic displacement of a god come to earth, but instead is rendered in totally human fashion. This portrayal leaves the ending appropropriately ambiguous. Although the characters and the action lack the dramatic intensity necessary for tragedy, the film does convey *pathos* especially well in the doomed character of Judas. When Jesus is transformed into a superstar, he becomes an idol—with an idol's feet of clay.

The title provided Jewison with a clue as to the film's universal meaning: "The title suggests two themes: Jesus Christ, reverent biblical; and then Superstar, hip contemporary. The approach I've taken was to blend the two themes."[77] The themes do not blend well. The iconoclastic impulse collides with the divine image of Christ, but the clash produces no new synthesis of meaning, and instead of a new insight, the film ends ambiguously.

Meyer Kantor suggested that the young identified Jesus was "every sacrificing man of God we ever followed, from Martin Luther King to Dan and Phil Berrigan," but that their weakness was that they were centers of cults and human at the same time. Judas is identified as one who sees "the very real goals of the movement being subverted into the worship of one man," while the Sanhedrin becomes those who cooperate with the enemy, the Romans become the Establishment they attempted to reverse.

The story taught them that in the matter of improving the human condition, there can be no miracles, no leaders who can rise up after dying, no man who cannot die, and above all, no man who can carry the whole load unaided by the people. In the matter of improving the human condition . . . we must all bear the cross. . . . It is a superbly made film about us, the ragtag army of the young who trudged across the sixties, trying to build a better world, succeeding sometimes and failing sometimes, and being human always.[78]

Kantor's article gives an important hint as to what happens in a secular age to the fundamental story of the Christian faith. *Superstar*, with all its moral relativities, suggests a world where supernatural rewards are no longer thinkable or even justified. The fundamental symbol is the *Via Dolorosa*, the way of the cross, not the Resurrection. The focus is on the ideals brought into action, rather than on the bearer of those ideals, Jesus the Christ. *Superstar*, by reinforcing the ambiguity, undercuts the moral authority of the Gospels, leaving an uncertain impression of a leader, and a diminished capacity to discern between good and evil, as well as increasing the personal responsibility to make moral choices in the absence of a normative story. The gap between it and the unambiguous *Ten Commandments* is stunning—an almost complete reversal of the role of the biblical spectacular.

NOTES

1. Sherman E. Johnson, "Exegesis to the Gospel of Matthew," *The Intepreter's Bible*, Vol. 7 (Nashville: Abingdon-Cokesbury Press, 1951), p. 571.

2. In *Salome*, Jesus' voice was heard, but the actor who spoke Jesus' lines was unseen.

3. It is difficult to classify *Gospel Road* (1973), since it had very few commercial bookings and is generally unavailable for viewing.

4. *Cincinnati Enquirer*, November 16, 1961, p. 37.

5. Judith Crist, "A Story Too Great To Be Told?," *New York Herald Tribune*, February 21, 1965, p. 27.

6. "Substitutionary" theory suggests that Jesus literally died for the sins of the world. The "ransom" theory is that Christ's death is a ransom payment for all the sins of the world and that, therefore, God is satisfied when we make a confession in Christ, and his unlimited account pays for the sins of the individual who professes faith in him. The "moral influence" theory suggests that Christ is the model of human existence, and we come to atonement with God through emulating his behavior.

7. Ivan Butler, *Religion in the Cinema* (New York: A. S. Barnes & Co., 1969), pp. 48–9.

8. Reprinted in *The Critic* 20 (December–January, 1961–62): 64.

9. *Commonweal* 75 (November 3, 1961): 152.

10. The synoptic Gospels are Matthew, Mark, and Luke, which contain a great deal of common material. Most of Mark appears as the basis for the other two.

11. Metro-Goldwyn-Mayer, *King of Kings*, Program Book, University of Southern California Library, Los Angeles, California.

12. *Dallas Morning News*, November 16, 1961, p. 17.

13. *Time* 78 (October 27, 1961): 55.

14. *America* 106 (October 21, 1961): 73.

15. Ibid.

16. *The Sign* 41 (December, 1961): 47.

17. *Family Weekly*, December 25, 1960, p. 14.

18. *Films in Review* 12 (November, 1961): 548.

19. Dwight Macdonald, *Dwight Macdonald on Movies* (Englewood Cliffs, N.J.: Prentice Hall Inc., 1970), p. 428.

20. *Boston Globe*, October 27, 1961, p. 17.

21. Program book, *King of Kings*, no page numbers, University of Southern California Film Library, Los Angeles, California.

22. *Los Angeles Mirror*, December 12, 1961, p. 15.

23. *Films in Review* 12 (November, 1961): 547–8.

24. Macdonald, *On Movies*, p. 426.

25. Ibid., p. 492.

26. Marty, *Nation of Behavers*, p. 176.

27. Herberg, *Protestant—Catholic—Jew*, p. 198.

28. For an analysis of Christian themes in mimetic literature, I suggest Preston Roberts' article, "A Christian Theory of Dramatic Tragedy," in Nathan Scott, Jr., *The New Orpheus* (New York: Sheed and Ward, 1964); Scott's own articles, "The Bias of Comedy and the Narrow Escape into Faith" and "The Tragic Vision and the Christian Faith" in *The Broken Center* (New Haven: Yale University Press, 1966); and Nelvin Voss, *The Drama of Comedy: Victim and Victor* (Richmond, Va.: John Knox Press, 1966). All make viable arguments for a Christian interpretation of mimetic literature, but the question of the possibility of a Christian melodrama has, as far as I can determine, never received any theological attention.

29. *The Hollywood Reporter*, October 11, 1961, p. 3; *Boxoffice*, October 16, 1961, p. 2; *Motion Picture Herald*, October 18, 1961, p. 3.

30. *Life* 43 (February 25, 1965): 25.

31. "Dorothy McGuire plays the Virgin Mary—more as a symbol than as a woman, who never ages, never speaks, and merely shows on her face the sorrows of the mother of Jesus." *Boston Globe*, March 12, 1965, p. 12.

32. Macdonald, *On Movies*, p. 436.

33. DeMille used the technique very effectively in *The Ten Commandments*, placing lines reminiscent of New Testament quotations at strategic points throughout the film. One Roman Catholic reviewer complained of the use of "debts" in the Lord's Prayer, and "love" in place of "charity" in this context. Never does he seem to notice that Jesus never even spoke the latter passage.

34. Bruce H. Petri, "A Theory of American Film: The Films and Techniques of George Stevens." (Ph.D. dissertation, Harvard University, 1974), p. 210.

35. This was taken up in *America* 112 (February 27, 1965): 296.

36. Nino Novarese, "The Costumes for George Stevens' *The Greatest Story Ever Told*," *Cinema* (Beverly Hills) 1, No. 6 (1965): 18.

37. William Trombley, "The Greatest Story Ever Told," *Saturday Evening Post* 236 (October 19, 1963): 40.

38. *New York Times*, February 16, 1965, Sec. II, p. 40.

39. *Commonweal* 84 (March 12, 1965): 765.

40. *Time* 85 (February 26, 1965): 96.

41. George Stevens Productions (Culver City, Calif.), Press Release, December 31, 1962, University of Southern California Film Library, Los Angeles, California, p. 8.

42. *The Hollywood Reporter*, February 15, 1965, p. 3.

43. James Silke, "Interview with George Stevens," *Cinema* (Beverly Hills) 2, No. 4 (1966): 25.

44. Macdonald, *On Movies*, p. 436.

45. *Variety*, February 17, 1965, p. 20.

46. *New York Times*, October 30, 1960, Sec III p. 5.

47. Novarese, "Costuming," p. 19.

48. *New York Herald Tribune*, December 9, 1962, p. 17.

49. *Playboy* 20 (October, 1973): 12.

50. Ibid., p. 201.

51. For a fuller discussion of this trend, see Ronald Berman, *America in the Sixties: an Intellectual History* (New York: Harper & Row, 1968), Chaps. 5–7; William O'Neill, *Coming Apart* (New York: Quadrangle Books, 1971), Chaps. 8–9; Nicholas Von Hoffman, *We Are the People Our Parents Warned Us Against* (New York: Quadrangle Books, 1968); and Douglas Miller and Marion Nowack, *The Fifties* (Garden City, N.Y.: Doubleday & Co., 1977), Chap. 11.

52. *Film Information* 4 (July–August, 1973): 1.

53. Harvey Cox, *The Secular City* (New York: The Macmillan Co., 1965), p. 107; Gibson Winter, *The New Creation as Metropolis* (New York: The Macmillan Co., 1962), pp. 35–6.

54. *Variety*, June 27, 1973, p. 20.

55. *Films in Review* 24 (October 1973); *Catholic Film Newsletter* 38 (June 30, 1973): 1; *Chicago Tribune*, July 24, 1973, Sec. 2, p. 4; *Wall Street Journal*, August 17, 1973, p. 6; *Newsweek* 82 (July 9, 1973): 82.

56. *Los Angeles Herald Express*, July 15, 1973, p. 23.

57. *Los Angeles Times*, December 24, 1972, "Calendar" section, p. 29.

58. *Los Angeles Times*, July 15, 1973, "Calendar" section, p. 1.

59. The punctuation for the lyrics is that found in the record booklet of the soundtrack recording of the film.

60. *Cincinnati Enquirer*, July 15, 1973, Sec. 2, p. 5.

61. *Esquire* 80 (October, 1973): 44.

62. *Dallas Morning News*, June 24, 1973, Sec. C., p. 1.

63. John Dart, "Superstar vs. the Book," *Los Angeles Times*, July 15, 1973, "Calendar" section, p. 27.

64. Paul Tillich, *Systematic Theology*, Vol. 1 (Chicago: University of Chicago Press, 1951), 1: 109.

65. James Wall, "*Jesus Christ Superstar*: A Surprising Film Success," *Christian Century* 85 (June 27, 1973): 693.

66. *The Hollywood Reporter*, July 24, 1973, p. 3.

67. Wall, "Film Success," p. 694.

68. Marc Tanenbaum, "Passion Plays and Vilification of Jews," *Christian Century* 90 (September 5, 1973): 859.

69. *Chicago Tribune*, July 24, 1973, Sec. 2, p. 4.

70. *New Republic*, July 24/August 4, 1973, p. 33.

71. *Los Angeles Herald Express*, June 28, 1973, p. 14.

72. Wall, "Film Success," p. 694.

73. Tanenbaum, "Passion Plays," p. 859.

74. *Dallas Morning News*, Sec. C., p. 1.

75. *Newsweek*, p. 82.

76. *Chicago Tribune*, Sec. 2, p. 4.

77. Universal Pictures, Pressbook of *"Jesus Christ Superstar,"* Universal City, California, 1973, no page numbers.

78. Meyer Kantor, "Is Superstar About Christ—or About Us," *New York Times*, September 23, 1973, Sec. 2, p. 13.

7

The Epitome: *The Ten Commandments*

Popular religion explores the same fundamental themes explored by theologians, but the approach differs. Theologians are specialists—mastering biblical exegesis, church history, and philosophy. Popular religion, on the other hand, appeals to religious consumers. Theologians dwell on the intellectual and institutional differences, whereas popular forms are likely to receive their support from the general culture. For example, economic pragmatism in assigning denominations to start new congregations is called ecumenical cooperation.

There is no clearer example of popular religion in films than the work of Cecil B. DeMille. DeMille used religious language and imagery to describe his political and economic point of view. That they were close to what the American people of his era felt about religion may account for his popularity with the public, and his unpopularity with critics and theologians.

DeMille's father read from the Bible and often "a chapter from American or European history or from Thackery or Victor Hugo," telling his sons that the dramatist must be like a camera and record the truth to reach people's hearts.[1]

This daily application of religion, drama, and history shaped DeMille's thought. With the exceptions of two pictures he did with MGM in 1934, *Cleopatra* (1935) and *The Greatest Show on Earth* (1952), all his films from *Sign of the Cross* (1932) to his death in 1959 dealt with either the religious or American historical themes. He first merged these themes in *Samson and Delilah*, and brought them to an epitome in *The Ten Commandments*.

To DeMille, God was "that Mind behind the universe we see, of which *our* minds are like small reflecting sparks struck off."[2] He interpreted the Greek word *logos*, which biblical scholars have rendered "Words" (John 1:1ff), as "Mind."[3] He defined prayer as "thought contact with the Holy Spirit," and contended that each person was "entrusted at birth with a precious fragment of the Divine Mind to develop for good or evil."[4]

The Decalogue was the "natural law, the law of life revealed to man by God. . . . Beyond the Ten Commandments is savagery."[5] When we choose good or evil, retribution comes "not as a vengeful visitation of an arbitrary God: rather it grows *inevitably* out of his own acts, for the moral law is as much a part of the structure of the universe as the law of gravity."[6] This moral fantasy explains why the underlying archetype of DeMille's films is melodrama, in which some form of providence is always working in the trials and tribulations of the people, finally revealing a moral order.

The personal dimension of such a faith has its archetype in Christ. He hated the "effeminate, sanctimonious, machine-made Christs of second-rate so-called art, which used to be thought good enough for Sunday Schools."[7] He admired the strong will of Jesus who could take 40 days of fasting and prayer, his sharpness of mind, and his sensitivities to the natural world and sinners.[8]

After DeMille's death, Salt Lake City's *Deseret News* summed up what DeMille himself might have written about an individual's Christian values, praising his vision of the fantastic, his practical business sense, his attention to detail, and the stewardship of his film-making gifts. He was praised as not taking advantage of people in his personal dealings, as accepting and welcoming spiritual guidance, and for losing himself in causes greater than himself. "These qualities, taken together represent something of what we mean when we speak of the Christian man."[9] They are also qualities generally attributed to the successful American businessman.

His social ethic also centered on individualism. He contrasted it with his perception of communism, saying that "your 'needs' are not measured by a standard of what you are worth as a human being, but only by the standard of what you are worth to the government in power."[10]

The Protestant heritage places a high value on individualism. Luther and the Reformers argued for the primacy of individual responsibility. Paul Tillich wrote that the Protestant principle is "the divine and human protest against any absolute claim for a relative reality."[11] This definition has been taken to mean that the concept of individualism is sacred, and has supremacy over the state or any other institution that is meant to serve the individual. This interpretation covertly posits an anti-institutionalism in the American consciousness.

For DeMille, humans are responsible for history. Christian evangelism is the propagation of correct ideology, derived from the Eternal Mind, and given to us first through natural law and then through divine revelation. Without even hearing the message, humans are obligated to follow the

Law. All have the possibility of being saved, for natural law precedes revelation. DeMille summarized the meaning of history in the prologue to *The Sign of the Cross*, saying that the "sacrifice of martyrs who gave their lives on the bloodied sands of Roman arenas preserves for us an Eternal Truth. The faith born then is still available."[12]

Most of his impressions of communism were formed in a 1932 trip to the Soviet Union, where religion was suppressed in the emerging Marxist state. Along with his memories of hearing the Bible and American history read to him as a child, it formed his idea of social salvation. In words that, in a slightly different context, might have been used to describe Christianity, he told the Valley Forge Freedom Foundation: "God planted the wheat of freedom here in America—watered with the blood of our fathers and our sons—and gave us hands to reap it and make it bread for all mankind."[13] America's divine destiny is to bring "freedom" to the world. In another era, it might have been Christian destiny to bring the world to Christ, but DeMille used the nationalistic version, to "make the world safe for freedom." This task was both the mandate to the nation and the duty of Christians, supporting the extension of freedom to all the world.

Over the years communism, in DeMille's mind, took on more menacing proportions. During the McCarthy era, he sided with those who demanded that all directors sign the loyalty oath. Communists represented the forces of darkness, replacing the Nazis in this role, and he never examined the difference between these variant conceptions of totalitarianism. For DeMille, Stalin was the antichrist as early as 1949. By 1952, he was saying that the Iron Curtain is another Dark Age, arguing that "the enemy is able to assault and crumble the inmost citadel of the mind itself. There is no place to hide."[14] To DeMille's mind, Korea was an ideological war, and "in the struggle for the minds of men, the only bullets we can shoot, thank God, are the bullets of ideas."[15]

In opposition to the evil of communism, DeMille posed his conception of American capitalism:

Imagine a world in which the Ten Commandments were kept by everyone. . . . It would be a world of freedom in which the rights of every man were respected by every other man, his right to speak, his right to be silent, his right of assembly, his right of independence, his right to worship, his right to work, all branches of the individual's tree of liberty, spreading over all the land, giving its protection equally to all.[16]

Yet DeMille supported the Hollywood blacklist. In fact, Edward G. Robinson had just been taken off the blacklist when DeMille cast him as Dathan in *The Ten Commandments*, the insidious traitor who would destroy freedom from within the Jewish community.

DeMille believed the conspiracy was worldwide. Speaking to the London exhibitors, he told of a review in a Polish Communist newspaper that repeated the "identical words and phrases" of an American review.[17]

Beneath it was a doctrine of works. DeMille's melodramatic mindset had convinced him of the eventual and inevitable triumph of good, but he knew that evil had to be presented in an attractive and seductive fashion. He told of having done a good deal of work on a film about the Virgin Mary and then being brought up short by a priest's comment: "You simply cannot show anything evil in the same picture with the spotless purity of this subject."[18] DeMille answered in dramatic terms: "Drama means conflict. You cannot show the brightness of good unless you show it in contrast with the darkness of evil."[19] Furthermore, helping the individual to choose the good is the function of religion, which issues out into acts.

Motion pictures could "tell the story of our faith in the language of the developed and accepted professional motion picture techniques."[20] He believed that shooting *The Ten Commandments* on location would allow people who could not actually go to the Holy Land to "make a pilgrimage over the very ground Moses trod, to the very spot where he received the Law." He believed that, as a tool for moral education, it had no peer, and it was distinctly American: "Only the eternal principles of morality—written once upon tablets of stone and imbedded by our Founding Fathers into our American Way of Life—can rightly guide the next generation's choice of life or death, freedom or slavery."[21] It helps explain why he was so bothered by the attacks on his religious films. DeMille was convinced that in *The Ten Commandments*, he had a film that would help "unify the world." All American motion pictures "presented America to the world." They offered the opportunity to create a brotherhood of man. Thus, motion pictures brought a commonality of experience to people and transcended denominational lines.

DeMille was especially proud that in choosing Moses he thought that he had crossed denominational and religious lines, uniting Muslims, Jews, Protestants and Catholics. In a letter to *The Jewish Chronicle*, he wrote, "These three great religions face a common enemy today. But they also have a common bond in their devotion to one God revealed to Moses at the burning bush."[22] In the final analysis, he believed film had the power to bring people together in a crusade for freedom, "a means of welding together adherents of all three faiths against the common enemy of all faiths, atheistic communism."[23]

DeMille's films were deeply influenced by the events of the world, whether the great urban upheaval of his early work, the dislocation of the economy in his depression era works, or in his last works, the task of preserving a nation that had rewarded him and made him rich and famous through its capitalistic system.

In utilizing religion to claim supernatural justification for his own positions, he was hardly alone. The work of Robert Bellah on "civil religion" traces the roots of supernatural legitimation of the state from Puritan America and Thomas Jefferson through Martin Luther King, Jr. Robert Jewett and John Lawrence have tied this to popular art forms.[24] DeMille used his technological skill and the techniques of mass marketing to sell his ideas as entertainment. Film making, religion, and American values all run together in his thought. That people found his films so appealing suggests that they struck a responsive chord.

DeMille was fond of remembering that his father had studied to be an Episcopal minister until persuaded by his wife that a message that would reach hundreds in a church could reach thousands as a play. His son, Cecil, thought of himself in that tradition, fulfilling his father's vocation on a wider stage and delivering his message to millions across the world.

In *The Ten Commandments*, DeMille took the formulaic elements of both biblical and religious spectaculars, and welded them into his final and most fully realized film.

DeMille's second version of *The Ten Commandments* (his first was made in 1923) reacts to the controversies and contradictions of American society of the post–World War II world. It comments on international tensions, considers the continuing difficulty of developing a national identity for a pluralistic nation, addresses the problem of how the sacred and the secular are related at a time when supernaturalism was under serious attack, and tries to provide a sacred basis for the American value system. In 221 minutes, that is a prodigious task.

The film uses the formulas of both religious and biblical spectaculars. Much of the story is a fictional melodrama woven out of the years Moses spent in Egypt, which are not accounted for by the Bible. From the experience of the Burning Bush onward, the film builds on the biblical account, using themes established in the fictional sequences.

DeMille broke the script into seven parts; he had started developing scripts in broadly sweeping outlines with his sound films. There is a prologue about Moses being found by Bithiah, the Pharoah's sister. Starting with Moses as a prince in Egypt, DeMille established the rivalry between Rameses and Moses for Sethi's throne and Neferitiri's hand. The second movement focuses on the building of the city of Per-Rameses, and Moses' eventual discovery of his true heritage. In the third period, he becomes a Hebrew in Egypt, working in the brick pits, and finally killing Baka, the architect. Rameses delivers him into the hands of Sethi, and he is cast into the wilderness. The fourth stage is his life in Midian, his marriage, and the arrival of Joshua, which concludes with the Burning Bush and the Divine Commission. In the fifth, he goes to Egypt, performing signs and miracles, which ends with the Passover. The sixth section takes up the Exodus, Rameses' loss of the Egyptian army, and the final section dramatizes the giving of the Law on Mt. Sinai, the spectacle of the Golden Calf, and the entry of Israel into Canaan.

In the vast sweep and scope of the film, DeMille summed up all the themes that had interested him for more than three decades. His commitment to the American dream, his belief that America's destiny was part of a divine plan in history, and his feeling that this was the culmination of his own divine mission convinced him to pour all his hope, energy, and resources into the film.

During the filming, he had a heart attack but was back on the set the next morning, writing "that if my motives in making the film were what I thought they were, I would be given the strength to finish it." At 73, he had lived long enough to "have learned something about the ways and power of God; and long enough to make it not so very important if one's greatest effort turned out to be his last."[25]

It did turn out to be his last. Not only did he direct and produce *The Ten Commandments*, but he also became personally involved in its promotion and distribution. He felt so strongly about the film that he made a free print available to any prison and offered to distribute it free of charge in the Soviet Union if they would not censor it.

The film is constructed around two primary affirmations—the superiority of freedom over slavery and the superiority of faith over reason. DeMille liked to say that *The Ten Commandments* was his most modern picture, because the struggle between freedom and slavery was still being waged on the contemporary landscape.

Are men the property of the state? Are men to be ruled by law or by the whims of an individual? The answers to these timely questions were given some three thousand years ago on Mt. Sinai. . . . [The film's] purpose is to portray the state of civilization at the time when God saw that mankind was ready for the first proclamation of freedom under law—and to tell the story of the man whom God prepared to receive the Law.[26]

For him, the Communists were taskmasters, and it was necessary for the "Christian nations" to resist slavery and extend freedom.

To dramatize the struggle, DeMille creates an opposition between those who value human life and those who do not. In an early scene, a stone is being dragged by slaves; Yochabel, whom the audience knows to be the mother of Moses while he does not; is caught in it, about to be crushed. Baka, the Egyptian architect, tells Moses: "If we stopped moving stones for every grease-woman who falls, the city would never rise." Fathers and mothers are not honored in a slave system—a violation of the Fifth Commandment.

Joshua, who has struck an Egyptian to get to Moses in order to save Yochabel, is asked if he did not know that the punishment for the offense is death. Moses is impressed with Joshua's courage and tells him that he does not speak like a slave. Joshua tells him that men made slaves, not God. When Moses asks why this God does not free them, Joshua indicates that God will choose the time and "the man who will deliver us." Baka sees such talk as treason, but even as an Egyptian, Moses understands the yearning for freedom.

The theme of freedom is basic to DeMille's treatment of Moses. DeMille removes the responsibility for slavery from God, because slavery is a human institution (and thus imperfect), but even one who has been raised as an oppressor can understand the yearning for freedom presumed to be in all human hearts.

The theme is reiterated both positively and negatively several times. Moses is obedient to the commandments long before they are given to him. Standing in chains before Sethi, falsely accused by Rameses (breaking the Ninth Commandment) of fomenting revolution, Moses tells Sethi that he is not the Deliverer, that it would take a God to free the slaves, but if he could, he would deliver them. Sethi believes that this statement is an expression of disloyalty to him and asks Moses, "What evil has done this to you." Moses replies:

The evil that men should turn their brothers into beasts of burden . . . to slave and suffer in dumb anguish . . . to be stripped of spirit and hope and faith—only because they are of another race . . . another creed. If there is a God, he did not mean this to be so. What I have done, I was compelled to do.

Before he knows them as divine law, he understands that freedom and faith are integral to one another. This Law is part of nature, and one can know it intuitively. The Law is the supernatural justification of freedom.

The primary symbol of freedom's victory over slavery is the Exodus, and it is more central to the film than the giving of the decalogue. The Exodus is the film's high emotional peak. DeMille was a genius with crowd scenes; he had a sense of pageantry, yet paid attention to minute details. He hired whole tribes for the Exodus. He had 63 assistant directors, 20 of whom spoke both Arabic and English. Yet he would often stop and correct someone's clothing, or show people how they should move, even when the camera boomed to show the whole of the 8,000 people on the set.

Script directions reveal the importance of the symbolic effect he was trying to achieve:

A shofar trumpeter stands on a rooftop—his shofar at his lips—a heroic figure, symbolic of all man's yearning for freedom. . . . Aaron raises his arms toward the village crying in a ringing voice: "Arise, O Israel—behold the dawn of freedom!"

DeMille needed this symbolism to implant the theme of freedom emotionally as something more than an intellectual construct.

The scene also had another function. As the people stream across the screen down the Avenue of the Sphinxes, the narrator's voice says: "A nation arose—and freedom was born into the world." Freedom is not an individual's possession or an attitude, but is something conferred by God on a people. It is through Moses that God gives freedom to the nation of Israel. At the end of the film, Sephora tells him they carry the Law in the Ark of the Covenant, and that he is "God's torch that lights the way of the freedom." As Moses sends the people out across the Jordan, his final words are from Leviticus: "Go—proclaim liberty throughout the lands, unto the inhabitants thereof" [Leviticus 25:10]. In these words, DeMille completed the connection that he had been driving at for so long. They are the words inscribed on the Liberty Bell in Philadelphia. It is America's divine destiny to spread the news of liberty throughout the world.

DeMille believed that the giving and interpretation of the Law were the work of the Old and New Testaments, but that the working out of the Law in history was the work of nations. In a 1953 speech, DeMille said that the Soviet ambassador had spoken the truth when he said that the greatest power in the world was not the atom bomb, but ideas. "God planted the wheat of freedom here in America with the blood of our fathers and sons and gave us hands to reap it and make it bread for all mankind."[27]

Moses symbolically represents the forces of freedom, whereas Rameses represents the forces of tyranny. In the cold war of 1956, Americans thought of the Soviet Union as threatening personal freedom, and the audience was called to identify with the values of the Bible.

Many notable personalities endorsed his concept. Eugene Carson Blake, then president of the National Council of Churches, spoke of the film as "strengthening our whole conception of freedom and responsibility under God." Gerald Kennedy, Methodist bishop of Los Angeles, said that "one cannot see it without realizing anew that God is the guarantee of our liberties and the ground of our hope." The *New York Herald Tribune* editorialized: "The message of the freedom to think and believe according to one's own convictions is powerful beyond any yardstick measure."[28]

Although many have found the message of freedom close to the surface of the film, obvious symbols rarely have the power of subliminal ones—those that come disguised as "entertainment." The film gathers its ideological force through its formulaic conventions. DeMille always thought the story was primary, and his films never wandered very far from the formulas of the nineteenth-century Belasco theater conventions. It was his great gift to turn everything into melodramas in which good struggles with evil back and forth until good wins a final victory.

The film attempts to defend the American way of life by associating it with the sacred. Typical of this view is the treatment of Dathan, whose villainy is necessary, for after the demise of Pharaoh's army, Rameses and Neferitiri leave the film, and the only villain left is Dathan.

Throughout the film, Dathan has been a Jew with the mind of an Egyptian. He becomes chief overseer of the Hebrew slaves; the script describes him as a "human vulture, feeding on opportunity, with a servility which is but the mask for an insatiable ambition." Early in the film, he cooperates with Rameses to reveal the promised Deliverer. When Baka is killed, he informs on Moses in order to gain Baka's mansion and take Lilia as his concubine. He does not want to go on the Exodus, but is forced to go when Joshua places the lamb's blood over his door post to save Lilia from being stricken by the Plague of the Firstborn. On the march, he repeatedly calls for the Israelites to turn back and finally instigates the rebellion in the orgy of the Golden Calf. When Moses comes down from the mountain with the stone tablets, Dathan suggests that Moses carved the tablets himself to gain power over the people, telling them, "He showed you no land flowing with milk and honey. I show you a pot of gold!"

Dathan is the enemy within, Pharaoh's surrogate, and as such, is as destructive as Pharaoh. In the age of Joe McCarthy, when charges were flying that the nation was being destroyed from within by "godless materialism," Dathan is an atheist. He is the force behind the Golden Calf, whereby the people revert to their animalistic passions. This element of course fits perfectly with the sex and social responsibility cycle of spectaculars DeMille launched with *Samson and Delilah*.

In 1950, DeMille and a number of other directors tried to force a loyalty oath through the Director's Guild. Joseph Mankiewicz, the Guild's president, opposed it. In a meeting that went until after 3 A.M., the Guild voted to ask DeMille and the other members of the board to resign. His comment, according to Phil Koury, his administrative assistant at the time, was, "If you don't think our country is in danger, you should have been at last night's meeting."[29]

DeMille felt deeply about conservative politics and was deeply opposed to Americans who had flirted with communism. At the 1952 Republican Convention, he lobbied for Senator Robert Taft of Ohio. He spoke in behalf of conservative causes everywhere. His files contain a large book of conservative political speeches. In 1944, he refused to pay one dollar in dues to the American Federation of Radio Artists to fight a "right to work" proposition on the California ballot, a decision that cost him $5,000 per week as host of the Lux Radio Theater, and a blacklisting from radio and television for the remainder of his life, except for infrequent interviews and paid announcements. The next year he formed the DeMille Foundation for Political Freedom and campaigned for "right to work" laws in several states.

At a time when Americans felt very strongly about the Berlin airlift, the Alger Hiss trial, and the execution of Julius and Ethel Rosenberg as spies, Dathan suggested "the enemy within," who poisons the weak and the gullible. Whether or not the political connection was obvious to the audience, Dathan did represent a villain who was familiar to their experience.

American social values were glorified and other values vilified. When

Bithiah finds Moses in the bulrushes, Memnet, her slave, is opposed to keeping the child. Judith Anderson plays Memnet as a slave who considers herself an aristocrat. In American social mythology, it is not birth or station that counts, but accomplishment. Much of the enmity between Rameses and Moses derives from this equalitarian idealism. Rameses expects to inherit Egypt because he is the blood heir to Sethi, but Sethi proposes that the succession to power is based on "the best man to rule Egypt." He sets Moses to building Per-Rameses, and Rameses to finding the Deliverer. The audience identifies with the values that Moses embodies; one is judged by deeds, not by birth.

Success is given a great deal of attention. Rameses and Moses are equals before Moses' conversion. Both are princes of Egypt at the beginning, but Rameses is competitive, mean, and deceitful, whereas Moses is generous, kind, and open. When Moses returns from the wars in Ethiopia, Rameses demands that Moses command the Ethiopian king to kneel to Sethi. Moses refuses, informing him that the king is there in friendship—"as an ally to guard our southern gates." Being gracious to one's former enemies was something that Americans understood when the U.S. had aided the recovery of Western Europe and Japan.

When the Hebrew slaves complain that they are being starved and overworked, Moses decrees a day of rest—the secular equivalent of the commandment to obey the Sabbath—and orders that the temple granaries be opened. When Rameses warns him that the grain belongs to the gods, Moses replies, "What the gods can digest will not sour in the belly of a slave." Human needs are paramount, and a religion that does not feed humans is idolatrous and unworthy of respect. In this way, Moses already obeys the commandment to have no other gods before Yahweh.

Moses is generous almost to a fault. He tries to intervene for Rameses when Sethi hints that Moses will be his successor. Sethi tells Rameses that he has "accused your brother falsely," but Moses calls attention to the fact that "he is the son of your body." Even Sethi accepts the commandment not to bear false witness.

Later, after his journey through the wilderness, Moses does not eject the Amalekites from Jethro's well despite their ill-mannered attempt to take it over. Also, when he hears of Rameses' command to destroy the firstborn of Israel, the script says, "Almost daring to challenge divine justice, he grips the pillar in anguish," for Moses knows that Rameses will lose his own son, the future Pharaoh of Egypt.

Moses' powers are signs of his spiritual success. This created a problem with the death of the firstborn. DeMille transfers the responsibility for this plague from God to Rameses and, thereby, away from Moses. Henry Noerdlinger, a biblical scholar hired by DeMille to provide technical assistance, takes note of this development, justifying it with a verse from the

Qu'Ran "where Pharaoh says, as the plagues are brought about, 'We will slay their sons.' "[30]

Beyond the scriptural justification is a cultural one. To attribute this degree of vengeance to God challenges God's goodness, and if Moses is good, while God is cruel and ruthless, then Moses' righteousness before God is questionable.

Moses' foil is Rameses, whose solution to the building of the city of Per-Rameses is more cruelty to the "stiff-necked slaves" who "die more willingly than bend their backs in Sethi's service." Rameses suspects that Moses is hatching a political plot against Sethi, saying that his popularity with the slaves, and his friendship with Ethiopia and Goshen have placed Egypt in jeopardy.

Rameses is secretive and surreptitious. He hires Dathan to spy on Moses. Even when he spares Moses' life, he is moved by coldly rational considerations. He tells Moses, "I defeated you in life. You shall not defeat me in death." Then he casts Moses out into the wilderness with inadequate rations to perish.

Moses is a success in everything he tries. He is a great soldier, and a master builder; even in Midian, he is the first capitalist. When the sheik of Ezion raves about his tribe's wool bringing a rich price, Jethro explains that it is "because Moses has sold the whole shearing of all the tribes in one place at one price." He is successful, "because his words are truth—his trading is just."

Moses is successful because of his spirit. Obeying the commandments before he knows them, he is an even greater success in his ultimate defeat of Rameses. His motivation is pure. He does not do things for his own self-aggrandizement. He is even willing to become a slave "to find the meaning of what I am and why a Hebrew—or any man—must be a slave." When he is tempted by Neferitiri to return to his old life, he holds firm to his new-found ideals. Of his clothes, he says: "If they are stained, it is with the mud of slavery, and if they reek, it is with the stench of injustice," emphasizing the importance of *choosing* the good, for he could have chosen another way.

Although Moses' success is both material and spiritual, Rameses' success is simply worldly. He obtains both the throne and the woman, but eventually fails because he is an atheist. The only value he holds is power over others. DeMille saw the communist rulers in Rameses. He exulted at the disinterment of Stalin and likened it to the pulling down of idols. Communism denied spiritual values, but Jews, Christians, and Muslims put material things in their proper perspective. "They say that the things of this world are good but not the supreme good."[31]

Rameses' test with Moses becomes a struggle between the human will and the divine will. Rameses must be utterly defeated before he affirms that "His God—is God!" Ambition must be pure; success must not be pursued for the sake of power over others, or it will ultimately be defeated. Those who recognize the divine law in their hearts are the ultimate victors.

The evidence of his films suggests that DeMille simultaneously held both a Puritan and Dionysian morality. In *The Ten Commandments*, he equates sexuality with destruction, culminating in the orgy of the Golden Calf. Three women typify his view of sexuality—Neferitiri, Sephora, and Lilia. They represent the bad, the good, and the vulnerable woman.

Neferitiri is the evil temptress who tries to lure Moses away from his duty. She confuses "love" with "lust," and harbors real hatred. She is childlike and does not hesitate to murder Memnet when the slave threatens to expose Moses. When Moses tells Neferitiri that "there is a beauty beyond the senses," she is stupefield, because she understands only pleasure. Like Rameses, she is an atheist, scoffing at the gods, forever scheming to keep Moses with her, and when Moses rejects her, telling her he is bound to God and "to a shepherd girl," Neferitiri recalls Rameses' prophecy in the dungeon: that there can be another woman in Moses' life. She tells him she will see to it that his people never leave Egypt unless he comes to her; he replies that it is not in her power to decree. "Who else can soften Pharaoh's heart—or harden it?" she asks, and when his advisors suggest that Rameses let the Hebrews go, Neferitiri mocks him: "You told Moses to make bricks without straw. Now he tells you to make cities without bricks. Who is the slave and who is the Pharaoh?" In the end, Rameses is destroyed because Neferitiri has hardened his heart in her efforts to keep Moses in Egypt. Moses survives because he rejects the pleasure principle in favor of responsibility to God and to his people.

Neferitiri's foil is Sephora. She loves Moses. When her sisters fawn over him, she goes out to tend the sheep. She makes no demands on Moses other than his companionship. Her image is that of the woman who holds together the values of the social order. She exemplifies Michael Wood's perception that women propose "a world of children and homes and porches and kitchens and neighbors and gossip and schools. . . . When community is asserted, it is asserted by women."[32] Wood argues that women are what men are running from—a form of entrapment. Sephora stays neatly in the background for most of the film. Moses may be a constant husband, one who does not commit adultery, but his "real" life is anywhere but in the home.

Lilia is the vulnerable one. From the first, men lust after her. When Baka takes her to be his house slave, an elderly character remarks, "Beauty is but a curse to our women," and later when another slave dies for crying out against the injustice, he complains: "You rot our bodies—steal hope from our souls! Must you also shame and defile our women?" When Joshua is condemned to death for his part in killing Baka, Dathan makes a deal with Lilia that she will become his concubine in exchange for Joshua's life.

In most movies, such deals are never consummated, but DeMille does not save her from "a fate worse than death." Lilia remains pure because her spirit is pure, though her body is defiled.

When Joshua returns, she still keeps her part of the bargain as a woman of honor and integrity in the midst of a demeaning and cruel system. Furthermore, when she finds out about the death of the firstborn, she is happy that she will become one of its victims, pleading, "Don't save me from death, Joshua—save me from life!"

Even after they have reached Mount Sinai, Lilia becomes the proposed sacrifice. Dathan, who has lusted for her throughout the picture, losing her during the Exodus, attempts to exact a final sacrilege, but the suffering does not prevent her from achieving her final triumph—she becomes the wife of Joshua.

As in other biblical spectaculars of the 1950s, luxury is equated with lust and self-indulgence, weakening the moral fiber. The opulence of Egypt is pitted against the toil and poverty of the Israelites. The Golden Calf is used to establish the threat of sexual licentiousness to duty. The Production Code limited the depiction of the orgy, so DeMille used a voice-over, using works "derived from the Bible either in direct quote or adaptation."[33] The script comments that "everywhere Satan strums his harp of sin—but the payment will be death."

This licentiousness almost undermines the Israelites' freedom. Dathan gathers power again, because he understands the impure urges that Moses overcomes. The abandonment of self to the pleasure principle leads to death and destruction, whereas freedom must be constantly on the alert for backsliders. Those who live by the flesh will die by the flesh. By depicting licentiousness and luxury together, DeMille links the pleasure principle with materialism. Dathan is an atheist, and so licentiousness becomes the work of an atheistic materialist, a favorite description of Americans for the Soviets. We are undermined by the weakening of our moral fiber, a constant danger even for those who have seen the miracles of God.

Other themes of lesser importance sustain the theme of freedom. To a nation that believes the fundamental unit of society is the family, Moses is the dutiful son, the loving brother, the gentle husband and father, and most of all one who loves his God and his people. On the other hand, Rameses is involved in a loveless marriage, cares nothing for his father save the chance to succeed him on the throne, treats his people as servants, and is an atheist. His only real love is for his son. It is little wonder that Americans thought of Rameses as an alien and his Egypt as a place where freedom could not flourish.

Although the issue of freedom was easily portrayed, DeMille's other major theme was not so easily established. He wanted to demonstrate that freedom was built on faith rather than reason. He found himself attacked from both sides. On the one side, he was confronted with a naturalistic world view that found it difficult to accept the miraculous occurrences that it was necessary to depict—the Burning Bush, the crossing of the Red Sea, the giving of the Law. On the other side were Christian groups that demanded absolute literal adherence to the scriptures. In addition, there was the problem of making the motivations of the characters into an understandable and plausible action, consistent with dramatic conventions. The problems proved considerable.

DeMille set Henry Noerdlinger to the task of researching the film. DeMille demanded authenticity whenever he could have it. As a part of the publicity campaign, he had Noerdlinger compile a book, *Moses and Egypt*, from his ten years of research. DeMille sent it to every major library in the country. The cost of the research was estimated at 2 percent of the budget. Noerdlinger said he had consulted 950 books, 984 periodicals, and 1,286 clippings, collected 2,964 photographs, and utilized the facilities of 30 libraries and museums in Europe, North America, and Africa.

DeMille said he used research to add authenticity and conviction to the final cut, thus influencing the audience "into the belief that it is watching reality unroll itself on the screen."[34] Creating suspension of disbelief was crucial if he were to show that faith is superior to reason, and that faith in our ideals, though they sometimes seem to defy our experience, is the backbone of our political system.

It was a common theme for DeMille. He said that "if God is dethroned, man is reduced to a worthless molecule without independence, without dignity, without rights, without liberty—with only one duty: to serve the dictatorship with all his mind and all his heart and all his strength." The antichrist is Stalin, and if the Soviet Union is not to rule the world, America must stop him. "Even if we failed to choose the side of God, He has chosen us, in spite of all our faults."[35]

From the beginning, opinion was divided with regard to the pyrotechnics of the miracles. Some saw them as marvelous displays of things they had only read about, but many critics were bothered by their technical virtuosity. The great scenes seemed "mechanical," and lost "the quality of credulity." In reading them, they could be accepted on faith, but "the miracle suddenly takes on the quality of mythology and the disturbing thought creeps in that one all his life has believed in a fairy tale."[36]

DeMille was fascinated with what he could do with the optical processes available to him, but he was also aware of the trends in the culture that could undercut his film. The miracle sequences were attacked and supported in no consistent pattern—religious leaders were awed or disgusted; secular critics praised or blamed him. He was attacked and praised by both liberals and conservatives.

The way in which DeMille and his artisans dealt with the problem of the Burning Bush is instructive. Two problems had to be solved—how to portray the bush itself and how to present the voice of God. After discussing the varying options in the Old Testament, the Midrash Rabbah, and Eusebius, and finding that there were varying interpretations as to whether the Burning Bush incident even occurred or whether the voice of God spoke, Noerdlinger noted that "it is left to the viewer to grasp the meaning beyond the physical manner in which this revelation is materialized."[37]

To solve the problem of visualizing the Burning Bush, DeMille developed a bush with a golden glow.[38] That, however, does not convey the ideology that lay behind it. The script shows the delicate interplay between the literal visualization of a miracle and the modern attempts to convey the Scriptures in the language of science. "Its vibrating fire stems from a gold core in a corona of spectrum rays that seems of the very purest essence of light itself. It mantles the bush in a miraculous aura that glows without consuming."[39]

The voice of God raised other problems, because the voice had to be presented not only here, but in the giving of the commandments. They solved the problem by reference to the Midrash Rabbah, which says that God spoke to Moses in the voice of Moses' father, Amram, so as not to frighten him. So they decided on Charlton Heston's voice, pitching it lower. Moses returns to tell Sephora and Joshua of his experience at the Burning Bush, telling them, "He revealed His Word to my mind."[40] Since the experience is not witnessed by others, it is possible to believe that it was a psychological hallucination or to mythicize it to get at the meaning beyond the revelation.

For most of the audience, it seems that this treatment of miracles worked. For those who were moderately conservative in their theology, the spectacles were impressive and did not violate the Bible. For those who were somewhat more liberal in their approach, the optical processes gave just enough unreality when compared to the scope of the Exodus to let people ignore the literal visual sensations and think of the miracles in terms of their meaning.

The voice of God is also associated with the giving of the Law on Mount Sinai. Although some reviewers found the voice bothersome, there were enough pyrotechnics going at the same time that most of the audience probably did not notice the voice of God. The visual burning of the commandments onto the stone is so spectacular and Moses' reactions so diminished in importance that the voice coming through the echo chambers had little effect.

The attempt to portray the miracles plausibly was not totally successful. Rabbi David Polish commented that it resembled a "Disney cartoon" at times and found it "a piece of effrontery."[41] Polish sensed the disparity between DeMille's attempt to "influence the audience into the belief that it is watching reality" and the theological problem of belief. The justification of miracles in naturalistic terms is an intellectual problem. If disbelief cannot be suspended, the intellectual response clashes with one's enjoyment of the film. Biblical miracles bring with them the difficulty of making religion and miracles different than our everyday experience.

Tom Driver thought that there was a confusion built into historical religion, which uses specific times and places, tricking producers into believing that they need to recreate them as they actually were. The problem is the biblical "style," which although anchoring its narratives in the historical world, uses it to examine the relation between God and humanity. The biblical style usually uses a specific time and place, but "never describes the physical details of a scene, or it would defeat its own purpose."

Driver points to the problem that makes many of Hollywood's biblical films seem inartistic—the very concretion of the image. Driver takes the inner shaping of the emotional and intellectual life by stories that are universal in meaning but particular in detail to be the central fact of religion, producing a clash in the consciousness.

Arguing that this visual literalism undercuts the story, Driver laments that the religious component is left out of the film.

God [in *The Ten Commandments*] is never . . . a mystery which sends a man scurrying into his inner self searching for a place to hide and [DeMille's God] is not the God above all gods who is beyond thought and therefore must be apprehended though the imagination reaching out to meet his self-disclosure. The DeMille God is imprisoned in the DeMille style, which means the irrelevant minutiae of Egyptian culture and the costume director. He bears no resemblance to the Old Testament Lord of History.[42]

Driver's argument points out the difference between the theologically trained mind and the makers and consumers of popular religion. Driver seems interested in demythicizing along the lines of Rudolf Bultmann's program, which searched for the meaning behind the story. His reference to the "God above all gods" is almost a direct reference to Paul Tillich's argument in *The Courage to Be*.

On the other side, DeMille thought of what he was doing as providing a spiritual pilgrimage for Christians and Jews over the same terrain Moses trod, teaching the lessons and values that he had learned through his own biblical study and his reading of the American experience. Even though he undercuts the myth by trying to make it acceptable to the rationalist, his direction is toward leaving the myth intact. DeMille could not avoid the miracles, and because he believed so strongly that movies intensified reality, he believed that the motion picture was adding power to the old stories for a new generation.

In that vein, he treated the Pillar of Fire as a cross between a cyclone and an electrical storm, "a flaming spiral nebulae."[43] The opening of the Red Sea resembles a hurricane and a typhoon. A boy exclaims to a blind man, "The wind opens the sea," and the blind man reinterprets it as "God opens the sea with a blast of his nostrils."

As for the "finger of God" burning the commandments into the stone tablets on Sinai, Noerdlinger used Philo, relying on mysticism, "giving shape and tension to the air and changing it to flaming fire." In his imaginative construction, the flame becomes the finger of God.[44]

The rational explanations of these phenomena do not explain away the miracle. DeMille believed that God used natural phenomena to accomplish his purposes. Part of the trouble with Rameses is that his atheism is built upon rationalism. When Moses turns the Nile to blood, Rameses explains it: "When the Nile ran red, I too was afraid . . . until word came of a mountain beyond the Cataracts which spewed red mud and poisoned the river." He has explained away Moses turning of his staff into a serpent, as interestingly DeMille himself did, by noting that there are still people who can make the Egyptian cobra rigid. Noerdlinger points out that many of the plagues are naturally recurring phenomena:

At the time of the inundation, the Nile does carry minute animal life and/or silt from beyond the cataracts which can produce a reddish tint in the water. Frogs still breed in great numbers about the same time. . . . Flies and other insects can be a plague in Egypt to this day. The spread of all manner of disease is not a thing of the biblical past alone. Thunderstorms and hail do occur in the winter season in the Land of the Nile. Under a recent Cairo dateline the *New York Times* reported locusts destroying plant life in that city. "Even darkness may be felt" is another still existing phenomenon. It is the *Khamsin*, the sandstorm which can obscure the sun, or the *Zobaa*, a whirlwind which whips the desert sand to rise in pillarlike fashion.

Rabbi Hertz concurs with such views but stresses the miraculous intensification of these phenomena to illustrate man's impotence against God and God's judgment on the idols of Egypt.[45]

All these explanations drive toward a single conclusion, expressed in a single affirmation. Having seen his army destroyed, his land plagued, and his gods proven impotent, Rameses is brought to faith. Moses' victory is complete because this violator of human freedom must admit his error. "His God—is God," Rameses quietly exclaims. In the face of the facts (even though rationally explained for the unbelievers), God is the victor over all those who would be slave masters, and even the atheistic materialist must confess in awe.

Another set of attacks on the film dealt with its historical accuracy. In March, 1957, the Biblical and Archeological Research Foundation listed several errors they found in the picture. Five months before, *Awake*, the magazine of Jehovah's Witnesses, had listed several errors. In both cases, DeMille set his chief researcher to work. Although it was his policy not to reply to negative film reviews of the picture, DeMille did decide to launch a counterattack on those who questioned the film's accuracy. The producers and publicists decided not to respond to small magazines, and considered it useless to confront Fundamentalists "with our more liberal views and the facts established by serious and devoted Bible scholars about the Bible, its formation, its canon and its translations."[46] When the accusations found their way into a column in one of the San Francisco newspapers, however, the DeMille staff issued a four-page, single-spaced, point-by-point refutation.

The Biblical and Archeological Research Foundation contested the dating of the Pharaohs, the problem that although Moses ages 40 years, Neferitiri does not, his transposition of time about what happened with Dathan and the Golden Calf, questions about Joshua and Moses being contemporaries, and the identity of the woman who rescued Moses in the bulrushes.[47]

Noerdlinger's reply is a masterpiece of rational criticism. He charges the foundation with breaking the Ninth Commandment—"Thou shalt not bear false witness." Then he proceeds to quote archeological opinion, respected scholars who agree with him, traditions, and legends out of the Jewish heritage and the Qu'Ran. By the end of the piece, the foundation seems more accurately characterized as a schoolboy than as a scholar.

Hidden in the replies are serious issues, revealing some of the dynamics behind the making of the film. The film maker, Noerdlinger hints, has a different purpose and responsibility than the scholar has. The film maker needs to tell the story with imagination, and Noerdlinger does not hesitate to note that the only charge that is not a subject of disagreement by scholars is the one about Dathan, whom he suggests they have "telescoped" for dramatic effect. Hidden is the tension between dramatic construction and historical accuracy, as previously discussed in *The Crusades*. Most notably, this dramatic change is seen in the film when the responsibility for the death of the firstborn is transferred from God to Rameses. Noerdlinger and DeMille thought of themselves as being in the mainstream of religious thought.

In America, there was a growing discontent, an ambiguity and a confusion about the future. Speaking of the souring of the postwar revival, which emphasized commonness and peace with God, and downplayed conflict, Martin Marty concluded that it was self-defeating. Positive thinking did not eliminate the Soviet threat or bring the Second Coming. At the heart of the revival was adjustments to corporate America, suburban expansion, and peace of mind.[48]

Moses is believable because he was so modern, traveling from atheism to belief like many others of the 1950s. DeMille's solution to the dramatic problem was to turn Moses into an "everyman."

Moses is everyman—in his pride, his bitterness at God allowing evil to befall his people, and in his reluctance to do God's work.

The life of Moses was a life of struggle and defiance, of daring and sorrow, a life of love and battle, of sacrifice and murder, a life of achievement and disaster, humiliation and glory.

Moses was one of the world's greatest human beings—human to the point of sin, holy to the point of seeing God face to face.[49]

The human side provided the drama that DeMille was seeking. Moses must learn to disbelieve in Sethi's flawed vision, even while presenting Sethi as an honorable figure. He must sense in himself and resist a divine compulsion that mixes with his human tendencies, such as going out to become a slave with his people. Facing the mountain, Moses is told that no man has ever seen God, because to look on his face would mean death. Moses wanted to know "that He *is*—and *if* He is . . . to know why He has not heard the cry of slaves in bondage." Moses does not believe in God until he has met God in the Burning Bush. The miracle liberates him psychologically. When he comes down from the mountain, his vision is not of God as a substance among other substances, but as he says: "He is not flesh, but spirit . . . the light of Eternal Mind. . . . I know that His light is in every man." The spirit that Moses finds is a psychological expression, inoffensive to modernists and fundamentalists alike.

To present this human side of Moses, DeMille was careful to document his choices, so that the general public and even most professional clergy would be impressed. He had Noerdlinger research a number of leads—especially about the years from his childhood to his young manhood when he killed the Egyptian overseer.

They placed Moses in Sethi's court, dating the Exodus in the reign of Rameses II, 1301–1234 B.C.E. They noted that at Karnak, a figure of Rameses was carved over another figure, and decided they had justification for placing Moses on that original stone.

That and the fact that ascent to the throne was matrilineal allowed them to posit a triangle between Moses, Neferitiri, and Rameses.[50] DeMille had found what he was searching for. Dates for the Exodus range from 1400 to 1200 B.C.E.; perhaps Rameses did not like his portrait; matrilineage was only one means of succession. DeMille's formula for success included a love triangle—Richard, Berengeria, and Alice in *The Crusades*; Marcus, Mercia, and Poppaea in *The Sign of the Cross*; Samson, Miriam, and Delilah in *Samson and Delilah*. For DeMille, the triangle was eternal, the source of human conflict.

From the birth of Moses to the Burning Bush sequence, there are 25 verses in the Book of Exodus. DeMille expands those 25 verses to 171 pages of script, enough for a long film in itself. On the other hand, from the time of Moses' first interview with Rameses to the time of the Exodus, the Bible spends 202 verses, whereas DeMille devotes only 52 pages to this period nearly a third of them develop the triangular scheme between Rameses, Neferitiri, and Moses, which does not appear in the Bible.

DeMille saw the triangle relationship as necessary to explain naturally "how God hardened Pharaoh's heart," but it also serves the cause of dramatic probability. In addition, it explains that God had human assistance in causing the numerous deaths.

Even evil served God's will. Noerdlinger asks, "How can a man, a creature of God, make the choice between good and evil of his own free will, if God hardens his heart?"[51] DeMille's solution never really resolves the problem, but it transfers the total responsibility from God to share it with Rameses and Neferitiri, satisfying those in the audience who would have found such an arbitrary God incomprehensible.

DeMille believed that his *The Ten Commandments* gave the world a message of freedom built on faith. The nation always stood with those who were fighting for their freedom. The film suggests that a technological, rationalistic, naturalistic world view was valid only when it issued forth from a faith that was common to all Americans—a faith that glossed over the difficulties between Christians and Jews, a secularized, generalized religion such as that described by Will Herberg and others. It was rooted in the popular religion that abandoned particularities, a religion more deeply felt by Cecil B. DeMille than probably any other member of the movie colony. In the phrases of a discussion that would not take place for another decade, DeMille's popular religion was very much a civil religion.

NOTES

1. DeMille, *Autobiography*, p. 31.

2. Ibid., p. 433.

3. This God concept quite possibly had its roots in the Transcendental philosophy of New England. In his "Thoughts on Modern Literature," Emerson declared that "there is One Mind, and that all the powers and privileges which lie in any, lie in all." For Emerson, good and evil emanate from the self; there is a correlation between the human soul and outward reality; and God is revealed in every person. These concepts found their way into DeMille's theology. Ibid., p. 434.

4. *Hollywood Citizen-News*, March 24, 1958, p. 14.

5. George Sokolsky's column, *Los Angeles Herald Express*, November 30, 1956, p. 9.

6. DeMille, *Autobiography*, p. 251.

7. Ibid., p. 276.

8. Physical courage and strong bodies were important to DeMille all his life. He admired Charlton Heston for walking down the steep climb at Mt. Sinai barefoot over the hot cinders, and he was furious at Victor Mature for not fighting a trained lion so that he could get realistic close-ups. DeMille's Christian man was not effeminate in the slightest.

9. *Deseret News*, January 22, 1959, p. 10.

10. Cecil B. DeMille, speech to the American Red Cross, February 28, 1950. DeMille's private files, Los Angeles, California.

11. Paul Tillich, *The Protestant Era* (abridged edition) (Chicago: University of Chicago Press, 1957), p. 163.

12. Program book, *Sign of the Cross*, no page number.

13. Cecil B. DeMille, speech to the Valley Forge Freedom Foundation, February 22, 1953. Private files.

14. Cecil B. DeMille, speech to the General Assembly of the Presbyterian Church (USA), May 23, 1952. Private files.

15. DeMille, *Autobiography*, p. 423.

16. Cecil B. DeMille, speech to Public Relations Society of America, November 15, 1955. Private files.

17. DeMille, speech to the London exhibitors, May 9, 1957. DeMille's private files, Los Angeles, California.

18. Koury, *Yes Mr. DeMille*, p. 219 ff.

19. *Hollywood Citizen-News*, May 28, 1952, p. 14.

20. Ibid.

21. DeMille, speech to National School Boards Association, February 16, 1957. DeMille's private files, Los Angeles, California.

22. *The Jewish Chronicle* 115 (September, 1956): 17. He could become ecstatic over what the power of film could do in achieving unity.

> When I think of Samson appearing on the screens of the world and telling his faith in the invisible God in German, French, Italian, Spanish, Arabic, Hindustani, Bengali—I cannot help being reminded of that time when the Day of Pentecost was fully come and the many tongued multitude were amazed because—as they said—"We hear them speak in our tongues the wonderful works of God." (DeMille, Presbyterian speech.)

23. DeMille, *Autobiography*, p. 421.

24. Cf. Robert Bellah, *The Broken Covenant* (New York: Seabury Press, 1975); Russell Richey and Donald G. Jones, eds., *American Civil Religion* (New York: Harper and Row, 1974); Robert Jewett and John Shelton Lawrence, *The American Monomyth* (New York: Doubleday and Co., 1977).

25. DeMille, *Autobiography*, p. 429.

26. DeMille, speech to DeMille Jr. High School (Long Beach, Calif.), June 25, 1957. DeMille's private files, Los Angeles, California.

27. DeMille, speech to Valley Forge Foundation.

28. Publicity release, Paramount Studios. University of California Film Library, Los Angeles, California.

29. Koury, *Yes, Mr. DeMille*, p. 303. Koury tells the story as an outsider. Joseph Mankiewicz's recollections are found in Peter Bogdanovich, *John Ford* (London: Studio Vista Press, 1967), p 19.

30. Henry Noerdlinger, *Moses and Egypt* (Los Angeles: University of Southern California Press, 1956), p. 47.

31. DeMille, speech to Public Relations Society.

32. Wood, *America in the Movies*, p. 42.

33. Noerdlinger, *Moses and Egypt*, p. 44.

34. Cecil B. DeMille, "The Values of Research," *Variety*, January 5, 1955, p. 3.

35. DeMille, speech at the First Congregational Church, Los Angeles, California. DeMille's private files, Los Angeles, California.

36. *Parents Magazine* 41 (December, 1956): 114. *Atlanta Journal*, February 8, 1957, p. 15.

37. Noerdlinger, *Moses and Egypt*, pp. 23–4.

38. DeMille, *Autobiography*, p. 430.

39. *The Ten Commandments*, Script, p. D–17.

40. DeMille, *Autobiography*, p. 431.

41. *American Judaism* 6 (January, 1957): 25.

42. Tom Driver, "Hollywood in the Wilderness," *Christian Century* 73 (November 28, 1956): 1390–1.

43. Script, p. F–45.

44. Noerdlinger, *Moses and Egypt*, p. 40.

45. Ibid., pp. 28–29.

46. Henry Noerdlinger to Ann del Valle (public relations), March 14, 1957. DeMille's private files, Los Angeles, California.

47. *San Francisco News*, March 8, 1957, p. 13.

48. Martin Marty, *Righteous Empire* (New York: Dial Press, 1970), p. 259.

49. DeMille, speech at DeMille Jr. High School.

50. DeMille, *Autobiography*, pp. 412–3.

51. Noerdlinger, *Moses and Egypt*, p. 27.

8

The Demise of the Biblical Spectacular: John Huston's *The Bible*

In 1961, when Dino deLaurentiis decided to make a film version of the Bible, the first Jesus film had not yet been released. He had completed *Barabbas*, a box office failure. Originally he had intended to make the story of the entire Bible, but eventually settled on the first 22 chapters of the Book of Genesis.

He wanted to have great directors do the film, Robert Bresson, Orson Welles, Luchino Visconti, and Federico Fellini, with John Huston supervising the entire picture. Huston's vision was that "the picture should describe man's emergence from the mists of mythology and legend into the first light of history," which would begin with the Creation and end with Abraham, the first historical figure in the Bible.[1]

Huston was known as a director who could transform Westerns, private detective, and other generic works into personal visions, whereas the others were *auteurs*, men who made very personal films. Biblical spectaculars, on the other hand, had been primarily formulaic. Huston set about the task of transforming the formulaic conventions into a personal vision.

The film, which cost $18 million to make, returned only $15 in domestic profits, and while it probably made a small profit worldwide, its box office performance was disappointing. Critical reactions were as mixed. Professor Harvey Cox suggested a "new pastoral classification: corrupt for adults, fine for children."[2] Yet *Commonweal* noted the ambivalent reviews:

The diversity of reviews ran the gamut from "breathtaking in scope and grandeur" and "as fine a version of the Old Testament as we shall ever see in the movies" and "stunning production" down to "literal pictorial representations" and the "film vulgarizes a host of sublime images" and "dull" and "Sunday school pageant mood" and eventually two critics who must have sat side-by-side: "something for everyone" and "it has something in it to offend everybody."[3]

The film frustrated expectations. Critics who spent years panning the spectaculars of Cecil B. DeMille found virtues in his work when compared to *The Bible*.

The greatest departure from the formula was the dramatic construction. Although Huston, deLaurentiis, and Christopher Fry, the scriptwriter, did not hesitate to make a film in "the grand style," they operated within a framework dictated by the Scriptures. To Cox, Fitzgerald, and others, this limitation seemed literalistic or "fundamentalistic," relying upon "literal reenactments and the sheer sonority of Holy Writ."[4]

George Stevens' *Greatest Story* had changed the archetypal pattern with disastrous effects at the box office. In Stevens' hands, the formula with its basic conflict between good and evil was overcome by his determination not to blame the Jews and his ambiguous presentation of Roman evil. *Greatest Story* could not make up its mind whether to be a spectacular or something else, and consequently ended up confusing its audience.

The critical response to *The Bible* shows this same confusion; expecting another biblical spectacular, the critics found a personal film on a gigantic scale, ranging from comedy to tragedy, segmented and held together only by sketchy genealogical relationships and the assumption that the audience had a residual familiarity with the stories. Huston tried to warn the public, making numerous personal appearances around the country, often repeating the same comments, that the movie was a work of art, asking audiences to approach it with a questioning spirit, rather than a reverent one. He aimed it at a liberal audience, those who understood that the myths it was based on were used to "account for our origins and the world around us."[5]

The structure was that of an art film. Choosing not to tie it together by a dramatic concept, scriptwriter Christopher Fry took the approach of treating the story as an ancient myth rather than the founding myth of the Jews and Christians. This freed Huston to interpret the film in a variety of visual styles. Between the different styles, the confusion over the genre, and the struggle between experience and belief, the film had a ready-made list of enemies.[6]

The material's familiarity worked against it because Fry's construction was logical rather than dramatic. This kind of film had never been popular with American audiences, and film makers had not attempted a "logical" spectacle since D. W. Griffith's *Intolerance* a half-century before. Nevertheless, Huston, Fry, and deLaurentiis decided to try.

Fry wanted to create a script that moved from its poetic origins to the beginnings of history.[7] The film that emerged redefined the problem of the biblical spectacular. Instead of reshaping the story, adding fictional events, or selecting events from different versions of the myth to fill out and make a narrative as DeMille, Ray, and Stevens had done, Fry wrote a script that stuck literally to the biblical narrative.[8] He made no attempt to offer scientific evidence for the miraculous and often incongruous events.

Many who had praised this technique in a small-scale Italian film about Jesus, *The Gospel According to St. Matthew*, believed this refusal to impose interpretations clashed with the modern spirit. Harvey Cox called the film "Gnostic" and charged that the treatment was designed to avoid giving offense to many religious groups. That certainly was a motive with numerous other religious films, since religious pressure groups could often convince some segment of the general public not to see a film. Fry, however, attributes his decision to the study of myth. He wondered what the Tree of Knowledge of Good and Evil meant or whether Eve historically ate the fruits of the tree, bringing death and sorrow. Was the Fall a punishment for sexual knowing? In the end, it means death and separation, disobedience to the laws planted in human nature, and self-consciousness (knowing our nakedness) and loss of God-consciousness. "Thoughts such as these couldn't be introduced into the film or we should have found ourselves making not a film of the Bible, but a biblical commentary."[9]

Cox argued that if someone entered the theater confused about "alleged conflicts between genesis and geology, or concerned with the theological meaning of the creation narratives, Mr. Huston turns him away without a word." Cox, known for his work as an interpreter of theology and culture, did not consider the possibility that Fry had based his script on studies of myth that were just beginning to be disseminated here in the works of Northrop Frye, Mircea Eliade, Claude Levi-Strauss, and others. Fry's script resists interpretation.

The film was deceptive. At its simplest level, it seemed to visualize Bible stories or "Sunday-school pictures." When one looks at what is visualized, however, *The Bible* is primarily a visual experience.

Pointing a camera is making an interpretive decision. Huston and cinematographer Giuseppe Rotunno decided to shoot the pre-Fall scenes on stock that had previously been exposed to a board painted gold, giving that section of the film a golden hue. This naturally affected audience response. When the film makers chose to have a blonde Eve, they obviously were not choosing a Chinese or African audience.

Richard Schickel, noting that the film did not have a conventional dramatic tension and that ties between segments created a chopiness, with the stories lacking physical and psychological detail, suggested that Huston and Fry "made a virtue of these defects, retaining the simple folkish quality of the tales," which he thought was courageous. He described it as a "semidocumentary trip through the folk-explanations of our beginnings," using the occasion to note the difference between scientific explanation and inspiration. "It is infinitely to the credit of the men who made *The Bible* that they sensed this fact and built their awesomely absorbing film around such a simple premise."[10]

Schickel's interpretation echoes Mircea Eliade's definition of myth as a "complex cultural reality" that places the sacred in the world of time and existence, revealing paradigmatic models and rituals for our activities.[11]

From this perspective, *The Bible* is like other spectaculars, attempting to provide norms for human behavior. Instead of providing an explanation, however, the stories are presented as myths, using the techniques of modern film making and the symbols of modern culture to tell that story. This was against the mainstream of American religious film making, which concerned itself with breaching the gap between the supernatural God and a world explained by science.

In retrospect, the film seems prescient about the time that lay in the immediate future. Segments of American culture were becoming aware of the contradictions imposed by modernity. Ethics were changing because of the advance of science. When presidential candidate Barry Goldwater suggested "defoliating" the Vietnamese jungles, some felt an unexpressed horror that the United States could create a desert out of a jungle through technology.

A countercultural movement led the attack on rationalism. Disgusted with the world they had inherited, citing racism, sexism, and exploitation of the world's resources and people, many young people rejected the majority culture and fled to communal groups to create new subcultures. Theodore Roszak argued that technocracy had become totalitarian, even to the level of shaping the mind in its image.[12]

Roszak noted that we tend to assume that technology can be made into programs to solve our problems, that the rational answers to our problems are not far off, and that the experts should be allowed to run both business and government, ridding us of the irrationality that holds us back.[13]

This technocracy is built on a rational world view, with science opposed to myth. On the other hand, Lewis Mumford was arguing that the new technocracy was an updated version of the ancient world view of Egypt and the Sun God. The new science, starting with Copernicus' calculations about the stars, diminished humans' respect for themselves as unique in the universe. Science had raised empirical thought to a sacred level. Thus, science becomes an ideology, providing both the means and the justification for a totalitarian control over all human existence.[14]

The counterculture's reaction was to abandon Saks Fifth Avenue and Bonwit Teller for Goodwill and the Salvation Army resale shops. They emphasized "being" rather than "doing." They began reading horoscopes and the *I Ching*, taking up magic, and making up outrageous acronyms to describe themselves (e.g., WITCH = Women's Internationalist Terrorist Conspiracy from Hell).

The students were shocking because of their antipositivist, antiscience feelings. Science was seen as the lackey of the military industrialist complex, failing to support life-affirming activities.

Whole classes protested the epistemology of science as well as its intellectual dominion. Students believed the Establishment claimed to be rational, but shows it was not. This supported one of the central truths of all religion, that man is more than a creature who reasons.[15]

Fry, Huston, and deLaurentiis thought it unnecessary to provide rational explanations. They were looking for sources of meaning and hope that a rationalistic society could not offer.

The archetype of melodrama, with its careful posing of antagonistic forces and its portrayal of providence working benevolently, appealed to a much less ambiguous time and world view. Although melodrama had the capacity to evoke *pathos*, it could not stir the imaginative world that myth stimulates. *The Bible* shattered the archetype of the biblical and religious spectacular; the film was not a moral fantasy that ordered the world according to human desire; rather, it presented the story of the beginnings with Old Testament clarity. The God of *The Bible* is an alien, primitive deity who tempts human beings and then chastises them for succumbing to temptation. This God is not a tolerant American parent, nor does he have the sentimental love for humanity that marked earlier biblical spectaculars.

Ernst Haas, a still photographer, was commissioned to spend 18 months searching the world for footage that would spell out the fundamental themes of the Creation story—darkness and light, water and earth, flora and fauna.

Fry's script called for a timeless succession of images. Repeatedly, the scene titles call for "At No Time (e.g., EXT. A BARREN PLACE: AT NO TIME)." The script emphasizes the universality and the continuing character of creation. Haas had been considering photographing natural phenomena for a book illustrating his theory that the world is in a state of continuing creation. This matched the conceptions of deLaurentiis and Huston, so they agreed to let him handle the Creation sequence.

The succession of images in these sequences throws the viewers back on their own consciousness. In one sense, it was an homage to the avant-garde underground film makers. Images are spliced together to evoke feelings. The camera zooms and flows, and the waters shine in elegant shafts of light piercing the screen from above. The colors are muted until the light shines; then they take on brilliant hues. Fry suggested that the voice-over should be "intensely human, and yet as though formed out of the vibration of the music," but the voice is in fact Huston's—as if he is informing us that in *this* Bible, he himself has proprietory rights of creation.

The visually stunning opening segment pairs the scientific account and the Judeo-Christian myth of beginnings. It uses natural symbols and visuals of the modern world to suggest the universality and believability of the biblical myths. According to Fry, the heavens at first are supposed to appear to be a void, which gradually becomes the Milky Way. This image imposes a human construction on the formless universe, because the viewer orders the images into a familiar pattern. Fry says that it should mingle natural and transcendent (heavenly) images in order to suggest a pattern of the unity of heaven and earth.[16]

In this prescientific world, lions and lambs stand together in pre-Fall harmony. The plants are lush and abundant, and the seas are filled with fish gliding gracefully through the blue waters. The images are spliced to create a harmonious whole, a world without humans where there is no tension among the elements of nature. The pre-Fall harmony of the natural world is set in opposition to the human structures—the Ark, the Tower of Babel, the charred ruins and human skeletons of Sodom.

In this world, innocence was plausible. It did not conflict with science because it used these images to demonstrate the essential harmony between nature and continuing creation.

Fry inserts Genesis 2 at the point where man is created.[17] He uses the image of dust for Adam's creation, symbolically powerful because of its prominence in the funeral liturgies of the synagogues and churches. The camera dollies in on the dust, revealing what looks like a dry stone hidden beneath barren dust. The wind, representing the spirit of God, blows over the dust until a man is slowly unearthed.

There is the sound of a sigh, the last grains of dust are blown from the man's lips, and they part. He takes an inhalation of breath, and exhales it in a sound of life. His eyes open, [CU OF ADAM'S EYES: they reflect and stare into a radiance which would be unbearable, except to a man in the state of complete innocence.][18]

As Adam rises, his hand reaches up in the classic pose Michelangelo used in his painting of Adam in the Sistine Chapel. The colors in these scenes seem to have been produced by an orange filter but modulated into washed-out browns and beiges to capture the feel of man's creation out of "the dust of the earth."

These colors change dramatically when the film enters the Garden of Eden. The tone changes to a hazy gold, the result of shooting with stock that had been exposed to a board painted gold. The animals are not afraid of Adam; he is one of them, but the other creatures are in pairs. Once again the scene has a double meaning—Adam's loneliness is reemphasized when he sees his image in the water dissolve as he reaches out toward it, yet at the same time, it recalls the story of Narcissus, the man of ultimate self-will.

The search for an actress to play Eve raised some questions. The color of her hair was chosen because Huston thought that the "blonde" color of her hair suggested innocence. He also attributed a "navel" to her, though she was born of a rib, and to Adam as well. The idea of innocence required small breasts and blue eyes, and no affectations.[19]

In interviews, Huston sounds unsophisticated, but the decision was political, the result of numerous letters sent to deLaurentiis calling for a blonde Eve. The aesthetic preference for a Nordic strain still predominated in the West, and the film was being made primarily for an American audience. An ambiguous nonsexuality as symbolic of innocence has a long history in Western culture, informing everything from the greatest paintings to the Miss America pageant.[20]

Much was made of Adam and Eve's nudity. There was virtually no way to satisfy anyone. Nudity was not yet common in American films. Too much nudity would emphasize their sexuality, and thus undercut their innocence prior to the Fall. Yet too little nudity would have the same effect. The solution was to disguise it by careful placement of the camera, naked buttocks, long hair glued over Eve's breasts, and so forth.

The industry had been anxiously cheering over the dilemma this put the Roman Catholic church into if their National Catholic Office of Motion Pictures condemned the film. The film industry was still angered by the Office's decision to use their "condemned" rating for *The Pawnbroker* because of a scene in which a prostitute bares her breasts, unlocking a whole series of painful memories in the former concentration camp victim.[21] Well into the 1960s, biblical films continued to lead the fight against censorship.

Eve is created while Adam is in a deep sleep, and as she stands before him, he reaches out to her as he did toward his own image in the water. Eve is shot against a haze of light; there is some suggestion that Adam is reaching out to his own alter image, but he finds that she is real, and they become one. The scene conveys the Greek conception of the incomplete self reaching out for completion, a widespread idea in America. When Adam offers fruit to Eve, Huston visually lays the groundwork for the opposite gesture in the Fall sequence.

At this point, Huston and Fry return to and complete the Genesis 1 cycle, showing the day of rest and the bounty that God has given Adam and Eve.

As the Fall sequence begins, Adam and Eve are in harmony with nature. A leopard sleeps nearby, and the Garden's lush vegetation has no weeds. A crystalline river winds around the Tree of Knowledge of Good and Evil in a long gentle arc, and the tree is filled with golden fruit. Although they are prohibited from eating the fruit on pain of death, Fry notes in the script that "death is a concept beyond their imagination."

Huston adds symbols of awakening sexuality—a nightingale singing, horses gamboling in the Garden, and a long shot of Adam and Eve emulating the playfulness of the horses. Eve's encounter with the serpent contrasts with this playfulness. A light undulating motion against the tree indicates the presence of the serpent. When Eve picks the golden apple and bites into it, Huston shows a close-up of the pleasure on her face. When Adam comes, she does not gaze at him directly; her carriage seems less hesitant. She changes from an innocent to a seductress, and instead of the golden sunlight bathing the film, this section is photographed in shadows and darkness.

Whatever the film maker's intentions, the film here suggests that sexuality was the basis of the Fall. It tries to convey a difference in the quality of sexuality before and after the Fall, but the earlier images leave the impression that the Fall is a natural passage as the childlike, dreaming innocents become the fully sexed creatures who clothe their bodies with fig leaves. When the golden haze dissipates, the film takes on natural color.

The curse on Adam, Eve, and the rest of creation is symbolized by a wind. It is a harsh, angry, howling wind that develops into a storm. The trees become copper-colored, as in autumn. Outside the Garden is a stony desolate landscape, where Adam and Eve must now live. The scene cuts to Adam's primitive "house," and Eve screams in childbirth as the fierce wind blows outside. They cover the child with an animal skin, noting now their alienation from the animal world.

The sequence visually sets the stage for what is to come; the viewer must make the logical connection. The loss of paradise and alienation from God are inevitable. The stark contrast with the natural world of the Creation scene, the loss of the golden age, and the stark images of deprivation are visual metaphors of existence. The film attempts neither to discount our alienation from the natural world nor to explain it. By their very nature, men and women are destined to succumb to temptation. No explanation is made for the evil that befalls them; the only choice is to accept it.

The setting for the Cain and Abel sequence is stark and barren. From a low angle, Abel is seen lifting up a lamb for sacrifice. The angle elevates his character. A close-up of Cain's hands shows him taking back some of his grain sacrifice. The smoke from Abel's sacrifice rises, while Cain's lurches downward, crackling and hissing. After Cain clubs Abel to death, he realizes what he has done, freezes in horror, and then runs.

The rejection of Cain's sacrifice still puzzles Old Testament scholars. The general consensus is that the story reflects the tension between farmers and semi-nomads, those who offer fruits and those who offer animals. Fry made the situation contemporary, noting that the distinction between shepherd and farmer in the social order was significant, but difficult to portray without destroying the story's simplicity so he made an emendation, in which Cain offered his gift grudgingly, "because it was expected of him and it was safer to stick to the 'rules,' while Abel made his with his whole heart out of his love of God."[22]

As the sun sets, Adam's face, hardened by his toil, looks anxiously for Abel. A high boom shot, with the camera acting as the eye of God, focuses in on Cain, booming lower as Cain stands with his arms crossed over his head. Cain receives the second curse, and the scene cuts to Adam, suddenly finding his dead son. Cain's flight approximates the earlier flight of his father and mother, who brought death into the world. Cain has added murder to the catalogue of sins. Fry suggested the makeup for the mark of Cain, resembling "a man struck by lightning left with the mark of a blasted tree," referring to the tree in the center of the Garden.

Throughout the whole segment, Fry and Huston use the natural world symbolically. Lightning is God's weapon; the desolate tree is the mark God leaves on Cain. The atmosphere, shot in long establishing shots, suggests the barren land they inhabit, in contrast to the dynamic natural world of the Creation sequence or the golden opulence of the Garden of Eden. Barrenness is the consequence of the Fall, and the knowledge of death leads inevitably to murder.

A montage suggests the development of civilization. At first we see a settlement of tents and then a potter throwing a jar. A musician playing a primitive harp follows, then a man at a forge develops metal, and a plow tills the ground, creating fertile fields. The metal, however, becomes a sacrificial knife plunged into a body, which is then replaced by another victim, while the first body is thrown like trash onto a heap of other bodies. Sacrifice becomes the social form of murder, and civilization is corrupted.

Huston and Fry undercut these images by their treatment of Noah. Huston, the director, met his match in Huston, the actor. His conception was comedic, and he had wanted Charles Chaplin for the role. Given the introduction of the ritual sacrifices, this section of the film, although coherent in isolation, changes the tone of the entire movie.

Huston and Fry had intended to present Noah as a simple yet canny man. Huston told Lillian Ross that Noah was "the child figure in the Bible"—a bit absurd—and that he was trying for a poetic humor.[23] In isolation, it is an interesting conception. The biblical story lends itself well to such a treatment, for as Huston notes, it is absurd. In the middle of Israel, far from the sea, Noah is told to build an Ark roughly 500 feet in length and three stories high. Noah visualizes the absurdity of such a command as he paces out the length and then looks at the vista incredulously.

As Noah and his sons build the ark, cretins gather to laugh and mock him. The composition of the shot seems truly inspired, with bizarre makeup and animal skeletons used as jewelry, and animal skins as clothing. Huston sets up the dichotomy between Noah, friend to all, who reestablishes the unity of the human and animal worlds, and these murderous and evil people. Huston, however, goes too far, undercutting the power of the scene with Noah hitting his finger with a hammer, evoking a cheap laugh.

Later his sons begin to doubt and, responding to public ridicule, ask to work at night on the Ark. Noah's mythic faithfulness, however, is the harbinger of Abraham's historic faithfulness in offering Isaac. This God demands obedience, not questions. The tests of faith seem capricious and oblivious to human feelings. In Noah's story, the consequences to him and his family are merely humorous; in Abraham's story, they are heart-rending.

The loading of the Ark produces another memorable vista—a long framing shot with the nose of the Ark occupying the right foreground, looking something like a gigantic minaret as a much smaller Huston leads a procession of animals. Playing on his ram's horn, he is followed by the zebras, elephants, camels, giraffes, and hippopotami. The turtles are the final animals to board, but the sight of polar bears and penguins seems to stretch the absurdity to its breaking point. This lyric sequence does not prepare us for the next, in which the people of the earth are drowned while the animal kingdom is preserved. Once again the sequence seems eclectically composed, the panning shot showing twisting bodies frenetically clawing at the Ark. These shots are crosscut with the tragic reaction of Noah's family to their plight. The humor and lyricism work against audience response to the world's destruction, and consequently, the Deluge does not evoke a tragic catharsis of fear and pity.

Humanity and the animal world are restored to a pre-Fall unity. The animals do not feed on each other, but are nourished by each other's milk and the vegetables Noah has brought aboard. However, the necessity of portraying the long period of waiting slackens the narrative pace, though there is a moving scene when Japheth realizes that the world will be changed and they will be alone on earth. The family's spirits are raised by the birth of a kid, starting life anew in the world. When they finally leave the Ark, the music, which has been silent since the destruction of the earth, begins again, and the animals begin to frolic off together, suggesting a new Eden.

Feeling lost in this bewildering new situation, Noah departs from the Ark to find that the water animals and the birds are still with him, and he sees the sign of the new covenant, the rainbow.

The sequence conveys a confusing message. On the one hand, Noah is too delightful—the man who seems simple but who obeys God with child-like faith. On the other hand, the image of blood sacrifice—of the ravenous mob—establishes the dissimilarity of ancient people and modern humanity. The people are drawn too broadly for us to connect with them—those who live off the flesh, bone, and fur of the animal world, and those animalistic demons. The humor becomes slapstick and is anchored neither in tragedy nor in heroic *pathos*. The lyricism with which Noah and the animal world are portrayed harkens back to the Eden segment without giving adequate justification for the implied connection.

Interesting by itself, the Noah segment seems so out of synchronization with the rest of the film that it detracts by calling too much attention to itself.

The conception for the Tower of Babel is taken from the ancient Babylonian form, the Ziggurat, but it looks like the archetype for the Leaning Tower of Pisa. Scaffolds lead up the leaning tower, which has flat, asymmetrical but hexagonal stones of concrete set one on top of another. The Tower extends beyond the picture frame, and the ramps leading from one level to the next are arranged counterclockwise in order to emphasize the insanity of the venture. Fry wanted to avoid making the audience enamored of the beauty and boldness of the Tower, lest God's punishment seem sad or unjust.

Huston creates a visual tension between the mythic description of the Bible and the laws of nature (in this case, architectural principles).[24] Sensing that the Tower will fall, the audience is struck by the foolishness of human pride, just after it has perceived the wise foolishness of Noah.

The character of Nimrod extends this conception. Nimrod and his entourage are first seen from the vantage point of the Tower wading through people gathered around the structure. A close-up shows that he wears dark eye shadow, that his eyebrows are painted, and he is ornately dressed. When he bends his bow to the heavens, Huston cuts to the clouds, and the arrow disappears into them. Then the clouds darken, the wind howls, the air is filled with dust, and the atmosphere begins to threaten a tornado. Huston chooses an oblique shot tilted at a low angle to represent the terror. The workmen are all robust but heavy men, physically and spiritually flabby. Nimrod defiantly yells at the master builder to stand his ground, an echo of the pride that caused the Fall, but no one understands him. Scrambled voices fill the screen, and Nimrod stands looking at the people who break up into defensive bands. Their inability to communicate marks the beginning of their belligerence. To a nation that had been hearing Lyndon Johnson urging it to "reason together" to solve the issues of war and race, these diffused voices must have had a familiar sound.

The Abraham sequence represents about one-third of the script. It is the most complex sequence and deals with three separate stories from the patriarch's history. Huston and Fry weave them together skillfully. The first concerns the barrenness of Sarah and the advanced age of Abraham, who needs a son in order that God's promise that his descendants will populate the earth be fulfilled. The second recalls Lot's sojourn in Sodom and Gomorrah, and the destruction of those cities. The last involves God's demand that Abraham sacrifice Isaac.

God promises Abraham an heir and commands him to leave Ur to accept the task of nationhood. For the first time, one of the enduring themes of the spectacular is presented. The fall from myth into history is also the story of the sacred trek to nationhood—the beginnings of the promise to the Jews of their divine mission. Leaving the city, they sojourn like "strangers on the earth." During the journey, Abraham's people have a vision of the promised land, but the Canaanites inhabit it. Abraham tells them that God's will is beyond their understanding. They have been promised the land in peace, so they must wait for God's promise to be fulfilled.[25]

At this point, Sarah's theme is introduced. As Abraham walks to Sarah's tent, he sees children playing. A tender love scene follows, with quotations from the Song of Solomon, but the scene ends with the narrator announcing that Sarah is barren, which jars because of the passionate scene just played out. As they prosper in the land, Sarah's barrenness contrasts with the increasing richness of her garments, while shots indicating the fertility of the land are crosscut with others showing Abraham's growing despair over his lack of a son. When he and Lot divide their retinues with the elderly Abraham going to the high country, he complains bitterly to God that he has no offspring. The childlike faith of Noah becomes the angry faith of Abraham—faith without belief, faith filled with doubt, faith without the expectation of fulfillment.

In a surrealistic scene, Abraham has a vision of God as a smoking flame devouring his animal sacrifices. The camera is mounted on a crane and dollies down to a shot in which Abraham, dressed in black, seems to be a part of the shadows. Abraham awakes, and we are not sure whether he really has had a vision of God. This is part of the strategy to move from the mythic realm, where God is one of the participants in the drama, to the historical realm, where God appears only ambiguously.

Hagar's pregnancy follows a scene establishing both the custom of the maid servant bearing the barren mistress's child and a reaffirmation of Abraham's and Sarah's mutual love. Hagar proves herself unworthy when she smiles insolently at Sarah and rubs her pregnant belly. Later she gives Sarah a dried fig, keeping a ripe pomegranate for herself.

A battle scene interrupts Ishmael's birth. Abraham frees Lot from the warring kings using a strategy similar to that of Gideon in the Book of Judges. This sequence is disturbing, because it disrupts the narrative tension of the developing triangle between Abraham, Sarah, and Hagar. It seems that it is included to explain the changes of names—from Abram to Abraham and from Sarai to Sarah—and to reward Abraham's prowess at war by the promise of another son from his barren wife. Dramatically it is distracting; apparently, the film makers wanted a battle scene to give the segment additional scale for the spectacular screen.

This reaffirmation of the promise tests Abraham's faith; Hagar wants him to declare Ishmael his heir, but Abraham waits for the expected heir. Hagar tempts him to reject his faith, saying, "The years have gone by and the promise is not fulfilled. Now with Sarah, the wife, the time of child-bearing is over." Abraham remains firm in his faith.

Three angels visit, and one of them goes off to Sodom to destroy the city. After another lengthy sequence, in which Lot's wife is turned to salt, the film returns to show the birth of Isaac. The Cain theme is reintro-duced—jealousy of the new brother, but it receives historical treatment and is no longer a mythic paradigm. While Isaac is carried and passed among the tribeswomen, Ishmael grabs a doll. As Sarah complains to Abraham, asking him to send Hagar and Ishmael away, the film cuts to Ishmael breaking the doll and hastily burying it in the sand. When Abraham reluctantly casts them out, Hagar carries her own child over the barren sand, as if the curse that Ishmael held in his heart toward his brother and Hagar's delight over Sarah's barrenness has been paid back in kind, but they miraculously find water in the desert.

The thematic movement of this extended narrative establishes Abraham as a faithful man with a great capacity of love for his kindred. Under Huston's direction, the scenes between Sarah and Abraham are played with tenderness and sexual passion in order to establish their historic hu-manity as opposed to the mythic distancing of earlier characters. The se-quence breaks with the previous segments, which move from naturalistic mythic (the Creation) to displaced romance (Tower of Babel). The images of sand and sea, and the change in makeup from the grotesque to the surreal to gritty reality visually inform us that we are now in the world of experience. The dramatic climax of the film, the trip to Mt. Moriah, de-pends on Huston's establishing Abraham's faith in the midst of his doubt and despair.

Fry and Huston link the destruction of Sodom with the journey to Mt. Moriah. Faced with the necessity of dramatizing the well-known story of the archetypal evil city and the partial fulfillment of the covenant with Noah not to destroy the earth, Fry and Huston inserted it just prior to the birth of Isaac.

Overall, the conception of the Sodom and Gomorrah scenes lacks the power of the story itself. They are presented sparely and abruptly, as something that cannot be omitted but also something that interrupts Abra-ham's story. The angel allows Abraham to bargain with him, allowing that he will not destroy the city if Abraham is able to find "ten righteous men."

Huston seems to have taken his visual clues about vice and licentiousness from Fellini rather than DeMille. The city is filled with scarlet lamps sig-nifying prostitution, and a group of drunken men try to get Lot to send the angel out to them, presumably for homosexual intercourse. Lot goes so far as to offer his daughters in place of the angel. One feels the justification of Harvey Cox's remark that "the brief scene of an excited maiden kissing a goat hardly seems sufficiently vile to merit the mushroom cloud that God visits on the fated city."[26]

The mushroom cloud appears to Lot's wife in a subjective shot:

We see what she sees: a glimpse of hell between the bottom of the slope and the crushing smoke clouds. . . . Lot's wife . . . raises her arms above her head in a gesture of terror, her face is convulsed, and her body twists in an agony of effort to turn and escape. But she cannot. She becomes fixed in this attitude, as wisps and cloudlets of flame-lit smoke swirl past her.[27]

The significance of the shot seems inconclusive, but it does suggest that the atom bomb both attracts and immobilizes us, making it impossible for humans to get beyond the terror. Dramatically, however, the shot looks like an interpolated comment to suggest contemporary meaning for the film.

The final sequence is the most dramatically powerful of the film. It begins with the camera holding in a close shot of Abraham's staff as he lays out the genealogy of his family, the first genealogy given by a human, emphasizing that the film is now in history. Then the camera pulls away to show Isaac, who takes the proffered staff from Abraham as though "he takes the future in his hand."

Once again, the angel speaks to Abraham in the night, as in the sound of the wind. Abraham awakens and walks through the night, listening, and the voice tells him that he wants Isaac as a sacrifice. As in the Kierkegaardian paradox (*Fear and Trembling*), Abraham has trouble believing what he hears. He thinks that the God he has worshipped and obeyed would not give him a son only to take him away. Later he cries out "No . . . no . . . no!" and lets out a howl of defiance, but he is forced by his own past to trust that which he cannot understand, and he decides that the voice that has led him to the land and made promises to him of a child is the voice that now speaks to him.

After the painful farewell to Sarah, who intuitively senses what Abraham is going to do, they go through the ruins of Sodom. This section was actually shot on the lava-strewn slopes of Mt. Etna in Sicily. "In this stark landscape, fragmented and overturned monolithic statues and huge stones block the archways and stairs of devastated temples, palaces, and houses."[28] As Abraham tells Isaac the story of Sodom and remarks that all the inhabitants of the city were destroyed, Isaac asks him, "Were all the children also wicked?" Huston cuts to a skull lying on the charred ground, and a snake moves swiftly out of it and slithers away. Huston seems to suggest the doctrine of original sin by this visual comment. American religious movies have steadfastly denied the doctrine because it emotionally complicates rather than solves the problem of the goodness of God. Abraham immediately says, "Shall not the judge of all the earth do right?"—more an agonized plea in the midst of ambiguity than a statement of faith.

The mountain itself is shaped like an altar. Abraham and Isaac prepare the ground for the sacrifice, and Isaac asks where the sacrifice is. When he realizes that he is the sacrifice, he is terrified at first, then looks plaintively at Abraham, and asks, "There is nothing that he may not ask of thee?" Abraham replies, "Nothing." As Abraham raises the knife to strike, he places his hand over Isaac's eyes and looks sternly toward the heavens as if he is defiantly saying that he is doing this act against his will, challenging the justice of God.

The voice of God, which informs him that he may instead offer another sacrifice and which commends him for his faith, almost denies Huston's conception of the scene. The final shots show the sun setting across the hills, and the small figures of Abraham and Isaac traveling toward their home.

Steven Farber called the sacrifice scene "excruciating."

Even knowing the outcome, I think any viewer is likely to wince at the cruelty of the story he was once told to accept as a high-minded lesson. Huston uses vast panoramas most effectively in this sequence to suggest the loneliness and precariousness of men against the power of an indifferent natural world and its "benevolent" God. And the final image, after the substitution of the ram for the boy, of father and son embracing against the landscape dominated by God's voice, provides a tentative, poignant hope for human life oblivious to divine decrees. . . . The form would seem to have a tremendous potential—only a film of almost insane breadth and intensity can effectively criticize our traditional myths of origin.[29]

Not all were enthralled. One evangelical Christian reviewer complained that Abraham's God is not "as much as a gentleman as I," and feared that the film would be taken as "Gospel truth" or "not to be seriously regarded; or like myself, just go away sad."[30]

The film challenges the American religious experience. It is not that the film makers have misshaped the Old Testament God so much as that they have presented God without any of the conventions that serve to placate American feelings about God. This God, in both the mythic and historical phase, presents himself as other, incomprehensible, wiping out the earth, destroying cities, cruelly testing the faithful. The American God always has a plan in mind, punishes wickedness, and rewards righteousness, but God is off-screen, not so painfully immediate as Huston makes him. The American version of God is understandable and a "gentleman."

Huston does something very radical—questioning the very nature of God. He is aware of the difficulty of translating the earliest myths into something that the mind can comprehend, pointing to the profound mysteries that resist rational interpretation and assimilation. His film is as distinctly "other" as his God. At the same time, the ethical concern of the biblical spectacular is pushed to the limit because of the operations of God in this absurd world. The conception is one that resists the possibility of normative moral statements, because the God on which they are based is so radically "other."

Pauline Kael's summary suggested that many religious people have learned to take the stories metaphorically.

The movie undercuts this liberal view by showing the power (and terror) of these cryptic, primitive tribal tales and fantasies of the origins of life on earth and why we are as we are. The God of wrath who frightens men to worship ain't no pretty metaphor.[31]

NOTES

1. Lillian Ross, "The Bible in Dinocitta," *The New Yorker* 41 (September 25, 1965): 201–2.

2. Harvey Cox, "How to Kill God," *Look* 30 (October 18, 1966): 104.

3. *Commonweal* 85 (October 21, 1966): 79.

4. *New York Times*, Sept. 26, 1966, Sec. 2, p. 1.

5. *Chicago Tribune*, July 3, 1966, Sec. 5, p. 9.

6. Cf. *Atlanta Journal*, December 22, 1966, p. 35, for a good analysis of the controversy.

7. Christopher Fry, *The Bible* (screenplay) (New York: Pocket Books, Inc., 1966), p. 5.

8. There are some deletions of events and a few connecting links supplied, but generally there is nothing that radically departs from the biblical record.

9. Fry, *Bible*, pp. 5–6.

10. *Life* 61 (October 7, 1966): 22.

11. Mircea Eliade, *Myth and Reality* (New York: Harper Torchbooks, 1963), pp. 5–8.

12. An excellent study of the way the mind is shaped by the culture of technology is found in Peter and Brigitte Berger and Hansfried Kellner, *The Homeless Mind* (New York: Random House, 1974), which explores the roots and effects of modernization of consciousness from the perspective of sociology of knowledge.

13. Theodore Roszak, *The Making of a Counter Culture* (Garden City, N.Y.: Doubleday and Co., 1969), pp. 9–11.

14. Lewis Mumford, *The Myth of the Machine: The Pentagon of Power* (New York: Harcourt, Brace, Jovanovich, 1970), p. 28–30, 106. The religious argument of the "Sun God" is remarkably plausible. In more recent thought, cf. Morris Berman, *The Reenchantment of the World* (Ithaca: Cornell University Press, 1981).

15. O'Neill, *Coming Apart*, p. 255.

16. Fry, *Bible*, p. 22.

17. In Genesis 1, male and female are created concurrently, but Fry uses the second account, in which Eve is created from Adam's flesh.

18. Fry, *Bible*, p. 28.

19. This is documented in "Problems in Paradise," *Newsweek* 64 (September 14, 1964): 90.

20. cf. Jewett and Lawrence, *The American Monomyth*, chapters I & IV.

21. *Variety* reported industry reaction:

> Presumably it was just as necessary to photograph Eve from the front as it was to shoot the girl in *The Pawnbroker* from the same angle, and Msgr. Little would not enter into a discussion of how if bare breasts in the film were capable of being "sanctified," it follows that they are always unacceptable in other contexts. (Scriptural origin of the situation is the presumed difference—ED.) It is expected that a more favorable rating for *The Bible* may encourage more distributors to challenge the Catholic Office on nudity in the future.
>
> But some industry-ites were hoping that the Catholic group would ask 20th Century Fox to make the cuts. "This would have been a perfect chance to challenge their power," one producer said recently. "Fox could have held out and seen if they could give a condemned rating to the Bible."*Variety*, June 1, 1966, p. 50.

22. Fry, *Bible*, p. 8.

23. Ross, "Bible in Dinocitta," pp. 202–3.

24. Fry, *Bible*, p. 100–1.

25. It is difficult to tell whether Huston and Fry were commenting here on the state of Israel in modern times. Certainly the promise claimed by the Israelis stems from this promise, yet the film makes no great attempt to portray the Canaanites as Arabs.

26. Cox, "How to Kill God," pp. 104, 107.

27. Fry, *Bible*, p. 150.

28. Twentieth Century Fox, Production Notes, p. 12.

29. Steven Farber, "Spectacles 1967," p. 13.

30. *The Christian Herald* 89 (October 1966): 15.

31. Pauline Kael, *Kiss Kiss Bang Bang* (New York: Bantam Books, 1968), p. 163.

9

After the Spectacular

The Vietnam War split the nation and its institutions. In mainline Catholicism, Protestantism, and Judaism, the dividing lines were drawn not over theological beliefs as much as whether the nation was righteous in its pursuit of the war. The discussion of "civil religion" demonstrated that from the earliest American period, the nation used religious symbolism to describe itself and its mission.

At the same time, the evangelical churches began to assert themselves in the public arena forcefully for the first time since Billy Graham had run his crusades in the large arenas of American cities in the 1950s. The election of Jimmy Carter as president in 1976 was a harbinger of the growing political power of the evangelical movement. In the rural South, Nazarenes and Assembly of God members turned out to vote for a Christian president who seemed to have the older values that the Washington-based politicians lacked.

Most of the nation, struggling to digest the lessons of the Vietnam War, wanted to put divisiveness behind it, yet divisions were burgeoning to the surface almost everywhere. Some Catholics and Protestants were becoming charismatics. Black congregations headed for otherworldly renditions of black culture as the civil rights movement faltered, whereas others, having learned the lessons of the 1960s, continued to function as the base of an expanding black independent political movement.

Exhausted by their internal political divisions over race and peace, and facing internal pressure to continue to open the range of opportunities for women, the mainline churches had little energy for rethinking their theology or mission, and entered a phase in which internal order—adjusting to the new definitions of the preceding decade—became paramount. The great ecumenical movements of reconciliation—the Vatican Ecumenical Council II and the Consulation on Church Union—languished, but the forces that they had set in motion could not be reversed.

In that same era, technology had finally transformed television into the true mass media. Most people's information about their world came from television. The series provided mythic glue for conversation; television characters became archetypes by which people explained themselves to one another. All over America, movie theaters were closing or moving to small multiplex screens. The movie palace, built to give the common person a place in their neighborhood where he or she could feel like royalty, decayed, became roach-infested, and finally was too costly to run for the diminishing audiences.

The American spirit, no longer feeling grand about itself after finding out what it had hidden from its consciousness with regard to minorities and women, and having frittered its treasure and children in a disastrous war in Southeast Asia, had little need for spectacle. The big screen had no grand place for a people feeling like losers.

At the same time, the small screen discovered the miniseries. If spectacle could not be great epic moments thrown on a giant screen in the dark, it could become longer on the small screen. People could commit to watching for longer periods of time than two hours; therefore, the topics could be bigger. When the 12-hour *Rich Man, Poor Man* went into production, television executives had decided that audiences could be "hooked" in their homes for a whole week. It was their version of the spectacular, and its archetype was clearly melodrama. Through a set of trials and tribulations, the series explored the American character as it went from urban immigrant experience through suburbanization, attempting to understand our national character and how we ended up a divided nation.

Franco Zeffirelli was first contacted about doing *Jesus of Nazareth* in 1973. The idea had been suggested by Italian network television (RAI) at the instigation of three Catholic producers—Emilio Gennarini, Emanuele Milano, and Fabiano Fabiani—and then found its way to British producer Sir Lew Grade.

Having seen all the films on Jesus, Zeffirelli found his resistance breaking down because with six hours of television, he had a "subject of incomparable worth, which had too often disappeared into empty rhetoric."[1]

Grade, a Jew, told Zeffirelli that he had an opportunity to tell the story in a new way to the contemporary generation, giving him time to develop the narrative, and that at a time when all the traditional values and ideals were in crisis, "we can perhaps remind people what they are foolishly and wickedly losing."[2]

The crisis was the continuing decline of the West and its confidence—

national budgets out of control, Third World countries freeing themselves from colonial intervention, yet having difficulty sustaining themselves, and the sexual revolution's readjustment of individual and institutional values (e.g., the church's stance on baptizing children born out of wedlock).

Zeffirelli saw it as an opportunity to set Jesus within a Jewish framework, recalling Paul VI's *Nostra Aetate*, which noting Christianity's Jewish heritage, stated that Catholic theologians should understand and respect Jewish theology. It officially absolved Jews of being Christ-killers, stating "what happened in His passion cannot be charged against all of the Jews, without distinction, then alive, nor against the Jews of today."[3]

Anthony Burgess, author of *A Clockwork Orange*, wrote the first draft of the scenario. Zeffirelli knew the difficulty was making a human Jesus, realizing that believing in Jesus as God had been ingrained into the culture. After delivering his draft, Burgess had to contend with the biblical scholars the producers had provided. Burgess had put the words of Jesus into the vernacular, which Zeffirelli felt undermined the mystical character of his Italian Catholicism.

Zeffirelli wanted to invest every action of Jesus with both human and divine attributes. In the end, Suso Cecchi D'Amico produced a script that satisfied Zeffirelli, but did not offend Burgess.

The script was not the only problem. Television could invest his film with sufficient length to impress an audience, but it could not overwhelm people with sweeping vistas, such as Stevens' *Greatest Story*, or the political action of Ray's *King of Kings*. The vistas were replaced by verisimilitude, mud huts, dusty villages, and cameras panning the landscapes.

The size of the screen dictated many of his choices. Television makes the close shot more powerful and vastly reduces the effect of the extreme long shot. Unable to place his cameras far away from his characters to tell his story in global terms and too respectful of them to push in on them except in the late scenes, Zeffirelli settled for a middle distance, emphasizing the relationships between the people. Although it works well for the ecumenical motivations and the intention to emphasize Jesus' Jewishness, it forces him to isolate Jesus eventually in closer shots at the end as he faces his assigned destiny alone, virtually sequestered from his family and his disciples. As he stands before the Sanhedrin, he is in isolation, and the visual tension volleys back and forth between him and Caiaphas, while the Sanhedrin is crosscut in reaction shots to the drama played out before them.

Whether the script presents Jesus as a Jew is a matter of debate. Zeffirelli stated that he wanted to "underline that he inherited an enormous spiritual patrimony from the Jewish world which stimulated him to renew the scriptures."[4] The eventual Christian religion was for many years seen as a reform movement within Judaism, much like those parties struggling with the Roman occupation and the dispersal of Jews cross the world.

The script included many Jewish rituals, particularly in the part of the story featuring Mary and Joseph. The Annunciation, the Jewish customs of the village regarding Mary's pregnancy, the dancing at the wedding, the dedication and bar mitzvah, and even the *mechitzah* (barrier) at the synagogue owe a great deal to the research done on Judaism. The Last Supper is set within the Passover tradition, and the various parties within Judaism (Zealots, Pharisees, Saduccees) are delineated with more care than was ordinary. Zeffirelli had told the Israelis that as a good Catholic, he not only wanted to re-evoke the story of Christ, but also to clarify the reasons for Christ's decisions that he thought would overcome the tragedy of anti-Semitism.[5]

Nevertheless, Hyam Maccoby pointed out the anachronisms of the project. He noted that Jews did not wear Arab headdresses and that the religion depicted was a "mixture of 'Oriental' mumbo jumbo and medieval Jewishness." He complained about the Yiddish accent, suggesting that it showed a "resignation to persecution that seemed as out of place in first-century Palestine as *borscht*-circuit comics." The film even used eighteenth-century Hasidic melodies from Poland. In the end, he suggested that Jesus' Judaism owed more to *Fiddler on the Roof* than to Jewish studies.[6] However, in popular culture, it made its point very effectively.

Burgess and Zeffirelli highlighted the political context. The Zealot revival, which would produce a revolution in the next generation, the strains of Roman occupation, and the puppet government all take up a great deal of screen time. Producer Labella's idea was to set Jesus "between two historical plans—the Roman and the Jewish—and achieve by reflection as much historical accuracy as possible."[7]

The Christian Century reviewer, Charles Henderson, thought that the kingdom Zeffirelli's Jesus preaches is spiritual, obtained through individual conversion. Jesus says that "men must change before kingdoms," and Judas is the one politically oriented, confessing at the end that Christ had always said that "the heart is what is important." Henderson suggests that the film urges separation from the world and its politics, an attitude then current in the church, eventually advocating a retreat from the political process and public life.[8]

Henderson may have presented too strong a case, though one cannot deny its presence in the story. Burgess wanted to clarify the role of religion in politics, particularly how it played itself out in history. Pilate is convinced that the Sanhedrin stands between him and the radicals. Although the Sanhedrin consider Jesus dangerous religiously, Pilate makes his decision politically.

The Nazareth sequences at the beginning of the film thus take on the burden of positing the religious world view of the beginnings. A curious interposition happens, however. The sequences that carry the Jewish message are based on Catholic piety. Zeffirelli finds his Jewish world view in Mariology.

He shrouds the Annunciation in mystery, letting Mary and Anne both doubt it. Mary alone receives the message, while the soundtrack records only Mary's answers. Zeffirelli argues that in the Judaism of that period, every male child might be the Messiah or female might be the mother of the Messiah. He argued that the concept was necessary because Mary could not be understood outside the context of Judaism.[9]

His modification of tradition, however, also included quasi-scientific concepts. He quoted parapsychology, suggesting that Mary was "particularly receptive to spiritual vibrations," being careful not to turn Mary into an ecstatic woman, but only "attuned and receptive to a transcendental message." His goal was to overcome Renaissance paintings and turn her into an "ambivalent mixture of the mystery and the divine light."[10]

Zeffirelli anticipated that the Nativity would be controversial. Mary appears as an exhausted and frightened teenager experiencing a painful labor in a dirty stable. Appealing to modern sensibilities, Joseph assists with the birth.

Part of the problem of this juggling of Catholic piety with Jesus' Jewishness is the scholarship involved. Zeffirelli used the work of Pierre Loisy and Charles Guignebert in the construction of the film. They both offer a good deal of insight into the historical Jesus and are thus valuable resources for the Jewish world, but are skeptics with regard to Catholic piety. Moreover, Lord Grade wanted the Jews and Muslims included, while not wanting to offend Protestants. Finally, one could not ignore the political and cultural discourses present in the age, especially feminist analysis, and a final compounding was nonideological. Zeffirelli left out Thomas' rejection by Jesus because he felt it lacked credibility and pushed the series too close to a Hollywood epic.[11]

Signs of that struggle are included in the scenes with Mary Magdalene, who is depicted first as an worn-out prostitute led to transform her life by Jesus. For long periods, she exists just inside the frame in long shot, but at the trial before Pilate, she prominently screams when the crowd chooses Barabbas, and at the cross she lies to the guard that she is family, which is confirmed by the company of women attending the body—including Mary the mother of Jesus and Mary of Bethany. When she comes to the house where the disciples are waiting to announce that he is risen, Thomas utters, "Women's fantasies!" Peter, however, believes her, because Jesus had predicted it. Thus, Mary is first to believe, an opinion prominent in feminist Christian literature.

John the Baptist is used to fuse the political and religious messages. Herod looks on him as a "mystic revolutionary," essentially harmless. He attacks Herod because he is morally indignant at the king and for having married Herodias, his brother's wife, endangering his eternal soul. John's religious intentions are thus politicized, a harbinger of what will happen to Jesus.

Peter's prominence is also motivated by Catholicism, a simple man who tells Andrew, "Don't put him in my way! You are used to John the Baptist, you are one who believes in these things. I am a fisherman, I believe in the nets, in my boats. Leave me alone, leave me in peace!" Zeffirelli describes him as "an angry disciple much like a faithful dog that doesn't know how to resist its attraction to the master."[12]

The film's high moment is Jesus' narration of the parable of the prodigal son at a Fellini-esque party at Matthew's home. Peter, boiling with hatred, stands outside, while Matthew and his friends are clearly moved by the story. The inside of the home has a fire creating the warm hues, while Zeffirelli composes Peter in blues outside. The reconciliation of opposites and the overcoming of personal enmity suggests the evangelistic power of the parable.

The long form allowed Zeffirelli to explore the characters as archetypal humans. Besides Matthew and Peter, unusual screen time is devoted to Simon the Zealot, Thomas, Nicodemus, Joseph of Arimathea, Mary Magdalene, and the sisters of Lazarus. In such a long form, the audience needs them to identify with.

The choice of Jesus is always a problem. After considering and rejecting Dustin Hoffman and Al Pacino, he looked for something in the eyes. He was considering Robert Powell for Judas, when he decided to test him for Jesus. Zeffirelli describes him in mystical phrases: "sense of miracle," "a transportation of matter," an "aura not his own." A seamstress looked into his eyes and exclaimed, "But he is Jesus!"

Zeffirelli suggests that spirit and philosophy are part of Christ's divine nature, whereas his humanness includes "his parapsychology, his miraculous powers, his political charisma."[13]

Yet Roy Larson thought "Robert Powell as Jesus looked too much like every Jesus picture I'd ever seen on Sunday School walls."[14] *The Times* of London was even less charitable:

Of all the many faces of Christ, indeed, the one we would surely never have acknowledged is that one, the wandering rabbi down from the sour hills with the Torah in his head and wild figs in his stomach. . . . Zeffirelli's film showed us the dreamy miracle-worker but balked at angels and the voice of God in the baptism encounter.[15]

The main critical community remarked on both the strength and frailty he gave to the character and his incisive line reading.

Burgess decided that Judas would have to be "remade from scratch." Burgess' image was that of "a decent American college boy," convinced of the divinity of Christ, but politically innocent. To play the role of the scoundrel, he invented Zerah, a scribe who dupes Judas into thinking that he will present Jesus before the Sanhedrin so that he can convince them he is the Messiah.[16] Burgess believed the traditional descriptions of the betrayal—greed, ambition, jealousy, fear—did not give him enough reason. This solution makes Jesus' calling of Judas seem less a bad choice and breaks away from the determinism insisted on by the Bible. Finally, it does not require political motivation within the disciples or the Sanhedrin, but instead places it on Zerah's ambition for power. Zeffirelli linked Zerah with Stalin's Yagoda, Hitler's Himmler, and Napoleon's Fouche, suggesting it was part of every power system.[17]

This Judas is very modern—the good boy gone bad, the protestor against his nation's policies. Zeffirelli finds Judas ubiquitous—the intransigent pedant, teaching error. He suggested that his modern counterpart is the intellectual who ideologically manipulates politics and the media.[18]

To deal with the culpability of the Jews for the Crucifixion, the film splits the Sanhedrin. Nicodemus finally is too late in concluding Jesus is the Messiah. Because of political motives, Pilate offers the people a choice between the scorned, tortured Jesus, symbol of national humiliation, and the rebel Barabbas.[19] Jesus is seen as someone who agitated the country, brought Jerusalem to the brink of rebellion with his attack on the temple, and betrayed his own followers by surrendering without resistance. That was not the Messiah they were following, and thus Zeffirelli lays the blame at the feet of Jesus. Yet even this emendation, which Maccoby attributes to the awakened conscience of Christians to the "criminal consequences of Christian anti-Jewish teachings," leaves the Jews as representatives of "uncomprehending humanity."[20]

The Crucifixion sequence shows the influence of Mariology. The *Pieta*, a significant theme in Italian Catholic art, plays a prominent role. The Crucifixion sequences were appropriately gruesome as befitted the modern style, and the arduousness of the shooting schedule exhausted Powell and the crew. The weather turned bad, and Powell had to endure the cold almost nude. Olivia Hussey dreaded the sequence and, when it had to be performed a second time, went into hysterics. Anne Bancroft (Mary Magdalene) slapped her, Bancroft and Zeffirelli literally threw Hussey into the scene, and she collapsed on Powell's body while the rain drizzled on them, creating an emotionally resonant shot, which Zeffirelli decided to keep in the film.

The growing disjunction between science and religion continued in this film. Although *Superstar* and *Godspell* had banned the supernatural from their films, it became apparent that a Catholic film could not dodge the issue. The film decided to clearly establish the presence of a world beyond experience, and Zeffirelli early on establishes the miraculous in the Virgin Birth.

Zeffirelli notes that the Creation story in Genesis has been "verified scientifically—the order indicated in the account being accurate but the time periods contracted, as is often the way in the Scriptures." Joseph is the first to have faith, telling Mary, "I believe you, I believe in this mystery." Zeffirelli took off after his potential critics. "Those whose minds are shut to reasons of the spirit are always looking for petty material motives, shabby reasoning, in terms of human speculation, to explain human history, while every page of the Gospel is permeated with poetry and a most fervid faith."[21]

He also establishes Jesus as a healer, raising the daughter of Jairus from the dead, curing the man born blind, healing the man who is crippled, feeding the 5,000, and bringing Lazarus back from the dead. Visually, nothing new is tried, but neither is there an attempt to disguise the miracle to hint ambiguity. The man's limbs become straight, Jairus' daughter rises and kisses Jesus, the baskets of bread and fish seem to fill themselves, and we see Lazarus close in a shroud. Sometimes, as with Lazarus and the lame man, the miracles are allegories, whereas at other times they are simply signs.

Zeffirelli's sentiments about the miraculous are quite clear. "If you do not accept the mystery of the Resurrection, neither can you accept Christianity." He ended the film with a test shot, frustrated at his inability to find a way to film the Thomas material or the visit in the Upper Room. The film ends with Jesus as the returned friend in a medium shot, Peter and John leaning toward his breast, followed by a tight close-up of Jesus, telling them not to be afraid, for he is with them till the end of time.

Bob Jones III, president of South Carolina's Bob Jones University, read that Zeffirelli had said that he would portray Jesus as "an ordinary man— gentle, fragile, simple." Jones concluded that the program would deny Christ's divinity. Without seeing the film, he labeled it blasphemous. When others joined him, nearly 20,000 letters were sent to General Motors, which had paid $3 million toward the cost of the film. GM dropped its sponsorship, sacrificing its investment.[22]

There is no doubt that Zeffirelli and his scriptwriters had decided to make a movie about the Messiah. All the contemporary political references and all the intentions about making Jesus a Jew aside, the film is always reverent about Jesus. Zeffirelli had questioned Burgess' script for using a modern vernacular, suggesting that Burgess's language interfered with Christ's essential characteristics of charisma and mysticism.[23] When Jesus is asked if he is the Messiah, there is no equivocation as in Matthew or Luke; he simple answers, "I am."

However, the conservatives found that they indeed had a large power of censorship. In the next few years, they would flex their power, forming the Moral Majority and entering electoral politics in a significant way, and with their growing influence in the television market and high discipline of their followers, they were able to invest large sums of campaign funds and deliver large segments of voters to the candidates of their choice.

The furor surrounding Martin Scorsese's *The Last Temptation of Christ* might have well been triggered when Jones convinced General Motors to pull out of its sponsorship some 12 years before. The Roman Catholic church had already been involved in an attempt at condemnation when it took issue with Jean Luc Godard's *Hail Mary*, a modern rendering of the metaphysical meaning of the Nativity story just about the time when the only Christmas controversy was whether to display Nativity scenes on government property. Aside from a few showings in major markets and a few pickets, the controversy was by and large confined to France and Italy.[24]

Franco Zeffirelli joined the fight. He wanted his film *Young Toscanini* withdrawn from the Venice Film Festival because Scorsese's film was included.[25] Mother Angelica, who had a Catholic cable network program, saying it portrayed Jesus "as a wimp," threatened eternal damnation for those who saw the film. Several bishops in major Catholic centers, without having seen the film, discussed banning it.[26]

Pat Buchanan, a national columnist and former speech-writer for President Ronald Reagan, was outraged at the "cultural polluters pumping this celluloid sewage" into the theaters for money, and linking them with college professors, the ACLU, and "an ideology that has caused mankind more death and suffering than Adolf Hitler." He wondered whether the constitutional guarantees should cover those who "routinely portray American soldiers in Southeast Asia as psychotics and sadists, and now, even mocking Jesus Christ as a confused lustful wimp."[27] The Greek Orthodox church joined in picketing the theaters, having opposed the book by Nikos Kazantzakis in 1956.

The evangelical right was the most vociferous and adamant in trying to prevent the film's release. In 1983, just weeks before principal photography took place, protests had convinced Paramount to withdraw from the project. As the film neared its release date, Bill Bright of the Campus Crusade for Christ offered to buy the negative and prints in order to destroy them. Universal replied in an ad in the *New York Times* that

In the United States, no one sect or coalition has the power to set boundaries around each person's freedom to explore religious and philosophical questions whether through speech, books or film. These freedoms protect all of us. They are not for sale.[28]

Evangelical groups circulated petitions by the thousands in their churches, claiming over 3 million signatures. The spearhead was the local theater, and several large chains decided not to bid on the film, leaving several markets without exhibitors and few cities with opportunities for wide release. These groups also managed to get the cable networks to give it limited release, and convinced some large videocassette chains not to purchase the video. When weighed against the publicity that they engendered for the film, which never had great box office potential, their crusade seems to have substantially hindered sales. The film that spawned all this activity was caught in the middle of the American cultural debate.

The great technological breakthrough of the 1980s was the videocassette recorder. By 1989, two out of three homes had at least one VCR. Mass marketed first late in the 1970s, the VCR changed the economics of television and movies. Thousands of rental stores opened, including large chains, and the film distributors and studios with their vast warehouses of films supplied the eager dealers. The aesthetics of the TV set now became a concern for film makers, for by the end of the decade, videocassette sales and cable contracts accounted for nearly half of a film's revenue.

Roman Catholicism had its first non-Italian pope, a conservative who had decided that liberation theology, agitation over birth control, ordination of women, and acceptance of modernism had reached their limits. He wanted priests out of politics, and liberal Catholic writers, such as Hans Kung, had been banned from Catholic presses and not allowed to speak on Catholic campuses. This was at odds with the majority of the American bishops, whose careful study of nuclear warfare and the capitalist system had brought criticism from Roman Catholics of the established political right, such as William Buckley, Michael Novak, and Treasury Secretary William Simon.

The religious evangelical right had greatly multiplied their visibility and political awareness in the years since Ronald Reagan had become president and had spoken at the National Association of Evangelicals conference in 1984, telling them that he was sympathetic to their cries for a return to morality, supporting McGuffey's Readers in the classroom, school prayer, bans on abortion, antipornography legislation, strong anti-Communist measures in Latin America, and calling the Soviet Union an "evil empire." Several leaders had risen to prominence because of their television programming, such as Jerry Falwell, founder of the Moral Majority; Pat Robertson of the 700 Club and founder of the Christian Broadcasting Network; Jimmy Swaggart, an Assemblies of God evangelist; and Jim and Tammy Bakker, of the PTL Network.

By 1988, because of sexual and financial scandals, Jim Bakker had lost PTL. Jimmy Swaggart was caught with a prostitute in a voyeuristic setting in New Orleans. Oral Roberts, the longest-running television evangelist and faith healer, had told his audience that if it did not come up with $10 million, God was going to "call me home." The ensuing financial effect on all the television evangelists was devastating.

Paul Schrader, writer of the first two drafts of the film script, said that the film's opposition would make more money from the film than those who made it. "It is not accidental that the film has become the subject of recent fundraising appeals by the religious right . . . there is nothing like the ogre of Hollywood to spring open the pocketbooks of Christian America."[29] The campaign took place about the time that Colonel Oliver North was facing trial for funding Nicaraguan rebels against the socialist government of their country by selling arms to the Iranians and lying to Congress about it. These two items began to convince the television evangelists' audience to return.

The American landscape, however, had changed considerably in those years. The right agitated not only against supporters of pornography and abortion, the continuing Communist threat in the world, and the breakup of the family through the newly accepted sexuality of women, but against the world view that surrounded them. Although they were building elaborate satellite hookups with state-of-the-art broadcasting equipment, they were questioning the scientific thought that produced it. They persuaded states to pass laws that allowed the teaching of "creationism science," arguing that the science taught in public schools negated the Genesis account of creation, invalidating their claims of the inerrancy of Scripture and of special creation. These ills were described as the effects of "secular humanism" and, in many cases, identified with the national Democratic party.

One such group, the American Family Association, founded by the Reverend Donald Wildmon, a United Methodist clergyman from Tupelo, Mississippi, kept up a steady attack on the media and what they were saying about Christianity. He maintained that "Christian bashing" was done with impunity by the networks. Citing a 1982 research study on the beliefs of Hollywood executives, he proved that they were Socialists, wanted women out of the home, blamed society for alienation, and thought that minorities lacked education, but should not be blamed for it. With regard to sexual morality, 97 percent were "pro-choice" with regard to abortion, and 51 percent did not believe adultery was wrong. The profile showed that three-fourths of these executives were political liberals, but only 7 percent were regular churchgoers, whereas 59 percent were Jewish.

The television elite . . . believe that entertainment should be a major force for social reform. . . . According to television's creators, they are not in it just for the money. They also seek to move their audience toward their own vision of the good society.[30]

The anger expressed against liberalism came at a time when Americans were unsure of their role in the world. Although polls showed a slight majority of the American people favoring "pro-choice" over "pro-life," the nation continued working toward more restrictive legislation against abortion. The Democratic Congress and the Republican presidency came to a virtual deadlock over the Nicaraguan Contras, wavering back and forth in their support.

The nation was worried about its schools, its homeless, and its drug problem, but it was also worried about high taxes, affirmative action, and the trade deficit. The distribution of wealth was more uneven, with the middle class and wealthy better off during the Reagan presidency, and the poor faring worse, yet the evangelical groups continued to express frustration about their inability to achieve their political goals.

The theological subtext for evangelicals remains a belief that the scientific world view has undermined the faith. It has permitted doubt to become a major factor in religious discussion. It has been too permissive and, thus, has undermined God's confidence in the nation. The cure is belief in an inerrant Scripture that will change the sexual mores of the nation. It will restore the nuclear family to its central place as the bedrock of the religious community. Finally, it will lead to prosperity because of God's blessing on a righteous nation. What they want is a savior who will rescue them from their sinful situation. A human Christ cannot fulfill such a function.

The liberal subtext starts with religious pluralism. As Robert Bellah and his associates have pointed out,[31] the present age is defined by the attempt to define self within the matrix of a managerial and therapeutic *ethos*. Community, long a function of families, has broken down as a source of meaning. The family itself takes so many forms that only the sketchiest definition allows the word to be in common usage.

In this pluralistic situation, religion is more a source of community memory than a place of ethical and metaphysical questioning. Although ethics are important, the church's function of doing good deeds satisfies the moral imperative. A large majority of members look upon the church as a place of personal support.[32]

That kind of world view accepts the church as an institution that picks up the members' civic duties in the midst of the family's increasingly diminished time availability. They enjoy the fruits of their technology and would not put it away. Often highly educated, they have inculcated doubt as a methodology that leads to verification, and ambiguity as a condition of life. A human Christ appeals to them, because they are looking for a model for their own humanness.

Scorsese's Christ, based on the earlier Kazantzakis model, steps right into this gap. He searches for the God in Christ—for the source of his authority. Jesus plunges through his doubts, fears, and his own humanness in his own freedom, and in doing so obeys the will of God. In interview after interview, when asked if Jesus was God or a deluded man who thought he was God, Scorsese replied, "He's God, He's not deluded. I think Kazantzakis thought that, I think the movie says that, and I know I believe that!"[33]

At the protest in Chicago, one group was passing out leaflets asking, "Who is Jesus?" Jeffrey Mahan, covering the opening for a church newspaper, said that he did not think everyone needed to see the movie. "People who want to deal with the struggle of who is Christ will find it provocative. Those who feel they will be offended shouldn't go to see it."[34]

A number of the usual questions asked of Jesus films are inappropriate here. The film never considered an epic form; Biblical stories had become television fare by the 1980s. The one major biblical epic, 1985's *King David*, had faired badly at the box office. The best reception had been for Monty Python's *The Life of Brian*, a British satire about a baby born in a manger just down the block from Jesus in Bethlehem.

The film's scholarship was found more in the set design than the biblical text. Scorsese used Mesopotamian tattoos on Mary Magdalene, and filmed in Morocco for the sense of the burning sand, but because he was using a Greek novel rather than the New Testament as text, the usual research was so insignificant that the traditional dating of Holy Week is compressed into what appears to be three days, and no one seems to have noticed it.

There is no culpability of the Jews. Pilate decides that Jesus is dangerous, because he wants to change how people think and feel. When Jesus tells him that change will happen with love rather than killing, Pilate replies, "Either way, it's against Rome, it's against the way the world is, and killing or loving, it's all the same. No matter how you want to change things, we don't want them changed."

The film's first problem lies in Kazantzakis' novel. Kazantzakis defined sin as an inability to choose freedom. In *The Last Temptation*, Kazantzakis identified freedom with the choice Christ makes. Humans are tempted not to choose freedom because they want happiness, which freedom rarely brings. The spiritual comfort of family and home overcomes loneliness and brings happiness. That is why in the temptation scene the voice of the serpent is that of Mary Magdalene.

The choice that Jesus makes in the dream is the greatest temptation. This translates into the struggle of flesh with spirit, the centuries-old problem of Manichaeanism. As one Catholic commentator pointed out, Kazantzakis' Christ opts for a "world-denying, transcendentalist, and even sexist spirituality, in which sexuality, marriage, and domesticity appear as 'temptations.' "[35]

Paul Schrader's script and the later revisions do not attempt to approximate biblical language. Scorsese did not even attempt to disguise the New York accents of some of his players. Schrader told Scorsese that unless they were speaking in Aramaic, the dialogue was going to be the director's wrong version. Scorsese modeled Peter as a "rough guy from the docks," and some of the dialogue was intended to be humorous, such as when Saul asks Lazarus, "How ya feeling?"[36]

Nor does Scorsese attempt to disguise the fact that they are adapting a novel. Nevertheless, many criticized Scorsese as if Jesus should have spoken Holy Writ, rather than halting human words.

Most offensive to many was the way these words determined the portrayal of Jesus. Pat Buchanan was furious that Jesus was portrayed as "a confused, lustful wimp." When Judas asks, "Who will pay for your sin?" Jesus answers "I'm struggling." He says to a monk, "I am a liar, I am a hypocrite, I am afraid of everything." When he first speaks to the crowd, he begins, "Pardon me, I'm not very good at this." His mother invites him home because he is "sick" (presumably in the mind), telling him that she will take care of him. He keeps changing his mind about his mission, until Judas in frustration tells him, "Every day you have a different plan. First it's love, then it's the ax, and now you have to die," to which Jesus replies, "God only tells me a little at a time." He suggests that Judas' betrayal is the harder task and that he could not carry out such a loving plan. These are human struggles and do not reflect a divine savior with the Father, through whom all things were made.

Humanness is found in his growing awareness of God's plan; the idea's validity comes from the "adoption" theories, which suggest that Jesus became the Messiah at his baptism, when God announced, "This is my son, in whom I am well pleased!"

Willem Dafoe's Jesus expresses the doubts through a variety of hesitancies. He portrays Jesus not strident and self-confident, but first tortured by his fear that God has meant him for a savior (thus he makes crosses for the Romans to crucify Jews), and then hesitant in numerous gestures and voice modulations as he struggles with his growing awareness. There is no transcendent savior here, even as he sets himself for the cross and undergoes the physical tortures of scourging and Crucifixion. Because of that, God's will looks harsh, bleak, obscure and finally unjust. What could humans have done that would cause such a sadistic punishment?

The sexuality most offended the religious right. As Richard Blake noted in the Catholic journal, *America*, "The problem often lies as much in one's attitude toward sex as with one's reverence for Christ."[37] Scorsese had learned that sexuality is evil, even though it was the greatest gift of God, but he also learned from a priest that the one sexual thing he was not responsible for was a "nocturnal emission," which was an involuntary fantasy. He thought of the dream sequence in those terms, thus relieving Jesus of the responsibility for giving up his mission. He was only "tempted" to do so.

Conservative Catholics, however, seemed to identify with the evangelicals' criticisms, which found the scenes in which Jesus waited in the courtyard while Mary entertained her customers, the one of his making love to Mary Magdalene, and his subsequent arrangements with Mary and Martha offensive in the extreme. They were also bothered by Judas kissing Jesus on the mouth at the end of the film, partly because one can sense that there is passion in their relationship, though up to this point not identified as "sexual" passion.[38]

These points are all subsumed in the divine human struggle, which mirrors the debate in the early church. The question there was whether Christ was fully human or whether he was "like a human." When at Chalcedon, the formula became, "God of God, Light of Light, Very God of very God; Begotten, not made; Being of one substance with the Father." The struggles were not over, but the divinity of Jesus had ascended over the human.

Although each film maker had wanted to make Jesus human, their treatment constantly denied his humanity. The camera rarely breaks the reverence for Jesus; he is constantly shot at a respectful level, never too close, never too far. When Nicholas Ray uses large close-ups of Jesus' eyes or George Stevens focuses on his head, it only tends to confirm that the eyes are the window to the soul or that we must take these teachings with authority.

Scorsese pushes Jesus at us, forcing us to enter into his psychological state. His doubts show as do his wild mood swings. His anger is real anger; he upsets the moneychanger's booths twice; he turns on the beggars and the poor, telling them that they are selfish and that God will not help them. Scorsese's camera poses his head perilously close to Judas. Dave Kehr suggests that "what had been added is largely a matter of personal psychology—that is to say, of the 20th Century's own way of dealing with the eternal questions."[39] That forces our identification with Jesus, rather than making him a model of humanity.

Scorsese wanted Jesus to find his divinity and accept it. "The divinity doesn't give him much help along the way."[40] Scorsese used imperfections to accomplish this: the growing consciousness of his messianic character, the sexual feelings, the sense of failing his mother and Magdalene, his struggle with Judas, the ineptitude of the disciplines. Some protesters carried signs saying, "Christ is perfect" and suggested that an imperfect Christ is a mockery. "For if Christ is imperfect, where does that leave an ordinary sinner? Without hope of redemption, perhaps. The image of Christ's imperfections makes it possible for a man to sin."[41]

What is equally odd is Scorsese's treatment of miracles. Some of them stem from Italian Catholic morality. The scene of the bleeding heart offered to the disciples was alternately ascribed to David Cronenberg's *Videodrome*, Steven Spielberg's *Indiana Jones and the Temple of Doom*, and Italian Catholic piety. Scorsese suggested that it could be a mass hallucination, one engendered by him divinely, but he also points out that his grandmother had the portrait of the Sacred Heart, and he remembered from church a statue in which Christ's blood dripped into a cup held by an angel.

He treats miracle as an everyday occurrence, much as the Middle Ages treated it in paintings. At the Last Supper, when the wine and bread are distributed, they become the body and the blood. Scorsese said that "in a movie, you have to see it."[42] The miracle of transubstantiation is played without symbolism, yet Scorsese understood it as the "life force, the essence, the sacrifice." In this disjunction, Scorsese reveals the deep cleft in modern consciousness and Church doctrine.

Other miracles are treated in the same manner. He spits seeds out of an apple, and a fruit tree appears where he spat them. He goes to a wedding feast, and the climax is not changing water into wine, but Jesus dancing.

His treatment of Lazarus' resurrection resembles Zeffirelli's version rather than Stevens' *Greatest Story*. He poses him walking to the cave without announcement of his intention or of his meaning. He stands not confidently, but peering into the mystery he does not understand. People are posed in shrouds around the dusty cave. He calls forth Lazarus while the camera focuses on him from inside the cave framed against the dusty world outside. When he pulls his camera back outside, one suspects that Scorsese is going to follow Stevens' lead, to undercut the literal quality and transfer it to belief. Then, however, he shoots the shrouded Lazarus in a close, over the shoulder shot with Jesus, and Jesus, astounded at what he has done, asks God to help him.

Once again, the literalness stuns. The style is distinctly Scorsese, yet this treatment of miracle is more like Huston's *The Bible* than the other Jesus films. Although one may mythicize the Genesis stories, it is dangerous to do the same with a film about Jesus. The effect here is to reconcile the two intentions Scorsese brought to the film—that of making Jesus divine, while struggling with his own consciousness (humanity) of that divinity.

Judas is almost exclusively a device to highlight the struggle of Jesus. Both Richard Corliss and James Wall called the movie a "buddy" picture, referring to such films as *Butch Cassidy and the Sundance Kid* (1969), where the interest is in the relationship between two male protagonists. Wall, however, saw it as a fundamental weakness, the inability of Scorsese and Schrader to "reject their Hollywood experience,"[43] whereas Corliss saw it as a culmination to the films Scorsese had been making for a decade in which "two men, closer than brothers, with complementary abilities and obsessions . . . connive in each other's destinies."[44] This fits only a few Scorsese plots, such as *Mean Streets* (1973) and *The Color of Money* (1986). More often he deals with the isolated individual, pushed down the road toward destruction or salvation—symbolically the road to the cross and the Resurrection (*Raging Bull* (1980), *Taxi Driver* (1976), *After Hours* (1985), *Alice Doesn't Live Here Anymore* (1975)).

Judas is the opposite of Jesus. He is fiercely devoted to the Zealots as the movie begins. He has been told to kill the carpenter who makes crosses for the Romans. Later, as he reluctantly joins Jesus, they discuss their mission. Judas tells Jesus to go to the Baptist to find out if he really is the

Messiah, and once convinced of it, Judas rejects the Zealots. He is fiercely loyal, and this loyalty forces him to consider the convoluted plan that frees Jesus to fulfill his mission.

Scorsese gives Harvey Keitel a red curly wig and builds up his nose to look like "Fagin," an easy villainous target to go along with the infamous name.[45] Keitel's role is similar to that of *Mean Streets*, where he spent the film trying to save "Johnny Boy" (Robert De Niro) from the mob and his own self-destructive tendencies. It is almost as if *Last Temptation* gave Scorsese a chance to replay the core of that film in the relationship between Judas and Jesus.

For Kazantzakis, the hardest thing to do will always be the mission to which we are assigned. To betray his friend as an act of loyalty is an act that Jesus himself says is the harder choice.[46]

The scenes involving Paul are curious. In the first, he is Saul, a Zealot, demanding that Judas go on killing. Later, he kills Lazarus, which the Zealots take as proof of Jesus' miraculous powers, which in turn confirm his messianic powers. Curiously, there is little discussion of this in the reviews.

However, his role in the final scene is controversial. In the culminating moments of dream, Paul adopts an evangelistic style of preaching, sounding very much like a fundamentalist preacher. Jesus, now aged, walks by with his family. The angel tries to dissuade him from listening to Paul, but Jesus accuses him of lying to the people. Paul replies that he has created the truth and that Jesus cannot stop it—that the myth goes on despite the facts.

The scene received a good deal of criticism, though the clear intention is to start Jesus back into accepting his Crucifixion. It presents a modern version of the Grand Inquisitor's argument in Dostoevsky's *The Brothers Karamazov*, who suggested that the people's needs for miracle, mystery, and authority were more important than Jesus' emphasis on freedom. The Inquisitor argues that the church has had to "correct" the mistakes of Christ, and that the church really cared for the weak and suffering, much as Paul in the film seems to suggest that truth is not a factor in religion.

In the end, Judas shows him his mission. As Jesus lies dying, Judas brands him a traitor, telling him his place was on the cross, but instead he chose to be a man. He tells him that he loved him so much that when Jesus begged him to betray him, he did. "You, what are you doing *here*?" At that point, the wounds begin to bleed again. He sees through the angel's disguise and that he has been tricked by his own desires, expressed from the beginning of the film when Magdalene tells him that she hates God because God took her from him. Judas' last words to him are that if there is no sacrifice, there is no salvation, and as Jesus crawls out the doorway, the soundtrack brings up the sounds of the crowd again, silent since he went into his reverie, and Jesus happily finds himself on his cross, smiling as he overcomes his temptation with the words, "It is accomplished."

Scorsese's film trades on dualism—spirit versus flesh, vocation versus contentment. His imagery often involves mortification of the flesh as a way to salvation. In the early scene where he carries the cross of a condemned man up to Golgotha, he first puts on a belt where the spikes press in on his flesh. Scorsese frequently has his fevered heroes grasping for redemption in a bizarre act of love, such as Travis Bickle's attempt to save the child from prostitution by murdering her pimp. His characters inhabit the edges of the imagination; humanity is more complex and less lovable than the humanity portrayed by most other directors.

Scorsese is not comfortable with faith, but he cannot leave it alone. He is uneasy with popular religion as well. He mentions the image in Woody Allen's *Hannah and Her Sisters*, when Allen, having converted to Christianity, finds a 3D Jesus winking at him. Statues on dashboards and Jesus on black velvet lack seriousness and invite disrespect for Jesus.[47] Perhaps that is the reason for the humor in the film regarding transubstantiation and the bleeding heart.

Every generation finds in Jesus a savior compatible with its times. The gospel writers saw Jesus as the apocalyptic Son of Man, the new Moses, the cosmopolitan Savior of the World, and the cosmic Son of God, present with God from all time. In *Jesus Through the Centuries*, Jaroslav Pelikan explores 18 different cultural images of Christ, whereas Frederick Buechner's *The Faces of Jesus* looks at the way artists rendered him, and Theodore Ziolkowski details novelists' conceptions in *Fictional Transfigurations of Jesus*.

America is a pluralistic society, fraught with contradictions between scientific world views and those that stress traditional values. The nation's pluralism has been spread through the popular arts, which allow a variety of views wide circulation in the marketplace. The cultural landscape can be imagined in apocalyptic terms with the forces of light striving against the forces of darkness and despair, and it is not hard to move from there to evangelical Christianity and secular humanism as the contending forces, each side imagining itself as the forces of light. The other side is seen as leading to the continuing degradation of abortion, divorce, pornography, and socialism, or on the other hand, trying to negate the gains made by the social revolutions of our time.

Religion is not spectacular in films any longer, but neither is it insignificant. Scorsese's film catches the cultural contradictions in powerful and contradictory ways, and the ensuing battle over it illuminates the ways that people struggle for values in a pluralistic society.

NOTES

1. Franco Zeffirelli, *Franco Zeffirelli's Jesus: A Spiritual Diary* (San Francisco: Harper and Row, 1984), p. 5.

2. Ibid.

3. Walter Abbott, S. J. and Msgr. Joseph Gallagher, *The Documents of Vatican II* (New York: Guild Press, 1966), pp. 665–6.

4. "*Jesus of Nazareth* on NBC," Cultural Information Service (Vol. VIII, #3) March 1977, p. 5.

5. Zeffirelli, *Jesus*, p. 17.

6. Hyam Maccoby, "Jesus on the Small Screen," *Encounter* 49 (July, 1977): 43–4.

7. "*Jesus of Nazareth* on NBC," Cultural Information Service, p. 6.

8. Charles Henderson, "Zeffirelli's Jesus: A Theological Perspective," *The Christian Century* 94 (April 20, 1977): 6.

9. Zeffirelli, *Jesus*, p. 60.

10. Ibid., p. 72.

11. Ibid., p. 95.

12. Ibid., p. 88.

13. Ibid., p. 17.

14. Roy Larson, *Chicago Sun-Times*, March 31, 1977, p. 74.

15. Dennis Potter, "The Celluloid Messiah," *The Times* (London), April 10, 1977, p. 33.

16. *New York Times*, April 4, 1977, Sec. 2, p. 1, 36.

17. Zeffirelli, *Jesus*, p. 104.

18. Ibid., p. 87.

19. Ibid., p. 35.

20. Maccoby, p. 45–6.

21. Zeffirelli, *Jesus*, p. 64.

22. Lord Grade commented that GM found the program "so sensitive and beautiful that they think it would be wrong for a commercial company to take advantage of it."

23. Zeffirelli, *Jesus*, p. 38.

24. Chicago City Council banned the movie, which was showing at Facets Multimedia, a group dedicated to showing foreign and classic films to a miniscule segment of the film market.

25. There is a confusing report out of Rome that he called the film a product of "the Jewish cultural scum of Los Angeles which is always spoiling for a chance to attack the Christian world," which he denies, saying his comments were taken out of context, and which Sylvia Poggioli of National Public Radio seems to deny having heard, but reported as what ran in Rome's newspapers.

26. Cardinal Bernardin of Chicago urged people to see what the US Catholic Conference and the staff of the people in its Department of Communications recommended.

27. Pat Buchanan, " 'Last Temptation of Christ' is Affront to Christians," *Chicago Sun-Times*, July 28, 1988, p. 19.

28. *New York Times*, July 21, 1988, p. C19.

29. David Elliot, *San Diego Union*, August 12, 1988, p. E1.

30. *The AFA Journal* 13 (January, 1989): 9.

31. Robert Bellah, Richard Madsen, William Sullivan, Ann Swidler, and Steven Tipton, *Habits of the Heart* (New York: Harper & Row, 1985).

32. I am indebted for these insights to Bellah et al., *Habits of the Heart*, and Martin Marty, *The Public Church* (New York: Crossroad, 1981).

33. Richard Corliss, "Body . . . and Blood," *Film Comment* 24 (September/October 1988): 36.

34. *The United Methodist Reporter* (Northern Ill. Edition) 135 (September 12, 1988): 1.

35. George Scheper, "Jesus Wrestles with God," *Commonweal* 115 (September 9, 1988): 472.

36. Corliss, p. 38.

37. *America* 159 (August 27, 1988): 100.

38. Their petitions quoted scenes not in the film but probably in an early Schrader script, such as Jesus saying after a kiss by John, "His tongue felt like a burning coal in my mouth," his permitting of the child angel to watch him and Magdalene have sex, and his saying to Magdalene, "God sleeps between your legs."

39. *Chicago Tribune*, August 12, 1988, Sec. 7, p. A.

40. *Commonweal* 115 (September 9, 1988): 467.

41. David Denby, "Time on the Cross," *New York* 21 (August 29, 1988): 50.

42. Corliss, p. 42.

43. James Wall, "The Last Temptation: A Lifeless Jesus," *Christian Century* 105 (August 17–24, 1988): 724.

44. Corliss, p. 42.

45. Caryn James, "Obsession Became 'Temptation,' " *New York Times*, August 8, 1988, Sec. Y, p. 17.

46. Scheper, p. 472.

47. Mary Pat Kelly, "Jesus Gets the Beat," *Commonweal* 115 (Sept. 9, 1988): 467.

10

Conclusions

Secular critics rarely are impressed by religious films. In a review of *God-spell* and the Italian film about St. Francis, *Brother Sun, Sister Moon*, Joy Gould Boyum commented that "neither brings a trace of the devotional, of theological interest even to their subject matter."[1] Many of the films discussed in earlier chapters received similar judgments. Theological matters per se are never very close to the surface of these films. There is no attempt to explain the rapid evangelization of the Greco-Roman world or to give life to the disputes that racked the early church. The content of faith is brushed in with the broadest and most general strokes.

The conflict with Rome and the violent actions that emanated from it provided ample material for the drama film companies were seeking. The films never were interested in the early Christian community, with the notable exception of *The Robe*. What fascinated them was the persecution of that community. In the Jesus films, even the disciples are often bland or ill-defined, with the exception of Judas. When a film maker made a serious attempt to understand the attraction and persistence of the Christian community in the face of adversity, as in *Barabbas*, the film failed at the box office.

One possible reason for this indifference is that the church in these films is presented as embodying a "new consciousness," but it is not a "new" consciousness; it represents the consistent values of American society. The church as a moral community remains faithful to these values even in the face of adversity. The church conserves American moral values and social traditions. In every case where violent revolution is presented as an option to overthrow oppression (e.g., *King of Kings*), the revolutionaries are morally flawed and unable to bring about a just social order. The films emphasize Christian ideology, but the institution that bears the ideology, the church, is ignored.

Martin Marty commented that religion is presented in the media as "a pious overlay of secular values," and that "God is packaged, man is depersonalized, the American Way of Life is proffered."[2]

Throughout the period of this study, American religion was concerned with secular problems. In a world racked by hot and cold wars, American confidence in its own destiny was severely shaken. Emerging out of World War I as a great power with enormous influence, in little more than a decade, the United States suffered a massive failure of its economic system; this was followed by a second protracted world war, two small limited wars (neither of which it could conclude successfully), and a seemingly permanent condition of nuclear stalemate. The spread of communism and fears of an atomic holocaust altered American self-confidence. At the same time, industrial technology (and later informational technology) was reshaping social values.

In the light of these changes, that Americans might not find philosophical questions of the existence or nonexistence of God central is not surprising. Technology depends on a world with definite repeatable patterns, and American schools drill students in scientific method. The scientific world view appears to students as a given, but it also conflicts with concepts of God. Concern for the discrepancy between scientific and religious world views is built into the culture.

Nations tend to justify themselves by assuming that their power confirms their moral superiority. When this superiority is challenged, the nation must adjust to its claims. Religious norms are used to examine the nation's goals; the Old Testament provides many examples of judgment on nations and what they must do to secure God's blessing. Religion thus builds into its system a criticism of our national experience.

Finally, changes in work arrangements alter social arrangements, and values are adjusted to meet new conditions. For example, when the technology of delivering mass contraception is provided, the religious rules against premarital or extramarital sex are no longer supported by biological consequences, and moral questions are asked in a new context. Since American popular religion considers religion to be virtually identical with ethics, films with religious themes would naturally deal with ethical questions.

Biblical or religious spectaculars made use of religion to examine these tensions. They are only tangentially interested in religion per se, but to suggest they are not serious treatments of problems in the culture is to misunderstand them.

The theme of science and religion is perpetually present in the spectaculars. For the great part of its history, the metaphysical basis of the Christian world has been dualistic. The early church argued long and hard over the nature of "substance" in its attempt to understand reality, formulating questions about whether Jesus was "wholly God" or "wholly man." The world had a spiritual basis as well as a material basis; in special cases, as in the Resurrection of Jesus, the laws of nature could be overcome.

Attacks on dualistic metaphysics begin with the rise of science. Alfred North Whitehead argued that the scientific mentality "has altered the metaphysical presuppositions and the imaginative contents of our minds."[3] Science has been the chief source of secularization since the seventeenth century, but Aristotle had attempted to distinguish the teleological basis of chance and luck in *The Physics*, which was a means of bringing those elements under rational control. Scholastic thought, finding in Aristotle a cosmology that could be adapted to create some coherence between religion and experiential metaphysics, worked out elaborate alliances between Christian thought and medieval science. Later, faced by the challenges of the Enlightenment, then by the theories of Darwin, Freud, Feuerbach and others, and finally by the studies of comparative religions, a serious schism in thought confronted the church. The entire culture, based on what it thought was eternal values and unchanging principles, found that its educational system, which fed the engine of modernization, pitted the religious view of the world against the scientific world view.

Commenting on the effects of the Enlightenment, Peter Berger argues that Friedrich Schleiermacher's basing religion on experience makes dogma relative; for example, the rising expectations of the Third World come into conflict with the Roman Catholic teachings on contraception. The supernatural is compromised to make room in truth for both reason and emotion. "In other words, the theological enterprise now takes place with constant regard for a reference group of secular intellectuals."[4]

Although in popular culture and popular religion people do not think in these complex formulations, the foundations of the religious metaphysical world are constantly being eroded. Karl Barth flatly refused to discuss metaphysics. Paul Tillich asks the questions in a way not accessible to scientific ways of thinking. Rudolf Bultmann attempted to separate the Bible's dualistic imagery from its message, affirming the experiences from which the metaphors of religion came.

In that context, the films struggle with the problems of science and religion. The treatment of miracles, especially the Resurrection, forms the most significant problem of the biblical spectaculars. The attempt to find semi-scientific explanations for miracles is a tacit testimony that within popular culture, the problem is persistent and never quite manageable.

The Resurrection of Jesus presents the biggest problem, and those films that deal with the New Testament often devise ways to avoid it. None of the depression era religious spectaculars or *Quo Vadis?* deals with the Resurrection, and it is carefully avoided in *The Robe*, *Demetrius*, and *Ben-*

Hur. Salome ends with the Sermon on the Mount. The problem of depicting the Resurrection is found only in the Jesus films. In *King of Kings*, it may be a hallucination; *Greatest Story* emphasizes the empty tomb with the ethereal double images of a lap dissolve; *Superstar* eschews all miracles and leaves a shadowy figure crossing the screen for audiences to fill in as they like. Only *Jesus of Nazareth* uses the appearance in the Upper Room, and though they wanted to use the episode where Thomas touches Jesus, it is significant that they could not make the scene believable and left it out in the film. *Last Temptation* ends on the cross.

In the Old Testament films, the problem is lessened by overtly naturalistic interpretations. David placing his hands on the Ark and ending the drought, Solomon restoring the unity of Israel with an inspiration in a dream, and Samson's enormous strength returning are more in line with dramatic conventions than the problems faced by those presenting the story of Jesus.

The two films that present the most problems are *The Ten Commandments* and *Ben-Hur*. The miraculous cleansing of the lepers at the end of *Ben-Hur* dramatically adds a note of implausibility that is difficult to reconcile with the rest of the film. *Ben-Hur* works as a revenge melodrama and becomes a problem only when the naturalistic emphasis changes. *The Ten Commandments*, on the other hand, is so far removed from ordinary experience that many of the elements—for example, the opening of the Red Sea—are acceptable precisely because the audience is expecting a big show. Since its dramatic intent is clearly to elevate Moses, the defender of freedom, and to destroy the atheistic materialist, Rameses, the means by which it is done takes on the aura of a fairy tale.

The Bible presents its miracles undiluted, but the destruction of the earth by the Flood or Sodom by fire is presented in quite a different light than the destruction of Pompeii by Vesuvius. In *Pompeii*, the volcano erupts providentially to save a group of individuals and to punish others. The same is true with the drought and the rain in *David and Bathsheba*, and the earthquake in *Solomon and Sheba*. These films assume that a divine will uses the natural world to punish evil, but only in *Pompeii* is it suggested that nature will save the good. *The Bible*, by abandoning the archetypes and making no attempt to present scientifically plausible explanations for the story other than the wrath of God, gathers its force by refusing to try to explain things rationally or melodramatically.

By the time of *Jesus of Nazareth*, it was possible to hold on to a liberal audience with a naturalistic setting and miraculous healings. The healings are not merely psychosomatic, but involve untwisting of withering limbs and the resurrection of the dead (Jairus' daughter, Lazarus). The audience was left to its own interpretation; conservatives could treat it as literal; liberals could treat it as symbolic or metaphoric. The script and the camera do not bother with interpretations.

The Last Temptation of Christ pushes past all the barriers. Ruthlessly human, Jesus runs from God like Jonah. Yet he raises Lazarus from the dead, even though he has to hold his nose to ward off the smell of the rotting corpse. He plucks his heart out and offers it to the disciples. The transubstantiation is rendered complete with its embarrassing cannibalistic subtext. Scorsese pushes the metaphors at us, rubbing the audience's noses in these beliefs and forcing them to come to terms with all the contradictions of religion that seem so coherent when enacted in the ritual.

The biblical and religious spectaculars were not the only films to take up the cause. Both secular and religious horror films question the naturalistic world as they suggest the limits of rationality. Confronted with psychiatrists suggesting exorcism, the mother in *The Exorcist* asks incredulously, "Are you telling me to take my daughter to a witch doctor?" That is precisely what they are telling her through their obfuscations.

Americans seem to feel that rationality and naturalism illuminate the technological and manipulable side of human experience, but there remains an ineffable side that only the art forms can satisfy, which can then be put off as superstition or magic. Our minds seem to resist complete rationalization.

In a country as diverse as the United States, national purpose is difficult to sustain. At mid-century, Erik Erikson suggested that the forces in American life cause more extreme contrasts and abrupt changes than in any other historic period, and the forces have greatly accelerated in the interim. World War I destroyed American isolationism, whereas World War II, the Korean War, and the Vietnam War were of such vastly different character that they hardly seemed to have happened to the same nation. World War II had virtually universal support; Korea was sustained by a vague sense of international cooperation, and the lack of consensus or national purpose made mobilization for Vietnam impossible. *Jesus Christ Superstar*, through the sympathetic treatment given the character of Judas, suggests the difficulty of telling the difference between the good guys and the bad guys, much less coming to consensus about morality or national purpose.

In pluralistic nations, the cohesive forces are bound together by a set of symbols that support the authority of the state, to which the populace are emotionally bound. Without these symbols, national unity is difficult to maintain.[5]

One perceived function of mass communications is to develop a political consensus. Common symbols, stories, and myths supply some of the nation's social solidarity, but in a pluralistic society, such as the United States, there are no official models of religion. In this atmosphere, states and ideologies claim their own supremacy, so the popular art forms demean the opposition to make their own claims seem legitimate. Nazis portrayed Jews as depraved, rich, licentious, and seditious, paving the way for their national policies. Not long after, Nazis appeared in American films as cold, sadistic, and covertly homosexual to aid in the American war effort.

In the religious spectaculars especially, attitudes that were fundamentally associated with the American nation were presented as "Christian" values, whereas those associated with totalitarian regimes were "pagan." Although Marxism has traditionally appealed to historical determinism, American ideals have appealed to "Nature and Nature's God," and have used religious imagery to explain national purposes. As nation after nation adopted socialistic systems, Americans found films that presented the American way of life as God's will convincing. In the 1970s, that treatment was called "civil religion," but the discussion generally ignored the role played by the mass media.[6] The imagery of a divine destiny has been present throughout American history, though the difficulty of maintaining it has become more difficult as racial, ethnic, and sexual groupings have developed their own consciousness.

The wide consensus of *The Ten Commandments* with its posing of "freedom" and "slavery" as metaphors for the United States and Russia became impossible a decade later, as a film such as *Hawaii* detailed the way Americans had taken an Asian paradise and, by its arrogant insistence on its own cultural superiority, had wreaked havoc with the simple native culture, a metaphor for criticisms of the Vietnam War.

In the religious spectaculars of the depression era, American values eventually triumph, because they are in line with the revealed purposes of providence. In the cold war films, a shift takes place; the persistence of the Roman world domination for three centuries before its alliance with Christianity is ignored, and the assumption that one can be a Christian in the environment of Rome appears. If one must be martyred, it is with the knowledge that the martyr's blood hastens the day of eventual victory when all will be reunited in heaven, but in *Ben-Hur*, the identity of the righteous nation has become so confused that it is difficult to find an unflawed society.

In the 1950s biblical spectaculars, personal ethics and national duty were closely linked, suggesting that the moral strength of a nation depends on the personal ethics of its people, and even more so of its leaders. In the Jesus films, one assumes that there is a righteous way, given the overwhelming negative images of Roman rule, but the way of Jesus has a tendency to stand more as personal good than as a model of national righteousness. In both *The Bible* and *Superstar*, there is a strong sentiment lurking beneath the surface that there is moral chaos, because there is no real Divine Intelligence behind the world. In *Jesus of Nazareth*, one might expect the righteous nation to be Israel, given the interest in making Jesus a Jew, but metaphors for the nation never really appear, not even as deeply oppressed, and thus no model materializes. *The Last Temptation of Christ* offers no national discussion, because it so intensely focuses on the struggle of Jesus to define his divinity and mission.

Theological ethics attempt to understand the principles governing Christian behavior. In American popular religion, ethics have been synonymous with religion. Numerous commentators point out how religion has become concerned only with private issues and the consequent deteriorization of religious institutions. Morality offers itself like a menu of choices to be made by individuals. The idea of a fixed morality, offered by culture and supported by religious belief, is undercut by individualism, the loss of a transcendent world view, and cultural pluralism.

In a sacred world view, principles are divinely ordained, and govern both social and private behavior. With pluralization, however, the individual is confronted with conflicting claims. One Protestant church accepts card playing and another inveighs against it, whereas Catholic parishes accept raffles as a means of financing its charitable work. Christians separate over pacifism and just wars, birth control, and divorce. Secularization erodes the foundations of the divine cosmos, and that which was taken as part of the "reality" of things is redefined along with its symbols.

The most persistent theme in the spectacular films is that duty is preferable to pleasure. From beginning to end, a morality based on pleasure is considered seductive and corrosive. For a community or individual to remain righteous, one must reject the claims of sexual passion, wealth, aggression, revenge, and power as a matter of duty. At times, especially in the religious and biblical spectaculars up to the mid–1950s, this must be done even if one's fulfillment is in the afterlife. In *Sign of the Cross*, *The Last Days of Pompeii*, *The Robe*, *Samson and Delilah*, and the Jesus films, the protagonists die, whereas in *Demetrius and the Gladiators*, *Quo Vadis?*, and *Solomon and Sheba*, they are brought face to face with ignominious death. In *The Crusades* and *David and Bathsheba*, the protagonists have to risk their love, whereas the heroine of *Salome* risks her virginity and her lover must become an exile. The survival of the nation, the happiness of individuals, and the eventual triumph of the moral order all depend on the protagonists doing their duty. Only in *Jesus Christ Superstar* and *The Last Temptation of Christ* is that duty ambiguous.

Increasingly more attention was paid to the basis for ethical behavior, whereas the relativity of ethics became the implicit background for *Superstar*, *The Bible*, and *Last Temptation*.

Each film was conditioned by the historical, political, and intellectual currents of its time. The films of the 1930s viewed the depression as a failure of individual morality, and the confused state of international affairs as the result of unnecessary intervention in European affairs. The films of the 1950s, with the cold war and the growing concern of the nation's increased affluence, warned against abandoning older values or flirting with alien doctrines. The 1960s and early 1970s were a period of vast social change, and the films exhibit the lack of surety about moral perspectives. *The Bible*, *Superstar*, and *Temptation* questioned whether "Christian" principles were indeed anchored in a divine cosmos or whether they were just as relative as all other facets of existence.

One can only speculate about the reasons for the demise of the spectacular. The most obvious reason is the cost-to-earnings ratio. After *Ben-Hur*, no religious or biblical spectacular substantially increased the profits of the studio that released it. This seems to be part of the general decline of the genre. The cost of reproducing ancient historical periods with massive armies, expensive sets, and authentic costumes has become nearly prohibitive for movies. The last three films discussed (*Superstar*, *Jesus of Nazareth*, and *Last Temptation*) turned to natural sets and smaller crowd scenes, forgoing the lavish displays of wealth that typified earlier attempts.

There is a great deal of money in television, and consequently, historical spectacles have been transferred to television. In addition to *Jesus of Nazareth*, television has mounted *Quo Vadis*, *Masada*, and *The Day Christ Died*. The miniseries, however, is best suited for length, so such films as *Shogun*, *The Winds of War*, *Roots*, and *The Holocaust* have been the historical spectacles that survive in the memory, whereas *The Story of Peter and Paul* has limited appeal even in the "high" religious seasons.

The themes that fed the spectacular no longer seem to require treatment in "the grand style." Science and religion are a staple of the horror genre; unable to approach faith through rational justification or arguments from nature, the question of faith now concerns human frailty before the powerful dehumanizing forces beyond human control. Thus, in such a film as *The Exorcist*, faith is the only defense before the persistent irrational forces that invade our consciousness.

The possibility of "the righteous nation" disappeared with Vietnam. War films, which always suggested that the idealistic death of young manhood brought the resources of renewal to the nation, lost their innocence. The agreed-upon solution to the Vietnam War was that American soldiers should not have been asked to fight a war where the commanders were self-serving and inefficient, the people we fought for were morally corrupt, and the politicians kept changing the purposes of the war. The idea of a "divine destiny" for the nation has become implausible.

Ethical problems have been scattered into other genres. Comedies have always been a good source for exploration of social themes and ethics; comedies always represent 30% of the 50 best-selling films of any given year. The freedom of films to portray forbidden topics frankly has made it unnecessary to disguise the films with an overlay of religion. Probably the most influential development is the increasingly secular nature of the motion picture audience; for a large part of the audience, religion is only one way among several in which ethical problems may be approached. Certainly, it is no longer necessary to use the spectacular canvas to discuss morality, and made-for-television movies made from social dramas (e.g.,

The Burning Bed, Roe v. Wade) have taken over that segment with several films per season on each network.

The big spectacular effects of recent years have been action-adventure movies, especially those set in the future, such as the *Star Wars* trilogy, those whose roots are in popular culture (*Superman, Batman*), and lone-wolf heroes (*Rambo, Die Hard*) where the good and the evil can be clearly separated.

On the other hand, religion has moved into every genre. Historical dramas (*The Name of the Rose*) (1986), murder mysteries (*The Rosary Murders*) (1987), horror films (*The Omen*) (1976), and comedies (*The Life of Brian*) (1979) have all had their share of religious figures and themes.

Finally, the melodramatic archetype no longer seems appropriate for religious concerns, except in social melodramas (*The Thorn Birds*) (1983). The distinction between good and evil has become blurred; ambiguity is more central to our experience of religion. Television has taken over melodrama. When the line between good and evil is blurred, a supernatural providence is no longer believable.

Religious and biblical spectaculars filled the needs of Americans as the social changes altered the perceptions of the nature of reality, and legitimacy of national policy, and the basis of personal and social morality. The changes were so significant that they were dramatized across the spectacular screen, and millions of Americans patronized them, went back to see them in rerelease, and continue to watch them on television. They are part of a history that is past—a style that no longer suits the needs it once filled. These films were not "mere entertainment," and neither the praise nor the invectives thrown at them understood them. The themes continue to trouble, but in a highly divided nation, post–civil rights, postfeminist, post-Vietnam, post-Watergate, post–Exxon Valdes consciousness, they no longer fit the spectacular's formula.

NOTES

1. Joy Gould Boyum, "Religious Themes in Modern Movie Idiom," *Wall St. Journal*, April 13, 1973, p. 10.

2. Martin Marty, *New Shape*, p. 105.

3. A. N. Whitehead, *Science and the Modern World* (New York: W. W. Norton & Co., 1925), p. 10.

4. Berger, *The Sacred Canopy*, p. 159.

5. Reinhold Niebuhr, *Moral Man and Immoral Society* (New York: Charles Scribner's Sons, 1932), pp. 83–4.

6. In recent years, several books have addressed this problem. Among them are John Wiley Nelson, *Your God Is Alive and Well and Appearing in Popular Culture* (Philadelphia: The Westminster Press, 1976); Jewett and Lawrence, *The American Monomyth*; Gregor Goethals, *The TV Ritual* (Boston: Beacon Press, 1981).

Selected Bibliography

BOOKS

Abbott, Walter, S. J., and Msgr. Joseph Gallagher. *The Documents of Vatican II* (New York: Guild Press, 1966).

Aristotle. *Poetics*. Translation and Analysis by Kenneth Telford (Chicago: Henry Regnery Co., 1960).

Arnold, Matthew. "On Translating Homer," in *Matthew Arnold: Poetry and Prose*, ed. John Bryson (London: Rupert Hart-Davis, 1954).

Bellah, Robert. *The Broken Covenant* (New York: Seabury Press, 1975).

Bellah, Robert, Richard Madsen, William Sullivan, Ann Swidler, and Steven Tipton. *Habits of the Heart* (New York: Harper & Row, 1985).

Berger, Peter. *The Sacred Canopy* (Garden City, N.Y.: Doubleday & Co., 1969).

Berger, Peter and Brigitte, and Hansfried Kellner. *The Homeless Mind* (New York: Random House, 1974).

Bergman, Andrew. *We're in the Money* (New York: Harper and Row, 1971).

Berman, Morris. *The Reenchantment of the World* (Ithaca: Cornell University Press, 1981).

Berman, Ronald. *America in the Sixties: an Intellectual History* (New York: Harper & Row, 1968).

Bogdanovich, Peter. *John Ford* (London: Studio Vista Press, 1967).

Borchard, Edwin, and William P. Lage. *Neutrality for the United States* (New Haven: Yale University Press, 1937).

Butler, Ivan. *Religion in the Cinema* (New York: A. S. Barnes & Co., 1969).

Cawelti, John. *Adventure, Mystery, and Romance* (Chicago: University of Chicago Press, 1976).

Cox, Harvey. *The Secular City* (New York: The Macmillan Co., 1965).

DeMille, Cecil B. *Autobiography*, ed. Donald Haynie (Englewood Cliffs, N.J.: Prentice Hall, Inc., 1959).

DeMille, William. *Hollywood Saga* (New York: E. P. Dutton & Co., 1939).

Eliade, Mircea. *Myth and Reality* (New York: Harper Torchbooks, 1963).

Fry, Christopher. *The Bible* (screenplay) (New York: Pocket Books, Inc., 1966).

Goethals, Gregor. *The TV Ritual* (Boston: Beacon Press, 1981).

Goldman, Eric. *The Crucial Decade* (New York: Vintage Books, 1960).

Gow, Gordon. *Hollywood in the Fifties* (New York: A. S. Barnes & Co., 1971).

Greenberg, Harvey, M. D. *The Movies on Your Mind* (New York: E. P. Dutton, 1975).

Grimsted, David. *Melodrama Unveiled* (Chicago: University of Chicago Press, 1968).

Guyon, Rene. *The Ethics of Sexual Acts* (New York: A. A. Knopf Pub., 1948).

Handy, Robert. *A Christian America: Protestant Hopes and Historical Reality* (New York: Oxford University Press, 1971).

Haskell, Molly. *From Reverence to Rape* (New York: Holt, Rinehart, and Winston, 1973).

Herbert, Will. *Protestant—Catholic—Jew* (New York: Anchor Books, 1955).

Higham, Charles. *Cecil B. DeMille* (New York: Charles Scribners' Sons, 1973).

Inglis, Ruth. *Freedom of the Movies* (New York: Da Capo Press, 1974).

Jewett, Robert, and John Shelton Lawrence. *The American Monomyth* (New York: Doubleday and Co., 1977).

Jones, Peter. *The USA: A History of Its People and Society Since 1865* (Homewood, Ill.: Dorsey Press, 1976).

Kael, Pauline. *Kiss Kiss Bang Bang* (New York: Bantam Books, 1968).

Knight, Arthur. *The Liveliest Art* (New York: Macmillan Co., 1957).

Koury, Phil. *Yes, Mr. DeMille* (New York: G. P. Putnam's Sons, 1959).

Macdonald, Dwight. *Dwight Macdonald on Movies* (Englewood Cliffs, N.J.: Prentice Hall Inc., 1970).

MacGowan, Kenneth. *Behind the Screen* (New York: Delta Books, 1965).

Madsen, Axel. *William Wyler* (New York: Thomas Crowell, 1973).

Marty, Martin. *A Nation of Behavers* (Chicago: University of Chicago Press, 1976).

———. *The New Shape of American Religion* (N.Y.: Harper and Bros., 1959).

———. *The Public Church* (New York: Crossroad, 1981).

———. *Righteous Empire* (New York: Dial Press, 1970).

Mowry, George. *The Urban Nation* (New York: Hill and Wang, 1965).

Mumford, Lewis. *The Myth of the Machine: The Pentagon of Power* (New York: Harcourt, Brace, Jovanovich, 1970).

Nelson, John Wiley. *Your God Is Alive and Well and Appearing in Popular Culture* (Philadelphia: The Westminster Press, 1976).

Niebuhr, Reinhold. *Moral Man and Immoral Society* (New York: Charles Scribner's Sons, 1932).

Noerdlinger, Henry. *Moses and Egypt* (Los Angeles: University of Southern California Press, 1956).

O'Neill, William. *Coming Apart* (New York: Quadrangle Books, 1971).

Pfeiffer, Robert H. *Introduction to the Old Testament* (New York: Harper and Brothers, 1948).

Richey, Russell, and Donald G. Jones, eds. *American Civil Religion* (New York: Harper and Row, 1974).

Rosen, Marjorie. *Popcorn Venus* (New York: Coward, McLain & Geoghagen, 1973).

Roszak, Theodore. *The Making of a Counter Culture* (Garden City, N.Y.: Doubleday and Co., 1969).

Scott, Nathan, Jr. *The New Orpheus* (New York: Sheed and Ward, 1964).

————. *The Broken Center* (New Haven: Yale University Press, 1966).

Thorp, Margaret. *America at the Movies* (New Haven: Yale University Press, 1939).

Tillich, Paul. *The Protestant Era* (abridged edition) (Chicago: University of Chicago Press, 1957).

————. *Systematic Theology* (Chicago: University of Chicago Press, 1951).

Von Hoffman, Nicholas. *We Are the People Our Parents Warned Us Against* (New York: Quadrangle Books, 1968).

Voss, Nelvin. *The Drama of Comedy: Victim and Victor* (Richmond, Va.: John Knox Press, 1966).

Whitehead, A. N. *Science and the Modern World* (New York: W. W. Norton & Co., 1925).

Winter, Gibson. *The New Creation as Metropolis* (New York: The Macmillan Co., 1962).

Wolfenstein, Martha, and Nathan Leites. *Movies: A Psychological Study* (New York: Atheneum Press, 1970).

Wood, Michael. *America in the Movies* (New York: Basic Books, 1975).

Zeffirelli, Franco. *Franco Zeffirelli's Jesus: A Spiritual Diary* (San Francisco: Harper and Row, 1984).

ARTICLES

Boyum, Joy Gould. "Religious Themes in Modern Movie Idiom," *Wall St. Journal*, April 13, 1973, p. 10.

Buchanan, Pat. " 'Last Temptation of Christ' Is Affront to Christians," Tribune Media Services, July 28, 1988.

Corliss, Richard. "Body . . . and Blood," *Film Comment* 24 (September/October 1988): 36.

Cox, Harvey. "How to Kill God," *Look* 30 (October 18, 1966): 104.

Dart, John. "Superstar vs. the Book," *Los Angeles Times*, July 15, 1973, "Calendar" section, p. 27.

Denby, David. "Time on the Cross," *New York* 21 (August 29, 1988): 50.

Driver, Tom. "Hollywood in the Wilderness," *Christian Century* 73 (November 28, 1956): 1390–1.

Durgnat, Raymond. "Epic," *Films and Filming* 10 (December, 1963): 9.

Farber, Stephen. "Spectaculars 1967," *Film Quarterly* 20 (Summer, 1967): 12.

Green, Peter. "The Movies Make Hay with the Classic World," *Horizon* 3 (May, 1961): 53.

Henderson, Charles. "Zeffirelli's Jesus: A Theological Perspective," *Christian Century* 94 (April 20, 1977): 6.

Houston, Penelope. "The Theory and Practice of Blockbusting," *Sight and Sound* 32 (Spring, 1963): 71.

James, Caryn. "Obsession Became 'Temptation,' " *New York Times*, August 18, 1988, Sec. Y, p. 17.

"Jesus of Nazareth on NBC," *Cultural Information Service* (Vol. VIII, #3) March, 1977, p. 5.

Kantor, Meyer. "Is Superstar About Christ—or About Us," *New York Times*, September 23, 1973, Sec. 2, p. 13.

Kelly, Mary Pat. "Jesus Gets the Beat," *Commonweal* 115 (September 9, 1988): 467.

Larson, Roy. *Chicago Sun-Times*, March 31, 1977, p. 74.

Maccoby, Hyam. "Jesus on the Small Screen," *Encounter* 46 (July, 1977): 43–44.

Novarese, Nino. "The Costumes for George Stevens' *The Greatest Story Ever Told*," *Cinema* (Beverly Hills) 1, No. 6 (1965): 18.

Petri, Bruce H. "A Theory of American Film: The Films and Techniques of George Stevens." (Ph.D. dissertation, Harvard University, 1974).

Potter, Dennis. "The Celluloid Messiah," *The Times* (London), April 10, 1977, p. 33.

"Problems in Paradise," *Newsweek* 64 (September 14, 1964): 90.

Scheper, George. "Jesus Wrestles with God," *Commonweal* 115 (September 9, 1988): 472.

Silke, James. "Interview with George Stevens," *Cinema* (Beverly Hills) 2, No. 4 (1966): 25.

George Sokolsky's column, *Los Angeles Herald Express*, November 30, 1956, p. 9.

Tanenbaum, Marc. "Passion Plays and Vilification of Jews," *Christian Century* 90 (September 5, 1973): 859.

Trombley, William. "The Greatest Story Ever Told," *Saturday Evening Post* 236 (October 19, 1963): 40.

Wall, James. "The Last Temptation: A Lifeless Jesus," *Christian Century* 105 (August 17–24, 1988): 724.

Index

ABOUT THE AUTHOR

GERALD E. FORSHEY is Professor of Humanities at Richard J. Daley College, City Colleges of Chicago. He also taught courses on religion in film and television at Garrett-Evangelical Theological Seminary. Dr. Forshey is an ordained United Methodist minister, and has extensively studied both film and religious history.